Praise for *Hol*

"HOLLYWOOD CLOWN proves Jason Lassen has not only led a hilariously interesting life, he also knows how to write. It's a laugh-out-loud inside look at the world of celebrity parties where nothing is off-limits and nothing is too outrageous; the real surprise is the enormous heart and soul Mr. Lassen puts into this book. At its core HOLLYWOOD CLOWN is a survivor tale of a boy who grew into a man...dressed in costume."

—Bart Baker,
bestselling author of *What Remains* and *Honeymoon With Harry*

"A wonderful treat! Hilarious, salacious, and endearing. It reminded me of Bad Santa in a Barney costume. I enjoyed this book and the characters so much, I read it twice. And laughed out loud both times again and again."

—Michael Loynd,
bestselling author of *All Things Irish* and *Gossiping With a Witch*

"HOLLYWOOD CLOWN is no joke! Jason gives you the inside track of a celebrity kid party. You feel like YOU are inside the Barney or Santa costume talking to Billy Crystal or Robert De Niro! His stories are price-less."

—Barbara Deutsch,
Entertainment Industry Career Coach and bestselling author of
Open Up or Shut Up!

"Even the word "clown" gives some people the creeps. There have been many stories about struggling actors in Hollywood, but Jason Lassen takes you on a hysterical journey you will not forget. After nearly 1,000 kids' parties, we are lucky he can still write. Don't miss this entertaining and detailed account of the good, the bad and the ugly of the famous and not-so-famous kids' parties in Hollywood. This is the tell-all book other clowns don't want you to read!"

—John Farrentine,
Senior Producer/Writer, Bruno White Entertainment, Inc.

TO MR. SENATORE,
Friend of the Friend,
Thanks for your
Endless Support!

Hollywood
Clown

An inside look into the highly competitive and political world of
children's birthday parties of Hollywood's rich and famous.

Jason Lassen

I have changed the names of all the party companies mentioned in the book. I have changed the names of some individuals and modified identifying features, including physical descriptions of individuals, in order to preserve their anonymity. In some cases, composite characters have been created or timelines have been compressed or altered in order to further preserve privacy and to maintain narrative flow. The goal in all cases was to protect people's privacy without damaging the integrity of the story.

*This book is dedicated to my wife Annette, kids Isabel & Evan and parents Dottie & Albert.
Thanks for the endless support!*

Table Of Contents

Chapter 1

Peek-a-Boo, I See You…You Talkin' To Me?

Raised on a farm in New Hampshire, studied acting and film in college, graduated at the top of my class, and now I'm dressed up like Winnie-The-Pooh playing peek-a-boo with Robert De Niro! Just another adventure in my pursuit to see if it is possible to find love and happiness while seeking fame and fortune in Hollywood.

Mr. De Niro took another deep breath, looked around, exhaled, and covered his eyes with the palms of his hands. Removing them quickly he delivered his line, "Peek-a-boo!"

I was frozen. I couldn't believe he fucking did it! *Is this really happening? Am I really playing peek-a-boo with Robert De Niro? I'm tempted to pinch myself to see if I'm dreaming, but that isn't an option since I have big, furry gloves on. It's probably a good thing I can't; I wouldn't want Bobby De Niro to think I'm some sort of self-pinching freak. Or would I?*

Looking out of the quarter-sized eyeholes six inches from my face, I do a quick scan and there doesn't seem to be anyone else around. Only Julian, his dad, and I. Did I mention his dad is Robert De Niro? I'm the only human alive witnessing Robert De Niro playing peek-a-boo with Winnie-the-Pooh, and I have a front-row seat to the whole event.

Now, if anyone had told me when I woke up this morning my day was going to consist of playing peek-a-boo with Robert De Niro, I would've told them they were high. One thing I've learned over the years, in this town and for this Hollywood Clown, ANYTHING is possible. The beginning of my day, however, was anything but glamorous...

Ring!
Ring!
Before I even attempt to open my eyes I do a quick check of my crotch.
Ring!
Oh good, I didn't piss on myself, always a good way to start the day.
Ring!
I take a deep breath, and as I do, I feel the pressure build up in my head from the insane amount of alcohol consumed last night in celebration of yet another successful sketch show at The Comedy Store.
Ring!
I exhale; releasing the pressure in my head. Sweet relief.
Rin...
In the best possible voice I can muster under the circumstances, I say, "Hello?" And sound like an eighty-year-old chain smoker who's been stranded in the desert for a week.

"Jay? Hey, got a last-minute party for you. You want it? You could use the money, right?"

I hate when my boss, Nick, asks me that, he does it a lot. Of course I need the money; I'm a struggling actor in Los Angeles. Who does he think I am that I would be exempt from the tight monetary grasp our society has on me and my balls? I hope he doesn't think I'm doing this job for my health? Because I *sooooooo* am not. I despise doing last-minute parties; it always makes me feel desperate for money, but I always cave in and end up doing them like the party whore I am. I find I'm constantly reminding myself, *At least you're not a waiter.*

"Yah, I'll do it. Where is it?" I say into the phone's receiver, trying my best to sound enthusiastic and somewhat sober.

"It's at the Bel Air Hotel. What's that sound? Are you taking a piss and drinking?"

"Yup, a little hair of the dog you know. How old's the birthday child?"

"The paperwork doesn't say but it's a Big Party Productions gig." It's common practice in the kids' entertaining business for businesses to subcontract performers from other companies. Some people who own companies don't even have performers; they subcontract every job. This is one of those jobs, it just happens to be with one of the high-end, fancy Hollywood companies. "That's why I'm guessing it's for some sort of royalty because most of the info is being kept a secret. If it is royalty, money means nothing to them; they use it to wipe their asses so they tip big. That's good, right? You're gonna be Winnie the Po...I mean, a Honey Bear Type, so you need to come over and pick up the costume. I'll have everything ready for you."

No matter how many times Nick said that, it was never true. The costume, my bag of games, my information, none of it was ever ready for me to just "pick up and go." He's always mentally all over the place, I bet he has some sort of adult ADD. I noticed long ago if he really doesn't like someone he usually had their stuff ready for them. Hmm? When I go over he always gets distracted by something—another employee that's been waiting longer than I have, his wife commanding him to do her bidding at that exact moment, or any bright colors, it doesn't take much. I learned all this about Nick over time and unlike some of the other employees that would get pissed off, I always knew I would have to gather all the costume pieces myself. I don't mind, it's not like I have a girlfriend, plus Nick is a very funny guy and always has a beer or two for me. Speaking of, I down the one in my hand and head over to Nick's.

"Hey, Jay. Wow! That was quick; I haven't had time to get your costume out yet. You can do it. You know where everything is, right? Cool."

Like I said, NEVER ready. Nick went about doing other stuff in his garage-converted office while I gathered the tools of the trade.

I don't think he was even working on getting my stuff together; if he was, there was no evidence of it.

All the years I've been doing this, it still always creeps me out to see the costumes hanging around the garage liked freshly skinned animal pelts. Their lifeless heads adorning the walls like the trophy room of a demented children's characters hunter.

"That Big Bird was one tough son-of-a-bitch!" the great hunter would say before proudly continuing with other stories of his conquest. "Barney on the other hand, I got him on the very last day of kid's character season. Tracked him for three days I did before I shot him in the spleen. He begged for mercy with all that 'I love you' crap. So I gave it to him by shooting him in the throat. Still love me now?"

While I gathered the Honey Bear Type costume and the rest of the stuff I needed, Nick regaled me with the story of how he and his wife, Rachel, had done a party for the Sultan of Brunei. I have already heard the story a hundred times but Nick loves to tell certain party-related stories over and over again—some ad nauseam—this being one of them. Never one to pop other people's bubbles, i.e. a pushover, I listen to his story, once again.

"Hey, Jay, the last time we did a party for Big Party Productions, at the Bel Air Hotel it was for the Sultan of Brunei. He loved us so much he flew us on his personal airplane to Brunei for a week, to do another party. How cool would it be if the party was for some sort of royalty and they loved you so much they want to fly you to their country to perform? I would of course tell them it was me in the Honey Bear costume and would go instead of you."

"Who knows, Nick, maybe they would be so impressed with me they would ask me to marry one of the princesses—my choice, of course—and I'd become a prince."

"Ya, that would be cool, fucking a real princess and shooting a big load on her face. Don't forget Honey Bear's red shirt."

Every conversation with Nick ended up relating to sex or became sexual in some way. No topic or subject was safe from his twisted, perverted mind. Beanie babies—sex, rainy afternoons—

sex, sex—perverted SEX! This is one of the things Nick and I do have in common. Maybe that's why he likes not having my stuff ready, to be able to hang out with me, because I understand that side of him.

While driving to the Bel Air Hotel, Nick's story got me to thinking, *Since everything about the party, other than where it is, when I'm to be there, and who I am as a character, is such a secret, it has to be for some sort of royalty.* My head must be in the clouds with dreams of fame and fortune; I drove right by the hotel. It's not easy to spot, even if you're looking for it. It's very discreet in its outward appearance, unlike the Beverly Hills Hotel that slaps you in the face as you drive by it on Sunset Boulevard. The Bel Air Hotel is within a mile of the Beverly Hills Hotel on a small, humble road off of Sunset.

701 Stone Canyon Road. And I'm at 1551 Stone Canyon Road! How the fuck did I pass it? Isn't it a big hotel? I was confused. I turned around and found it. I pulled into the driveway and was met by a valet.

"May I help you, sir?"

"Is this the Bel Air Hotel?"

"Actually, sir, it's the Hotel Bel Air, if you want to get technical. It doesn't really matter to me, but I know some of the higher-ups get pissed off if you call it by the wrong name. How may I help you, sir?"

Let me rephrase that, I was met by a very polite and informative valet.

"I'm here for the party."

"Which party is that, sir?"

"I'm going to be a character for a party here at the hotel today." I pointed to my passenger seat that was currently occupied by the head of the Honey Bear Type.

The valet leaned forward to get a better view of what I was pointing to. "Ahhhh, look at that. You're Winnie-the-Pooh. Cool."

"Actually, sir, I'm a Honey Bear Type, not Winnie-the-Pooh. It doesn't really matter to me, but I know some of the higher-ups get pissed off if you call it by the wrong name. How may you help me, sir?"

He laughed. "Drive ahead, go across the street, go up the hill and park in the staff parking lot."

Boy, they sure are nice here. This IS a classy place.

I found my way to the staff parking lot and was lucky enough to find a spot with some shade under a few trees. I changed because I wasn't sure whether they would have a place for me to do so. I'm sure they had a luxurious suite just waiting for me to disrobe in, but I didn't want to inconvenience anyone so I changed outside in the parking lot.

The Honey Bear costume has really crappy vision; I have to walk very carefully and slowly in it. Imagine having a large ball made of hard plastic that is two feet wide. Now make a hole in the ball and put your head in it. Don't forget to make two quarter-sized holes about eight to nine inches apart that you can attempt to look out of. If you can picture that, you have just stepped into my office.

Crossing the road in this costume always scares me and today is no different. The parking lot entrance is straight across from the driveway of the hotel. Just south, to my left, was a bend in the road and people were flying around it. The only way to really see out of the Honey Bear head is to hold it up with your hands and try to get one of your eyes close to one of the eyeholes. Whoever designed this head obviously never tried it on to see whether they could see out of it, had eyes that were very wide apart on his own head, or just plain didn't give a fuck as long as the check cleared. I'm going to bet it was a combo of the first and last choices.

There are a few different types of Honey Bear heads; some have extra fabric around the hole where you stick your head so that it can be stuffed under your trademark red shirt. This prevents the real curious little kids from leaning against you, looking up, seeing and confirming for their developing little minds that you are, indeed, not real and that their parents are big, fat liars, who lie. The only way to get all the fabric under your shirt when you're

6

alone is to attach the shirt to the extra fabric and then put the shirt on at the same time as the head. It's a real pain in the ass and that's what I had to do that day.

"HONK, HONK!!"

I peered out of the right eyehole to see a car had stopped and the driver was waving me across the road. I cautiously started crossing the road. Just because someone to my left stopped doesn't mean someone coming from the north side of the street was going to follow his lead. I couldn't hear whether a car was coming because the head also does a good job of keeping noise out. The only thing I could hear was my own heavy breathing from struggling to keep my head up. I was right. A car was coming. They slowed down as they passed me and the driver yelled out.

"KIDS, WAVE TO POOH! HEY, POOH!"

I could make out two little faces from the back window waving to me. I waved back to them but was thinking, *If you love me so much why didn't you fucking stop for me, asshole?* After the car passed, my buddy the valet ran across the street over to me.

"Hey, Honey Bear, you're good to cross. I got someone blocking traffic for you."

I find it easier to get my version of Honey Bear's voice right if I start off every sentence with "Oooohh." In my best Honey Bear voice I said, "Oooohh, thank you. It's really hard to see."

"No problem. Follow me, I'll get you heading in the right direction."

I followed him and he led me to what looked like a stone bridge.

"Pooh, old buddy!" I heard a familiar voice yell, and then I felt a slap on my back. "How ya doin', buddy?" I know that voice. It was Stan, my friend who introduced me to the world of entertaining at kids' birthday parties. Stan turned to my valet escort. "I got him from here, thanks a spanks. Have a happy, happy, happy, happy, happy, happy, happy, happy, happy, day. Look, everyone, I'm holding my Pooh."

Stan is super cheesy and corny. Not only when he's performing either—all the time. It's just who he is and most people he performs for love it. I can only take him in small doses because, like most comedians I've encountered in this town who don't know how to "shut it off" and be normal for a minute, he's mentally exhausting and like the engergizer bunny, keeps going and going and going. It must be from all the booze, cocaine and low self-esteem. "Hi, Stan," I said, glancing out of one of the eyeholes, "What are you supposed to be?"

"I'm a Pied Piper," he said, doing a little dance and mocking playing a flute, or "pipe" if you will. "Isn't it obvious?"

"Not really. You look like a cross between Peter Pan and a leprechaun."

He laughed. "You kill me. Let's go to work." He took me by the hand and led the way.

"I have to ask, are we crossing a stone bridge?"

"Yah, it's trippy. Can you see the swans in the water under the bridge?"

"No. Are they real?"

"Here take a look." He led me to the side of the bridge so I could get a better look.

Son-of-a-bitch, he was right! There were seven swans-a-swimming in the water that flowed under the bridge. Once we crossed the bridge it was like we had crossed into a magical land covered in trees, flowers, and cobblestone paths. It was hard to believe we were only minutes away from downtown Beverly Hills. Stan found our contact person and she led us to the room where the birthday party was located. Once there she gave us our instructions.

"Ok, this is the room where the party is going to be. I need you, Pooh Bear, to stand here by the doors and greet the guests as they arrive. Pied Piper, I'm going to have you and the other Pied Piper float around entertaining the children as they arrive. Where is the other Pied Piper?"

"They're on the way." That Stan, always quick on his feet protecting his own.

"Good. When they get here you can fill them in on what's going on. Pooh Bear, you stay here, the guests should be arriving soon. Piper, you come with me." She was all business. Then again she is the coordinator for a Big Party Productions party and they treat all their gigs like major productions, complete with walkie talkies and a minute-by-minute breakdown of events. They are one of, if not the, biggest party company in town. So I wasn't shocked at our coordinator's "all business" attitude.

I did as I was told and stood out in front of the doors to the party room. Fortunately for me, I was in the shade under a canopy covered in vines and flowers. I waved to people as they passed me by.

"Hey, Pooh! I'm finally here."

It was our other Pied Piper, Lauren, a wannabe actress who works for Nick and his wife, Rachel, in the office of their party company, Fun Entertainment. I don't like her. When she first came to L.A., we flirted for a few months; when things got serious and naked one night after she invited me over to see her, she put a halt to our romantic relationship. Her putting the brakes on after I got her off and was waiting for reciprication isn't what bothered me. After that night she became a cold fish toward me and "didn't want to discuss it" adding, "can we keep this a secret just between us?"

I know she wanted to keep it a secret because everyone she knew in town up to that point worked and partied with me, and she didn't want to look like the bitch she is. She says she still wants to be friends and acts like nothing happened. That kind of behavior is more common in men, what kind of woman does that? A messed-up one, that's who. I would say a messed-up "actress" but that would be redundant.

It sucks. I wear my heart on my sleeve and when I have feelings for you they carry a lot of weight with me; if I love you, I really LOVE you, if I despise you I REALLY despise you. Dating in this town blows. Yah, to say I'm bitter is an understatement. Her loss not mine. Besides, she's not ready to give someone a chance to truly love her; she still has all the usual emotional baggage that comes with trying to be a working actor in this town. I should know, I've got some baggage of my own but actresses are a whole different ball game.

Maybe one day I can forgive her, but I'm a Scorpio and we hold grudges, so today is not that day.

I pointed to my invisible wristwatch to give her shit about being late. I wasn't sure whether she got the reference though; she's not the sharpest knife in the drawer.

"I know, I know." She did get it, I'm surprised. "Is the party in there?"

"Yup." Short and simple, she doesn't deserve any more or any less from me.

She went past me and into the door that had become my post. She got there just in time because seconds later our coordinator came running toward me. How did she get by me? There must be another way in and out of the party room.

The coordinator came up to me and spoke into one of my eyeholes, "Ok, Pooh Bear, our birthday boy is here. Just wanted to give you a heads up." Then she ran inside the party room, I'm guessing to let everyone in there know our secret birthday boy had arrived.

I saw a group of about ten or twelve people approaching me. As they got closer I realized I was right. The party *was* for royalty, Hollywood royalty that is. It was for one of the sons of Mr. Robert De Niro. *The* Mr. Robert De Niro. It's a good thing I was wearing a giant plastic head because my eyes bugged out and my jaw dropped. Then the unthinkable happened, he spoke to me. Me, Jason Lassen, from a small family farm on a dirt road in the hills of New Hampshire.

"Look, boys, it's Winnie-the-Pooh. Hey, Pooh. Say hi to Pooh, boys."

I got down on one knee to get on their level to be less foreboding to the two boys who were apparently twins, "Oooohh, hi, do you know who I am?"

"You're Pooh."

Who am I to correct two little boys? If they want to call me Pooh then I'll let them. But for all legal purposes I just want it to be known that I AM NOT Winnie-the-Pooh. I'm a Honey Bear who just happens to wear a red shirt, no pants, and looks like another bear with a friend named Piglet.

"Oooohh, is it your guy's birthday today?" I asked them.

"It's his birthday," Mr. De Niro said, pointing to his son, who was being held by his mother.

"Oooohh, it's your brother's birthday today. How old is he?"

"One. He's one years old," one of the boys said.

"His name's Elliot," the other boy added.

"Oooohh, wow. What are your names?"

"I'm Julian and this is Aaron, we're three."

"Yah, we're three," Aaron said as both boys tried their best to hold up their hands and show me what three looks like with their fingers.

"Oooohh, that's a lot. Can you guess how old I am? I'm this many." I held up my furry, gloved hands and rapidly contracted and extracted my fingers multiple times.

Laughing, they looked up to their dad, who is Mr. Robert De Niro, and said, "Pooh's funny, isn't he, Dad?"

"He sure is."

Validation from the young Don Vito Corleone; it's official, my life is complete.

"Let's go inside, boys, and we'll see Pooh in a little bit. Isn't that right, Pooh?"

"Oooohh, your dad's right. I'm going to stand out here as your friends arrive so they know where the party is. You don't want anyone to miss the party, right?"

"No," Julian said while Aaron nodded.

They all went inside while I stayed by the doors hanging out on cloud nine. *I just met Robert De Niro!* I kept repeating it over and over to myself, unable to grasp its reality. There are only a handful of celebrities that impress me and that I truly admire, he is one of them. And I just had a dialogue with him. You bet your ass as soon as this party is over and I get to a phone, I'm calling my mom and dad.

I continued to stand by the doors and greet guests as they arrived. Some I didn't recognize, others I did, such as Rene Russo,

Quincy Jones, Whoopi Goldberg, and Billy Crystal. *This is some guest list they got going on here.* I'm sure there were other guests who are celebs in their own right that I didn't recognize. My vision impairment didn't help. Along came another guest, I waved to her from a distance. It was a woman carrying a little girl. *That's a tall woman,* I thought to myself.

"Look, honey, it's Winnie-the-Pooh. You love Winnie-the-Pooh." The little girl, who didn't even look a year old, turned away from me and buried her face in the nape of her mom's neck.

The woman bent over to try and put her daughter down, but she was not letting go. She had her mom in a death grip and wanted nothing to do with Honey Bear/Winnie-the-Pooh. I knelt down on both knees and leaned slightly forward, testing the waters.

"Oooohh, hi, I'm Winnie-the-Pooh. What's your name?" I didn't want to confuse the already petrified little girl so I went with the label her mom had given me.

She squeezed her mother tighter and made a whining sound while she did so.

"Ugh, honey, Winnie asked you what your name is."

She whined some more, keeping her grip intact.

"Honey, look, he's nice."

The little girl turned her head around, moved the hair away from her eyes, and watched as her mother ran her hand down my red shirt and onto my furry arm.

"See, he's nice. Do you want to touch him?"

The little girl just looked as if she didn't know what to make of me. Her mom took her by her little hand and tried to coach her to "pet" the Pooh. She almost made it. She retracted her hand before she could complete the task. Her mother looked at me, defeated. That's when I recognized her—it was Uma Thurman! How did I not recognize her? It's really weird, it felt like a switch literally turned on and I recognized her instantly.

"Sorry, Pooh. Maybe later, right, baby? Thank you, Pooh."

"Oooohh, you're welcome. Have fun."

I couldn't believe I was felt up by Uma Thurman! I LOVE MY JOB!

Soon after what I will now always refer to as "The Uma Incident," the party coordinator came out and gave me the ok to go inside and join the rest of the party, with the precise direction to "mingle and play with the kids." That, I can do.

There were a lot of people there; I don't remember that many people walking by me while I was at my post out front. What I could see of it, the room looked to be around fifty feet long by forty feet wide, had tall ceilings and was decorated with balloons and streamers. I was impressed at how appropriate everything was for a one-year-old's birthday party.

There was nothing extravagant, gaudy, or over the top, which a lot more people than should seem to do, regardless of who they are or where they are on the socio-economic scale. You'd be surprised at some of the shit I've seen at one-year-olds' birthday parties. When it comes to their kids' happiness, people's IQs seem to plummet. The most outrageous thing I think they had there, other than having it at the Hotel Bel Air, was a moonbounce outside. Like I said, I was pleasantly impressed.

I continued to walk around, mostly being eye-candy. I saw Rene Russo sitting down with a little baby that looked to be only a few months old. *I didn't know she had a baby?* I think she has an older little girl. I'm not always that good at keeping up with who's having or had a baby in the world of celebrities. Whatever, I had a job to do regardless of whether it was her kid or not.

"Oooohh, hi. Can I sit and sing a few songs with you two?"

"Sure, Pooh, sit."

We sang *Wheels on the Bus* and *Twinkle, Twinkle, Little Star.* You know, the standards.

"Oooohh, thanks for singing with me today. I'm going to say 'hello' to some more kids."

"Thanks for singing with us, Pooh."

"Oooohh, you two have fun. Bye."

"Bye, Pooh."

She's really nice and easy on the eyes, if you know what I mean. She's a "hottie." Nothing gets my juices flowing like a sexy woman singing *Wheels on the Bus.* Hubba hubba.

I walked around some more and could see Whoopi Goldberg from where I was standing. I was dying to go up to her and tell her I used to deliver mail to her production office at the Paramount Studio lot when I worked in the mailroom. Her assistant at the time, Ron, befriended me and loved to chat.

One day while I was delivering mail, *Entertainment Tonight* was doing a story on celebrity assistants and they were featuring Ron. I was delivering mail and there was a camera crew filming Ron "in action." When I noticed this I stopped at the door so I wouldn't get in the shot. Ron saw me stop at the door entrance.

"Hey, Jason!" he called out.

He told the camera crew, "This is our fabulous 'male' man Jason." Ron loved the play on the words "mail" and "male" when it came to me, his "mailman." He used to tell me I was a very rugged, manly man and that's why he called me his "maleman."

Ron continued to talk to the director of the camera crew. "I have an idea, let's get a shot of Jason giving me my mail."

The cameraman said, "Ok, that would be great. Just come in and do what you normally do. Ok? And try not to look directly into the camera. Thanks."

"Are you ready for your close-up, Jason?" Ron asked.

"Sure," I replied.

"Ready when you are," Ron announced proudly.

I walked in and said, "Here's Whoopi's mail, Ron."

"Thank you, Jason."

The cameraman said, "That was great, thank you."

After I saw the segment on *Entertainment Tonight*, I put on my acting resume that I did "featured" work on *Entertainment Tonight*.

I seriously thought about going up to her and telling her that story. It was my first on-camera acting job in Los Angeles, and I wanted to thank her for having such a "cool" and understanding assistant who not only allowed, but invited, me to participate. Believe me, kindness out here in La La land is not as common as one may think. I decided against talking to her since I was dressed up in a costume and I didn't want to freak her out.

I continued my duties and watched Stan and Lauren go about theirs. They were lucky; they didn't have to wear a big head for the party like I did. All children's entertainers want the gigs where you get to wear a costume but don't have to be a hooded character. It makes the job a lot easier. The kids can see your face and you become more "real" to them and it lessens their urge to hit and punch an expressionless face. It's easier all around to communicate with everyone at the party. Plus you can see and hear everything around you. I just can't rave enough about doing non-hooded gigs. Generally, I'm much happier when I'm not in a hood and I do a much better job. If you really need to have that special hooded character at your party, you could have the entertainer do the last fifteen or twenty minutes in the hooded costume, mostly for pictures with everyone and the cake. Food for thought if you're ever planning a party for your kid.

"Hey, Pooh, how are you doing in there?" I heard a voice say to my right.

"Oooohh, I'm good. Thanks for asking." I repositioned my head to be able to put a face with the voice. It was Billy Crystal! I love Billy Crystal. When I was a little tike, I used to stay up late with my parents and watch him play Jodie Dallas (one of the first openly gay characters on American television) on the show *SOAP*. Before Jodie, I thought "gay" was something my cousins called each other when someone did something stupid.

I thought I heard him say he used to do hooded characters for Bailey Brothers Circus, and that's where he met his wife. Almost on cue, his wife came over to us. Billy turned to her. "I was just telling Pooh we used to do this type of work. Remember the circus?"

"Oh, I remember," she said, and I could see the recognition on her face.

"I can relate to working inside a hooded character in the heat. I really feel for you, I know it's hard work. Be sure to take a break and get some water."

"Oooohh, I will, don't worry. I'm waiting for the right moment."

"Now's a good time."

"Oooohh, you think so?"

"Yah, now's perfect."

His wife added, "Yes, you have to take a break. Have you taken one yet?"

"Uh, no."

"Then you have to. Billy, tell him he has to take a break."

"I told him to."

I figured if Billy Crystal said it was ok to take a break, it was probably all right to do so.

Billy asked me, "Where do you need to go to be able to take off your head?"

"Oooohh, they set a room over by the stairs where we could go and not be seen."

"Ok, you go and take a break and I'll make sure someone brings you a glass of ice water. Go, go."

I made my way to the cast changing room and seconds later I got my glass of ice water. The lady who brought it in told me, "One glass of ice water, compliments of Mr. Billy Crystal."

I chugged the water and was still hot.

The woman who brought me the water just stared at me with concern. "Are you ok? You're drenched."

I caught my breath, "I'll be fine, thanks."

"I'll bring you some more water. Hold on."

She left and came back with another glass of ice water. "Another glass of water for you, Pooh, this time, compliments of me."

I chugged it down and was still hot.

"Do you need another?"

"Nah, I'm good thanks. I think I'm going to go outside for a breath of fresh air."

"Now would be a good time. You have about ten minutes or so before they do the cake and I'm sure they are going to want you there for that."

"Good to know. Thanks."

"I'm going to get you another glass of water and I'll leave it in here for you, alright?"

"Sounds like a plan."

With that, I put my Honey Bear head back on and made my way through the crowd. One of the De Niro twins, Julian, saw me heading for the door.

"Are you leaving, Pooh?"

"Oooohh no, I'm just going outside for a minute."

"I'm coming with you, ok?"

We went outside and stood about ten feet from the door, roughly around the same spot I stood while I greeted everyone as they arrived. I was hoping to be alone so I could relax and cool off. What was I supposed to do, tell Julian Honey Bear/Pooh needs some alone time because he feels like he's going to spontaneously combust? Like Julian's daddy, I too am an actor, and will do anything for a role, including sacrificing my personal health and comfort. Talk about being a method actor.

I got down on my knees and sat in front of Julian, "Oooohh, are you having fun at your brother's birthday party?"

"I love you, Pooh."

"Oooohh, Pooh loves you too. Do you want to play peek-a-boo?"

He nodded his head in excitement.

"You first," he said, with the most enthusiasm I think I've ever seen from a child in anticipation of playing peek-a-boo.

I put my hands up to the eyes on the Pooh costume, took them away, and said, "Peek-a-boo." "Me next." He laughed as he put his hands up to his eyes and pulled them down quickly, "PEEK-A-BOO!"

I grabbed my chest and acted startled, "Oooohh my, that was a good peek-a-boo. You scared me."

We repeated the peek-a-boo drill a few more times. I heard the music and the party noise get louder then get quiet again. I'm going to deduce that someone just came out of the party or snuck past me quietly and went in.

I heard a voice say, "Here you are. What are you two doing?"

I looked up and saw Mr. De Niro looking down at us. I tried to remember whether either Julian or I had told anyone we were going outside. I don't think we did, I was kind of in a hurry at the time. I also couldn't tell whether anyone had seen us leave. *Curse you tiny eyeholes!* I hoped for two things; one, Julian's dad wasn't worried and two, that Mr. De Niro didn't have me "whacked" for not telling anyone where we had disappeared to.

"Daddy, Pooh and I are playing."

"What are you playing?"

"Peek-a-boo. Do you want to play with us, Daddy?"

"Oh, no that's ok, Julian. Daddy'll just watch."

Then, in that voice that no parent can resist, Julian said, "Please, Daddy!"

I think I actually saw Robert De Niro's heart melt. He took a deep breath and looked around, I'm guessing to see whether anyone else could see what he was about to do. He got on his knees next to Julian, directly across from me. It was like an old western showdown, who was going to draw first?

"Do it, Pooh," Julian requested and at the same time making a decision for us men.

I put my hands up to the eyes on the Honey Bear costume, took them off, and said, "Peek-a-boo."

Julian laughed. He looked at his dad and said, "Now it's your turn, Daddy."

"That's ok, you can do it."

"Pleeeease, Daddy!"

Mr. De Niro took another deep breath, looked around, exhaled, and covered his eyes with the palms of his hands. Removing them quickly he delivered his line, "Peek-a-boo."

I was frozen. I couldn't believe he fucking did it! *Is this really happening? Am I really playing peek-a-boo with Robert De Niro? I'm tempted to pinch myself to see if I'm dreaming, but that isn't an option since I have big, furry gloves on. It's probably a good thing I can't; I wouldn't want Bobby De Niro to think I'm some sort of self-pinching freak. Or would I?*

Looking out of the quarter-sized eyeholes six inches from my face, I do a quick scan and there doesn't seem to be anyone else around. Only Julian, his dad, and I. Did I mention his dad is Robert De Niro? I'm the only human alive witnessing Robert De Niro playing peek-a-boo with Winnie-the-Pooh, and I have a front-row seat to the whole event.

"Do it again, Daddy! Do it again!"

"Isn't it Pooh's turn?"

"No, you do it again, Daddy."

He did as he was asked. Sucker.

"Peek-a-boo, Pooh."

I was just waiting for him to say, "Peek-a-boo, I see you... you talkin' to me? Are you...talking *to* me?" I can't even describe what it was like seeing all this from inside the Honey Bear Type costume. The only thing that comes to mind is "very surreal." The whole thing is just very surreal. I decided to have a little fun at Mr. De Niro's expense, and upped the ante. I pulled Honey Bear's signature red shirt up over the costume's face, lowered it, and said my line," Peek-a-boo."

They both laughed. Julian looked at his dad, "Now you do it."

His dad started to put his hands up and Julian stopped him.

"No, Daddy. Do it like Pooh did."

"No, that's ok."

"Pleeeeease!"

The old drawn-out please trick. Julian was pulling out the big guns, yet again. His dad knew what he had to do. He pulled his shirt up from the bottom and put it over his face. Slowly he lowered it.

"Peek-a-boo."

"Now you, Pooh," Julian asked.

I pulled my shirt back up over my face, lowered it very quickly, and decided to have some more fun and changed the line just a little bit.

"Peek-a-boo-boo."

Without even being prompted this time, Mr. De Niro pulled his shirt up over his face and lowered it quickly.

"Peek-a-boo-boo to you, Pooh."

Was he on to my games now? Was he trying to one-up me? He had no idea who he was dealing with. I'm a pro at this. I could, and have at times, done this for hours. *What can I do next?* I thought to myself. I could turn around and turn back quickly and say "Peek-a-boo right back at you" and do a little jig.

The door to the party opened up and a voice yelled out, "Time to do the birthday cake, everyone!"

He was saved from further embarrassment, in front of no one. We stood up and Julian said, "Thanks for playing with us, Pooh."

His dad added, "Yah, thanks Pooh."

The three of us went inside and everyone gathered around Elliot. The staff brought out the cake and we all sang *Happy Birthday* to the birthday boy.

Before I left, Mr. De Niro shook my hand and said, "You're the real star here today."

He's such a nice, genuine guy. He even played along with Stan who went up to him and did a few lines from *Analyze This*, which had come out a few weeks earlier.

In the character's accent that Mr. De Niro did from the movie, Stan said, "Youuuuuuuuu. Youuuuuuuuuuuuuu. You're good."

Mr. De Niro just smiled at him and laughed half-heartedly. What a good sport. I would've punched Stan in the face. Even Stan's need to prove he can be annoying didn't stop Mr. De Niro's generosity.

Later on in the week, I went to pick up my paycheck from Nick. He told me the De Niro party gave each of us a $67 tip.

One to never miss an opportunity to gossip, Nick informed me Mr. De Niro was asking around for a Honey Bear costume he could purchase. It turned out both Julian and Aaron loved hanging out with Honey Bear at their brother's birthday party. With a little help from the children's performers community, Mr. De Niro was able to get his very own Honey Bear costume to parade around in for his boys. It's parties like this that make me lie awake in bed at night wondering, *Kids' birthday parties? I've been in the party performers' world for a few years now and it never ceases to amaze me. My guidance counselor never gave me this as a career option. How in the hell did a farmboy like me ever get here?*

Like any good story we should start at the beginning, where unbeknownst to me my life would change forever...

Chapter 2

How Does One Become A Purple Dino Type?

"You want me to be Barney? As in Barney the dinosaur?"

"We don't use *that* word in our profession, it could get us sued. We refer to him as a '*purple dino type*.' Now let's work on some balloon animals."

What the hell am I doing here?

Thus was my introduction into the world of children's birthday parties. A world I never knew existed. A world unlike any other I have or will probably ever know. Not only does it exist here in Los Angeles, but turns out to be a thriving, competitive, political, big-money business. Who would've thunk it? Not I.

Honestly, who moves to Hollywood in hopes of becoming a children's performer? I came out here for the same reason most people do; to make it big in the entertainment business. And I mean BIG. I wanted the fame, the fortune and to have one woman riding my dick and another sitting on my face while they discussed how talented, wonderful and overall fucking awesome I am. I mean really, who doesn't want that?

Reality hit soon after I arrived. It hit hard and seemed to hit repeatedly.

Once in town, I had headshots taken, got an agent and waited for the phone to ring. It didn't. I thought I was doing all the right things in all the right ways, why wasn't I getting auditions? This acting thing was a lot easier in college. The confidence I possessed upon my arrival faded fast and only got worse. I was three thousand miles from home and away from everyone I felt truly loved me; even though I lived with twelve of my friends from college in a two-bedroom apartment in Calabasas, I never felt so alone. They didn't have time for my worries; they all had their own to contend with and like me, were trying to make it in "The Biz."

I had no idea the extent to which my emotional state was going to be tested on a more personal level. Does anyone ever really know the path their life is going to take when they set out on a journey? If they did, how many would take those first few steps? I have always been up for an adventure and the unknown excites me to my core; little did I know the ride I was in for, or the series of events ahead of me that would change my life forever in ways I couldn't have ever imagined.

Within a few months of my arrival in L.A, my grandfather died and a friend who was going to move out here was fatally shot by an ex-boyfriend who had gotten her pregnant. It ate me up inside that I couldn't afford to go back for either funeral. I quickly learned being a broke wannabe actor SUCKS! To make matters worse, I called my girlfriend, who was still in college in New Hampshire, for emotional support only to have her tell me she'd moved on and was seeing someone else. My heart was crushed; I had thought this girl was "The One." I really needed someone to lean on emotionally and that someone was now gone without any type of closure to our relationship, other than that painful phone call. Something I regret to this day.

I love "love" with all its possibilities and seem to do better creatively when I have a muse to share my successes and struggles with. Unfortunately, to me Hollywood doesn't feel the same way I do; I dreaded being plunged into its trendy fake dating scene.

I picked myself up and forged ahead by taking the opportunity to look at my bucket list and cross something off it—travel. I depleted my savings and spent three months on a backpacking trip across Europe. A few of my friends thought I was crazy but I had no intention of putting a time limit on how long I was going to stay in L.A. and "try" acting. I'm in it for the long haul, California is now my home and I knew the television and film industry wasn't going anywhere and would still be here when I got back.

I returned a changed man. I felt focused and refreshed. I'm a people-pleaser by nature and always put other peoples' needs above my own. I decided it was time to please myself first, even if it meant at the expense of others. How L.A. of me! Love was the furthest thing from my mind; I was all set to get my acting career back on track. I got into a comedy improvisation group and for the first time since moving to L.A. felt like a real actor. I was reaching for the stars little by little and not even the Northridge earthquake deterred me. A handful of friends moved after the earthquake—it's nature's way of thinning out the herd here in Hollywood. Fewer actors equal less competition at auditions, so bring it on.

L.A. let me get a Monday through Friday job but being the bitch she is, wasn't done with me yet; unbeknownst to me the worst was yet to come. I don't know why she hates me so much but she just does.

Being a production assistant in this town is anything but glamorous but it sure does help getting to know the layout of the city. While sitting on the 101 freeway heading to drop off some tapes for the *Leeza* show in Burbank, I witnessed a woman do a swan dive off the Barham exit bridge right into traffic. She plummeted off the bridge and was hit by two cars ahead of me before someone finally stopped. The first car hit her so hard her right shoe flew off and landed about a hundred yards away from her body. Traffic came to a halt in an ocean of red taillights accompanied by an orchestra of screeching brakes. I slammed on my brakes and my car skidded under the flatbed of a semi truck. The truck was high enough that I didn't hit it with the front of my car, but when all was said and done the flatbed part was about six inches away from my windshield. Another car almost rear-ended me, but fortunately was able to swerve into the breakdown lane. I watched as a guy got out of his car and made a feeble attempt to cover the body with an old, brown jacket he had lying in the backseat of his car.

I was so close to the body I could've reached out and touched it. A skid mark of blood around three feet wide preceded the body and began to pool around the lifeless corpse. It was eerie looking at the skid mark. I had seen this much blood plenty of times while butchering pigs on the farm I grew up on, but knowing it was created by another human being who had been dragged about thirty feet under a speeding car freaked me out. I'm sure she was dead by the time she hit the pavement and before the first car hit her, much less the second one.

I found myself mesmerized by her long, black hair, made crimson with blood. She might have originally been blonde but at that point it was impossible to tell. There was a huge piece of her head—about the size of a softball—missing where blood and brains were oozing out and onto the pavement. Both of her legs were bright purple and swollen to the point where they looked like they were going to pop. One of her legs was bent sideways at her hip, snapped at the knee, and it lay parallel running up alongside her, her shoeless foot next to her face. It was a very unnatural position for the human body to be in, and this includes any contortionist I've ever seen.

I passed by the body and continued on my way to NBC to drop off my ever-important tapes.

That night I went home and couldn't sleep. So I drank. Then I drank more. I eventually fell asleep, not due to exhaustion but from intoxication.

It wasn't until the next day that what I had witnessed the day before really hit me. I was driving to pick up something REALLY important for the taping of the show that day (it's standard practice in the entertainment industry that everything is as important as brain surgery and needs to be done as quickly as possible). I was driving down Santa Monica Boulevard near the beach when my hands started to shake uncontrollably.

I pulled my car over and started to weep. Not just cry, but a full-on bawling fit. I felt claustrophobic and had to get out of my car. I sat on the sidewalk shaking and sobbing hysterically. I found myself getting angry with the woman who jumped. *She could've killed so many people with one stupid, foolish act of selfishness!* Then I became sad for her. *Who was she? Why did she jump? What was going through her mind?* Then I got angry again. It kept going back and forth like this for a while.

My boss, Chris, kept paging me because I was late with dropping off at the sound stage. I don't know how I did it but I got back in my car and drove to Stage 26 at Paramount, where we taped the show. Chris being the cool and understanding boss he is covered my ass and smoothed things over. He honestly was more concerned about my wellbeing than any stupid shit having to do with the show. For this, I am grateful to him. I didn't get behind the wheel of a car for a week after that. It made my job as a "runner" very interesting. The only reason I didn't get fired was because Chris had talked to Leeza Gibbons, who in turn met with me, and I filled her in on what had happened. She felt bad for me and worked something out with the bosses that were above both Chris and I.

I was given some vacation time and I used it to go home to New Hampshire. It was a nice, relaxing visit with very little driving around. I came back to Los Angeles feeling a little recharged and my parents were coming out soon so I had something to look forward to. On their second night here they decided to rent a room in a hotel at Universal Studios. The phone kept ringing all night and when we'd pick it up no one would be on the other end. An eerie sense of foreboding that something was wrong filled the room that night. The phone rang at 4:30am and woke us up. My mother answered the phone and we were all groggy waiting to hear who was on the other end.

"Allison?" It was my sister. "What's wrong?"

My mother started to cry and she NEVER cries. Up until that point, I had only seen her cry one other time in my life, and even then it only lasted a minute at most. She is the rock in our family; the anchor that the rest of us lean on, but even she was not prepared to hear what no parent or grandparent ever wants to hear. She was able to compose herself long enough to tell the rest of us why she was crying.

"Zachary is dead. He died last night," she said in an almost trance-like state, not believing the words that had to be forced from her mouth to the rest of our ears. "We have to get home."

Zachary, my three-and-a-half-year-old nephew, passed away. Back in New Hampshire it was a dark and rainy night and Zach had come down with croup. Not new to this, my sister knew what to do, she gave him cough syrup to help him breathe better and they both went to bed. Zach's dad, Brian, came home from work a few hours later to find him sitting on the couch coughing and gasping for air. He pointed upstairs and when Brian asked him if he wanted his mother, Zach nodded.

By the time my sister got downstairs he had fallen to the floor. Allison rushed him to the kitchen where she flung open the door to give him air. Brian called 911 but because they lived on the border of two towns, both towns responded then cancelled thinking the other town was on top of it. Zach's seven-year-old sister, Jasmine, sat on the stairs with their father watching the events unravel.

In the meantime, Allison moved Zach to the floor to perform CPR, as she was instructed to do by the 911 operator. My sister picked him up to move him to the floor; as she did he looked up to her and said, "Help me, Mommy. Please help me!" His pleas stopped so he could make one last statement to his mother, "I love you." And then he died right there in her arms. She could do nothing but just watch him leave this earth.

Allison rode in the ambulance on the way to the hospital praying to God Zach would cry and that the EMTs could still save him. They couldn't.

The worst thing that can happen to a family is to have to bury one of their children. I was the one who named him, he held a very special place in my heart and I was happy I had gotten a chance to see him a few weeks prior to his passing. We later found out our family was lucky to have him in our lives as long as we did, because his internal organs were not growing along with the rest of his body and his condition would've only worsened over time.

While everyone else packed I needed to go to work. Chris was no longer my boss and it was his replacement's second day at work. I walked up to my new boss and said very matter-of-factly with zero emotion, "My nephew died last night and I have to go home. I should be back in a few days." I wasn't asking for permission to leave, I was giving him the facts and if he wanted to fire me, I could care less.

"Sure, Jason, just let us know when you'll be back." What else was he going to say?

I didn't say anything back to him; I was running on autopilot. I had rehearsed what I was going to say to him on the way into work, so I could do it without crying. I wore sunglasses to hide my puffy eyes as a result of having already been crying for hours. I walked backstage of the *Leeza* show set and lost it. I was crying so hard my chest hurt and I was gasping for air. I fell to the floor in a ball next to a pile of lighting cables.

WHY? WHY? WHY? I never got an answer. It's times like these that make one question the existence of a higher power if they believe in one. Who could let this happen to someone so young and innocent? *He was a little boy for Christ sake!* I picked myself off the floor and drove home to pick up my parents.

My friend John, Leeza, and one of the other runners, Daniel, sent my sister money to pay for my nephew's headstone. Leeza and my friend John had separately sent flowers as well.

After the funeral I came back to Los Angeles feeling more alone than ever. To say I took his loss extremely hard would be an understatement. Life cut that short is unnatural. There truly is no pain as great as the pain forever felt from the loss of a child in a family. I don't wish its knowledge upon anyone; you are never the same person after. I never wanted to feel that loss ever again and looked into getting a vasectomy. My request was denied and all I got out of that appointment was a recommendation to see a shrink.

I found my own therapy at the bottom of a Jack Daniel's bottle. I had to drink every night so I would pass out, otherwise I wouldn't be able to fall asleep. I tried not drinking but I would cry so much I wouldn't sleep and would be tired all day. I preferred to be hungover and sad than tired and sad.

My daily routine became going to work, doing my time and going home where I would sit and play my guitar in the dark cursing God, eventually denouncing him and drinking Jack Daniel's until I passed out. I wasn't spending money on food so I was actually saving money during this time. I prayed for the day I wouldn't cry from the moment I woke up until I fell asleep or passed out crying. This was the beginning of a dangerous drinking pattern that became my norm.

Acting was the last thing on my mind and I quit my improvisation group. It was hard enough just getting out of bed every morning, much less forcing myself to feel funny. Love and acting didn't only get put on the back burner but removed from the stove completely.

I quit the *Leeza* show and bounced around from job to job while trying to get my head back in the game. I took a job working as an assistant director for the 1994 World Cup that lasted two weeks. I needed another job and got hooked up with one over at SDDS, Sony Dynamic Digital Sound, installing sound systems into theaters around the city. The higher-ups never liked me, especially after I offered to play Hollywood tour guide for our visiting introverted techies from Japan. They were looking for an excuse to get rid of me and I personally handed them one on a silver platter by finding a glitch in their system, "You can't work if there's nothing to install."

I put myself out of a job and didn't shed a tear for my old boss at SDDS when I heard he was forced to resign after a sexual harassment suit was brought against him. Karma is a bitch but always finds you. Ha!

Not being good at sitting around on my ass I landed another job quickly, this time in the mailroom at CBS. The happiness continued when one of my roommates broke up with one of our other roommates and because she refused to move, we were forced to move into an awesome house with a pool and waterfall. What really made this house special was its wine cellar/laundry room. Most houses in Los Angeles don't have basements because of earthquakes and we took advantage of the space and the five of us roomies formed a band.

Music has always been important to me and is very therapeutic. When I play my mind clears and I get very focused on the music; all the troubles in my life seem to fade away. I hadn't been in a band since college and I forgot how much I enjoyed it. We played house parties and if there were no parties to play at we would throw one of our own. Things were finally starting to look up.

It didn't last long.

One night, without any warning or signs of any kind, one of my roommates and fellow band member, decided to deprive us of his company and committed suicide. I couldn't have been happier. After three lonely, miserable, unsuccessful years in Hollywood, I finally had a good excuse to give up.

I was done.

I called my mother and told her I wanted to come back home.

"Sure you can come home for a week or two if you need to get out of L.A. for a bit," she said.

Frustrated, I told her, "I don't think you understand me, Mom. I want to move back home, *to New Hampshire*. I've fucking had it with this place!"

After a slight pause my mom said, "Why? Is it because of what happened? Because if that's the case, I got news for you: the same thing could happen here. That's life; you deal with it and move on. Here or there, life happens and you have to deal with it."

"It's a combination of things, Mom."

"Money, do you need money?"

"I'm barely getting by; my job doesn't pay enough to live out here. I don't know what I'm going to do."

"I'll loan you money, whatever it takes to keep you there."

I hesitated for a moment thinking about what my mother just said, then I asked her, "It sounds like you don't want me home?"

I'll never forget her response. "It's not that we don't want you home. There's nothing we would want more than to have you here. I just know you'd be miserable. And I would rather not have to go through seeing you so sad every day, moping around. Everything you've worked so hard for is out there. You belong out there and we'll do whatever it takes to keep you there. I tell you this only because we do love you so much."

So I stayed.

I wanted to stay true to myself and who I am. I never felt it directly, but there was always this pressure in the air to conform and be "trendy", to be "Hollywood." You have to wear the right shoes, drive the right car or as one of my friends and fellow L.A. transplants put it, "We live in California; we HAVE to live at the beach." I watched friends I moved out here with change and conform and succeed. Was their success due to their becoming prisoners to the pressures they felt from this town? There's no way to tell. Putting up airs and façades is not my thing but I figured I'd give it a shot, if it worked for them, why not me?

I hated myself.

I hated who I was and felt out of place.

I have a powerful creative side but an equally powerful practical side and they are always at war especially when I'm broke. I can't afford to fit in here.

I started to look for a second job. A friend and fellow comedian-lunatic, Stan, called and said he had a job opportunity for me and I should come over to his place to talk about it. Having no other prospects and being very desperate I went over.

"You want me to be Barney? As in Barney the dinosaur?"

"We don't use *that* word in our profession, it could get us sued. We refer to him as a '*purple dino type*.' Now let's work on some balloon animals."

Stan had asked me a year-and-a-half earlier if I wanted to "perform" at children's birthday parties. He was trying to appeal to my inner actor, since any chance to perform and get paid for it is a good thing to my kind. I had met Stan while doing dinner theatre, something I truly despise. He on the other hand loves it, that's why I took his first invitation to do kids' parties with a grain of salt. Times change and like I said I was desperate for work.

Stan went over some of the basic balloon animals I should know, such as a dog, a cat, and a horse. He also showed me how to make a hat, a sword, and glasses.

"You want me to dress up pretty for money? Sounds like you want me to be a whore?"

"So you'll do it?" Stan asked.

"Sure. It'll be a giggle."

"Ok, so I forgot to tell you one thing."

"What?" I asked, not knowing what to expect. This was Stan, after all, and anything was possible.

"My bosses want to meet you."

"I thought you were the boss?"

"I'm doing this party through another company and when I told them I had someone that could cover my shift, they balked a little bit and told me they *had* to meet this person before they would ok it. They just don't want a stranger representing their company. You understand, right?"

"Fuck it. Let's go, take me to my pimp." I needed the money.

It was pouring rain outside so we did rock, paper, scissors, to see who would drive over to his bosses' house. Come on, good old reliable rock!

As I was driving us over to Stan's bosses' house he informed me he lied to them about me.

"What did you tell them?" I asked.

"Well, I kind of told them you've been doing parties for a few years now. But it's ok, they'll never know. That's why I wanted to show you all the stuff at my house before we went to meet them. That way you'll kind of know what you're talking about. It'll be fine, they'll never know."

Finding the house was easy; it was the one with the big party going on. We had to park far away and trudge through the monsoon to the front door. Stan walked right in without knocking.

"They wouldn't be able to hear the knock anyway," he said, justifying his actions.

Stan introduced me to his bosses who were also his friends, Nick and Rachel. I had not shaven in over a month and I was pretty beat emotionally over my roommate's recent suicide. Let's just say I did not look my best and wasn't my usual jovial self.

Stan and I chatted with them a bit about the weather and other trivial things. Everything was going according to Stan's evil plan, that was until Nick asked me something I didn't know and Stan didn't prep me on.

"So what parachute games do you play?"

I had no idea what the hell he was talking about and I'm positive the blank expression on my bearded, weathered face showed it. My cunning improv skills kicked in to save me.

"Which ones do you like?" I asked him, hoping to get the heat off of me. It didn't work.

Nick went on to say, "Oh, you know, the regular games."

Damn him, putting it back onto me! He must have also taken improv classes. It was so painfully evident I had no clue what he was talking about that it was even killing me. I wanted to throw my hands up, call it a day, and say, "You got me. I have no fucking clue what the fuck I'm talking about! Thanks for playing."

Like I said, Nick knew I had never done a party before and now, not only was he messing with Stan, he was messing with me as well. He was like a cat and I was the prey he was batting around before he would put me out of my misery and kill me. But the killing blow never came. By this time, I was having second thoughts about the whole thing. I came up with an idea: I'll talk about something I do know.

"I make balloon animals."

"Really? Before or after you do the parachute?"

Son-of-a-bitch! Now he's just being cruel. Rachel came over to us and told Nick he had to go do something host-like. I like to think that in one way or another she felt bad for me and was trying to save me from the interrogation. Nick started to walk away from Stan and me to go do his wife's bidding. A few steps away he turned around, looked back at me, and said, "Have fun at the party tomorrow."

Stan was so excited. We pulled it off and got the blessing from the "godfather" himself. Stan didn't want to act suspicious so we stayed at the party for a few hours.

"Well, we should be going. Jason's got an early party to do tomorrow," Stan announced to Nick and Rachel as we were leaving. We thanked them for having us over to the party and we left. The rain was still coming down in buckets.

On the walk back to the car Stan patted me on the back and said, "Congratulations on a job in deception well done! You are officially going to be a children's entertainer starting tomorrow. How do you feel?"

"Wet."

I personally wouldn't go as far as to call it a successful meeting but it was done and over with. I wanted to be upfront and honest with them about everything from the beginning. I wasn't in the mood to lie. It's a kid's birthday party, not espionage. Stan expressed to me he thought they knew he was lying and suspected they were trying to catch him in a lie, by letting him refer someone they knew had no experience, in the hopes he wouldn't bail on a party for them ever again. This whole thing was very last-minute and suspect.

Did I mention I was desperate?

Back at Stan's place he showed me what the "parachute" was.

"OHHHH, one of those," I said with recognition.

It literally was a parachute, except instead of being army green it was rainbow colored, very child friendly. Stan got high and sang Billy Joel and Rolling Stone songs. And why not? He wasn't working the next day. In between songs and bong hits he showed me a game or two I could do with the parachute at the party.

I practiced some of my balloon animals. Stan looked up

occasionally from his bong to make sure I was doing them right. By this time it was around two o'clock in the morning. I was exhausted and Stan was higher than a kite. Stan double-checked my bag to make sure I had everything I needed and thanked me once again for "saving his ass." He could tell I was worried about doing a good job so to make me feel better he put the party in perspective for me.

"Doing parties is a great way to hone your acting and improv skills. You never know what's going to be thrown at you. You're an actor. Act like Barney."

"That's Mr. Purple Dino Type to you."

I was feeling the same way I do before any performance. Nervous. Why was I nervous? They're just kids! What's the worst thing that can happen?

I walked down the stairs with no idea what the adventure I was embarking on had in store for me—or that it would last the next several years and forever change my life.

I looked at the big Purple Dino head staring back at me in the passenger seat of my car. *Am I really going to be you tomorrow? In essence I'm now a professional clown. How the hell did I get here? Oh, that's right, desperation. Who knows, maybe it'll just be a one-time thing?*

Before tonight, my only knowledge of Barney came from my nephew Zachary. Oh, how I hated that Purple Dino! Believe me, the irony of all this is not lost on me. I knew Zach would be looking down on me tomorrow, smiling and laughing, getting a kick out of his Uncle Jay dancing around as Barney; spreading the love so many other three-year-olds have for that damn dino. I would give anything to have been Barney for him at least once.

His obituary read, "He loved music, books and Barney."

Chapter 3

The Church Of Satan

"Did I wake you?" Not waiting for an answer, Nick continued. He was a man on a mission. "Hey, Jay, are you available to do a party with us today? I'm sure you can use the money." He sensed me pausing and continued, "It's for the Spielbergs."

"Sure, when is it?" I'm a whore for cash, plus it would be awesome to meet THE Steven Spielberg.

Nick started to give me some of the details, but I had been working for him and his wife, Rachel, long enough to know that when all is said and done the plan will be to meet at their place. It always is. Predictable people they are.

"Cool, Jay, we'll call you later with all the details." CLICK.

He just hung up. No goodbye or nothing. Nick is his wife's little bitch. I'm sure she was riding his ass to just get the character they needed covered and worry about the details later. The party is for THE SPIELBERGS, after all.

I looked down at my half-full cup of coffee.

I wish I had milk.

It was during these lean times I learned to appreciate the simplicities of black coffee. Now, on to my next dilemma—telling my out-of-town guest I had to work that day.

I felt bad. She was my only friend from high school to ever visit me since moving to Los Angeles. I've had a lot of friends *say* they were going to come out to visit but they never made it. These promises were usually made in the midst of a drunken stupor.

Theirs, not mine, when they were feeling adventurous. I've had so many of them tell me, "You were so lucky to get out of 'cow' Hampshire." Luck had nothing to do with it. I got in my car, started it, and drove west. Easy.

Oddly enough, my visitor was my ex-girlfriend from high school, Sara. She was very understanding and excited for me.

"No prob, Jay. I know how bad you want to do this particular party. I'm flexible, in more ways than one. Hee hee, but you know that already."

It was also a bonus for me Sara didn't mind her coffee black. *Man, I have to go shopping!*

We altered our scheduled sightseeing for the day. She got in her bikini, which my other four male roommates enjoyed, and laid out in the sun, while I sat around waiting for "the call."

Well, the call never came.

I left messages for both my bosses at their home and on their cell phones. I was so pissed off they never called me. Not so much because it was a party for the Spielbergs and I was looking forward to doing it, but because I had a guest in town and she had to take a day of her vacation waiting around for me to hear from them.

They finally called me the next day to say things got crazy and they ended up doing the party with just the two of them. *Thanks for the heads up!*

Even after their lame-ass excuse of an explanation, it still bothered me they didn't call to inform me of their plans; just common courtesy, if nothing else. I don't get it; at times they can be extremely generous and other times they act selfishly without any consideration for others. At that time, I hadn't known them for long, but I grew to learn that was just a part of who they are. We can't change our friends; we just have to accept them for who they are. If we can't do that, they shouldn't be our friends anymore, but be demoted to "acquaintances." I felt indebted to them for giving me a chance during a dark time in my life so I allowed them to continue wiping their feet on me. To their credit, they did feed me regularly, thanks to Nick not liking leftovers. How can you not like leftovers? That's crazy!

I didn't mind the extra time with Sara; we discovered our feelings for one another were still there and toyed around with the idea of getting back together. Not an easy task since she now had a three-year-old son. She knew I wasn't going to leave L.A. and she'd have to move out here.

I dropped her off at the airport before heading off to a Barney gig I had at a church. We said our goodbyes and promised to further discuss the possibility of continuing our relationship.

I haven't been a fan of churches since I was a child. After my parents divorce, I lived with my father who found solace in becoming a born-again Christian and getting in good with the pastor and his family. One day after a service we were invited to stay and have dinner with the pastor's family, all ten of them. While my Dad hung out with the pastor and his wife, I played with the kids outside. One of the older boys had a sword and I asked if I could hold it. I took it in my hands, it was heavy and slightly rusted. I'm not sure why, other than I was an eight-year-old boy, but I placed it by my crotch, pointed it upward and said, "Look I have a sword dick!"

They all gasped and had looks of shock on their faces. I thought they were going to drop to their knees and pray for my forgiveness from God. The older boy immediately took the sword from my hands and said something to the tune of how I desecrated it. After that they all became mean to me, calling me names, excluding me and making fun of my "dirty" appearance. I was so hurt by this that the moment my Dad gave me the decision to go with him to church or stay home, I always stayed home. In my little mind, between my parents splitting up and how cruel those kids were, it was obvious to me that if there was a God, he hated me and I had no place in his house of worship.

Today will be my first time back in a church, other than for a wedding or funeral, and I was not looking forward to it.

I arrived early, as I always try to, and asked around for my contact person. I stood there waiting and looked around at the goings-on. They had game booths, an arts and crafts table, and donkey rides for the kids. The adults had the option to play bingo (a church favorite no matter where you live), a dunk tank, and ME, to babysit their kids for an hour. You're welcome.

I just need to find a spot to do my show when the time comes. *That spot over there looks good. I can make that work. Centrally located for easy adult and shy children viewing, without being too much in the way.*

"Hello, I was told you were looking for me. I'm the pastor here, how can I help you?"

"I'm your entertainer for today."

"You're our Barney? The kids are going to be so excited. They have no idea you are coming today. You're a surprise for Jacob, who's turning one."

"Is all this for him?"

"No, no, no. That's funny. We were having the event and the kids have been so well behaved lately we decided to surprise them with a little treat, and it just so happened that Jacob's birthday is today. So we figured, why not? Ya know."

"If there is anything special you want me to do, just let me know. I'll be right back."

"The kids are in the gymnasium awaiting their surprise visitor."

I told him I'd go to my truck to change and make a grand entrance.

"You're more than welcome to change in my office and it leads directly to the gymnasium. Would that be easier for you?"

The only thing to make this party easier for me so far would be if I gave the pastor my costume and he did the party.

I went to my truck, got my bag o' goodies and my costume, which luckily was in a big, black trash bag so if I was spotted by any children, they couldn't tell what I was carrying. I met up with the pastor and he showed me the way to his office. He led me to a door that opened to a hallway off of the gym. I could hear the children inside the gym yelling and screaming. We went though a few sets of doors before we came to an ascending staircase.

"It's right up here."

How appropriate, I thought to myself. "We must ascend ourselves to a higher place. His office." It just struck me as funny and gave me a chuckle. I take them when I can get them.

"Feel free to leave anything you want in here. The kids are ready when you are. Thanks again, this means more to them and us than you know."

I was left alone to change. I was so excited to see the pastor had a bathroom in his office. Before any performance, I always have to pee and sometimes poop. One time when I was doing sketch comedy we were doing a show without bathroom access and I had to shit like a madman. I grabbed an old box, threw some dirt in the bottom of it, found a nice private place backstage behind a curtain, and did my business. Gross? Maybe, but nature is one call you can't put on hold. We had a very important reviewer in the audience that night and I was very sick but as they say, "The show must go on!" And boy did it ever!

I'm glad I only had to pee; it would have been "unholy" of me to disrespect the pastor's shitter. Especially after all the kindness he had shown me. Once I was ready I descended upon my disciples.

I stopped once at the bottom of the stairs to turn on my boom box. That way I could enter the gymnasium at the exact moment when the lyrics of the song started.

Not yet, it's still the intro.

I could see though the gymnasium door window some of the kids could see me and were already running toward the door.

Almost there…and…NOW!

I opened the door just as the song started into its most famous lyrics among the two-year-old crowd.

"I love you, you love me…"

Giving the gym a quick once-over through my tiny eyehole, I was transported back to seventh grade gym class. This place IS what you think of when you hear the word "gym." It's got a small-town feel like the home court in *Hoosiers* or *Quantum Leap* when Dr. Samuel Beckett leaps into himself playing basketball in his tiny hometown school gym. It's a great episode. My mind wanders. Allow me to "leap" back to being a Purple Dino Type at a one-year-old's birthday party.

The parents as well as some of the children were sitting in chairs placed on the sides of the basketball court, as if they were going to watch a game. I started out by walking around and greeting the children. The kids sitting when I entered were not sitting for long. Before I knew it, I was in the middle of an ocean of screaming children. The sounds of the music emanating from my boom box had been dwarfed by the excitement of the children and the vastness of the gymnasium. I couldn't even hear it and it was in my hand! If I had to guess, I would say there were over fifty kids there, ranging from one to thirteen years old, and it was my job to entertain them all.

In a gymnasium.

In a Purple Dino Type costume.

Impossible?

Not for me, I would entertain them. That was my mission.

There were so many people at this party it was more of an event than a one-year-old's birthday party. Oh, that's right, it was an event first, a birthday party second.

The older kids started into me immediately. The song I entered to was still playing, and the song is only two-and-a-half minutes long. They're quick. They were all trying to pull my tail and not even taking turns. They were ALL trying to pull my tail at the same time. I was able to reach around and grab the tail and hold on to it myself. So, now I had my tail and boom box in one hand, and my bag o' tricks in another. My hands were full. I needed to drop something. The radio.

I was only ten feet away from the door where I had entered and noticed a few tables set up off to the side of me. I could see a P.A. system on one of the tables and figured that was as good a place as any to put my radio. We moved as a big blob of bodies toward the table. These kids had become part of me and they were not going to let their nucleus out of their sight or reach, even for a moment.

I was surprised no one, and by no one I mean any adult of the many to choose from in the room, was helping me. I could see a few adults out of my eyeholes but they were taking pictures, laughing, or just plain sitting.

Where did the pastor go? I thought to myself, trudging my way to a table to set my radio down. *Man, he bolted quickly!*

I set the radio down, stopped the music and yelled as loud as I could, asking the kids to help me get something out of my, as they called it, "Barney Bag." They were still surrounding me, screaming and yelling so loud no one could hear me. I couldn't get their attention verbally, so how about visually? I set down my bag and started to pull out the extremely large parachute I had in it. That got their attention.

A vast majority of the kids surrounding me seemed to be over seven years old, so we could play some cool games with the parachute. The idea of fun games gave me a glimmer of hope that I'd be able to get control of this party, get it back on track and give everyone the good time they didn't even know was possible. Lucky them.

The acoustics in a gym are not very conducive to regular ol' conversation and are near impossible from inside a big, hooded costume. I had to yell as loud as I could, and in my Purple Dino voice to boot. Yes, I am that dedicated to the façade. The kids had to put their faces right up against the mouth of my Purple Dino head to be able to hear me. They were so close I could smell their stank breath. *What have these kids been eating? Shit with a side of rotten corpse guts. WOW! Is that smell getting trapped in here as well? What the fuck? I hope I don't puke.*

I was able to communicate to one of the boys listening to my mesh-covered mouth and he yelled out to everyone what I wanted.

"BARNEY SAID FOR EVERYONE TO GRAB ON TO THE PARACHUTE!"

Thanks, kid.

I had to use my superior mime skills to communicate with these kids. I started to shake the parachute. They caught on to that one quick and followed my lead. They were shaking it very violently as if trying to inflict pain upon it. I stopped to see if they would stop. It took a few seconds longer than I wanted but they finally stopped. I kept doing this until I thought they finally caught on enough for me to let go while they were shaking it and go get the birthday boy, Jacob.

I found Jacob easily because I'm a professional and have trained myself how to spot the child of honor amongst a large crowd of children. It helped there were only a handful of kids who looked to be one-year-old. It didn't hurt he also had a red tee shirt on that said in big, yellow letters, "I'M THE BIRTHDAY BOY!" I started to escort Jacob and the young girl of twelve years old or so holding him to the parachute. I could see a very excited child running over to me followed by an adult I'm guessing is his mom. They came out of nowhere and now they were attached to my waist.

"I LOVE YOU, BARNEY!" The child's emotional outburst was followed by a big squeeze.

Man, this kid is strong! I thought to myself, gasping for air that still smelled of little kid breath.

All the other kids were laughing and pointing.

"Jimmy, let go of Barney so he can play. Jimmy. Jimmy," the woman said, trying to pry her Jimmy off of me.

"I LOVE YOU, BARNEY!"

I braced myself, and yes there it was—the squeeze. As his mom got him to let go I could see Jimmy has Down's syndrome. The mom was blushing and seemed mortified. I took Jimmy by the hand, led him over to the parachute and let him stand next to Jacob and I while we shook the parachute. We put Jacob in the middle of the parachute and sang *Happy Birthday* to him. I got into the middle and had them shake it so hard I would make myself fall. After a few seconds of lying down I would get back up and do it again. They liked that Purple Dino was falling and possibly hurting himself. Why do I think that? It was all in the way they laughed. I've done a lot of sketch comedy in my day; I know the difference between when the crowd is laughing with me from when they are laughing at me. Their laughter was more on the evil side than amused laughter.

I moved on to a game of parachute hide-and-go-seek by having some of the kids hide under the parachute, while the rest of us would lift it up and bring it back down. Easy enough. Or so I thought. While some of the younger kids were under the parachute, a bunch of the older kids surprised me and tackled me. This is very easy to do, since the Purple Dino Type head has zero peripheral vision. I tried not to fall down, as this was clearly their goal. I was doing really well, until this one huge kid got a running headstart and slammed into me. I could see "ol' chubbo" gearing up like a bull to ram into me. I never stood a chance. The floor of the gymnasium was slick, too slick for me to be able to stand my ground. I struggled to get free and got turned around.

My back jerked as I was hit and I was going down, HARD. My first instinct was not to put my hands out in front of me, like a normal person does when they are falling, but to hold my damn Purple Dino Type head on, so as not to traumatize these little monsters. My kindness came with a price. I came crashing down on the poor, little kids still under the parachute who had no idea of the ugliness that was going on above them outside of their multicolored draping. These innocent, little children who were, just seconds before, having a fun time with Purple Dino. Now he was squashing them. I'm sure they were traumatized. I can almost guarantee we'll be seeing them on *Dr. Phil* in ten years in need of therapy.

"I don't know what happened, Dr. Phil. One moment we were all laughing and the next…the next…the next all I could hear was screaming."

"It's ok, son. As part of your therapy we brought the man behind that costume here to the studio so you can tell him how he hurt you."

"He's here?"

"Yup, let's welcome Jason Lassen to our show." I enter to a hostile studio audience.

"BOOOOO!"

"HOW COULD YOU? YOU SUCK!"

"YOU LOOK LIKE YOU DRINK!"

"Calm down, people. So, son, what do you want to say to this man?"

"I...I...I..." Long thoughtful pause. "I FUCKING HATE YOU! YOU RUINED MY LIFE!"

"I'm sorry, I was blindsided and..."

"Now it's time for you to get yours." The boy gets dressed up in a Purple Dino costume and throws a rainbow parachute over me, leaps off a high dive and lands directly on me. He gets up, jumps up and down on me repeatedly, yelling, "I DON'T LOVE YOU! I GOT CANCER BECAUSE OF YOU!"

My screams for mercy are drowned out by the sound of the crowd's hunger for blood.

I whisper to myself, "I was ambushed. I do love you. Why?"

Like I said, my mind tends to wander at times. Back in reality... there were crying kids under me and laughing kids on top of me. I rolled off of the kids under me and got them out from under the parachute. The kids who had jumped me were a little disoriented from me yanking the parachute out from under their feet, and I was able to escape their clutches. It was so difficult getting up and holding on to my head at the same time. Once back on my feet, I looked around and the parents were not even concerned with what was going on. Did they *not* see what just happened?

I needed a second to collect my thoughts and to "speak" privately with the perpetrators who tackled me. Without saying anything (not that anyone would have heard me anyway), I sprinted as fast as I could, heading for a set of doors on the opposite side of the gym than I had entered from. They led outside to a courtyard where more classrooms were located. As I expected, the kids thought I was playing a game and some of them followed me. The nice Purple Dino Type voice went away and out came a deep, angry voice.

"Listen up, you little fucking bastards! Lay THE FUCK off me. I'm trying to do my fucking job! I don't come to your classroom and kick and hit you while you're trying to do your schoolwork, do I?" is what I wanted to say, but it came out more like, "You need to be nice to me. If you're not nice to me I'm going to leave."

Surprisingly, this seemed to not really have the effect on the children I was hoping for. The leader of this pack of dreadful children spoke.

"We're not going to be nice to you until you take off your head and tell us who you are."

Tell you who I am? They must think I'm someone from the church dressed up as a Purple Dino Type. Which, if you ask me, makes their behavior even more inexcusable. What kind of satanic church is this?

While the leader was distracting me, one of his cronies snuck up behind me and tried to unzip my costume. I turned around to deal with him only to find it was a *her*. What happened to sugar and spice and everything nice, bitch?

"Hey! What are you doing?" I shouted.

She just smiled and said nothing. I felt this little hand by my neck, and without thinking or looking I just raised my right hand and grabbed me a little wrist.

"Hey now, there will be none of that," I told them.

Another kid was actually holding up the kid whose wrist I had because he was too short to reach the bottom of the head of the costume. They were evolving. Stacking themselves for the attack like African fire ants attacking a water buffalo. They just kept coming from all around me. Now all the kids were making their way outside. It was worse out here than inside. At least if I'm killed inside someone will find me eventually. Out here, my assailants might drag me off to where they do Purple Dino Type sacrifices and my lifeless magenta body may never be found. I bumped a few of Satan's spawn as I made my way back inside. Not by accident either, I may add.

I went over to the parachute to put it away. As I was gathering it, the older kids made their way back inside and several were now pulling on my tail. This costume was not meant to handle that kind of punishment. I kept picturing the tail ripping off, leaving a huge hole in the back of the costume, and exposing my white, hairy ass. *Damn, I should've worn underwear today.* I got an idea. I let myself fall backwards. I might have felt bad if it was only one kid on the receiving end of two hundred twenty-pounds, but my weight was being distributed between several of them, like when a sideshow freak lays down on a bed of nails. That worked out to be about thirty pounds per child. They could handle it. Boy, were they ever surprised!

"Oopsie daisy, Barney fell." Ha, ha, ha, ha.

Now I was having fun.

Actually I wasn't. All right, I was having a little bit of fun falling on them, but a very little bit. I hated to do it, just to teach them a lesson, but it had to be done. No one else was doing anything. I thought parents were supposed to get "paternal" and protective of their kids when they saw their offspring getting fallen on. Nothing. I wanted to run over to one of the adults, shake the hell out of them, and check for a pulse.

I got myself up and told them again, "If you are not going to be nice to me, I AM GOING TO LEAVE!"

"We don't care! Just show us who you are!"

What is their obsession with knowing who I am? I looked around and once again the parents weren't doing anything. Fuck it. I'm leaving then. Obviously I'm the only one that gives two shits that I'm here.

"Bye, kids."

I'm a firm believer in not making empty threats. If you say you're going to do something, fucking do it. Kids know when you're bullshitting them. I don't play that game. I picked up my parachute and just carried it to get my "Barney Bag." They tried to pull my parachute away, but Purple Dino Type pulled a little harder than they did. I had to pull out "Man Strength" on them. Man Strength is commonly known among children performers as a last resort when all else fails. You stop being gentle and use your regular strength at 60-80% to let the kids know you are serious. It's usually reserved for early teens or adults that are a pain in the ass. These kids were in a large group so in my opinion, they could handle Man Strength.

I went back up to the pastor's office and locked the door behind me. Once inside, I took the Purple Dino Type hood off and shook my head in disbelief. The kids were outside the door banging on it and yelling.

"COME OUT AND SHOW US YOUR FACE!"

I looked at the clock. Twenty minutes had gone by since I started the party. I was scheduled to be there for another forty minutes.

"COME OUT AND SHOW US YOUR FACE!" they demanded.

I was not going back out there. At that point it became a battle of wills. I was not going to let them see my face, no matter what it took. I was just waiting for them to leave so I could do the same. The banging on the door got louder due to them now kicking it.

"COME OUT AND SHOW US YOUR FACE!"

Where were these kids' parents? I started to get out of my costume so when the coast was clear I could make a clean, quick escape.

Then there was silence.

It was an eerie silence, like the calm before the storm.

I heard an adult voice but couldn't make out what it was saying. It sounded like the adults in a *Peanuts* cartoon. "Whaa Whaa Whaa. Wa. Wha Wa Wha Wa."

About time, I thought to myself.

"Children, what's going on here?" the voice asked, close enough to the locked door for me to clearly make out what was being said.

The kids all talked over one another, spouting off lies I'm sure, but I could clearly hear one say, "Barney's locked himself in your office and won't come out and play with us."

"Children, go downstairs while I talk to Barney. Now, please. Thank you."

The doorknob jiggled and I heard a voice say, "Barney, are you in there? Open up. It's me, Pastor Myers."

I put my Purple Dino Type head back on, as I WAS NOT going to let any child see my face. This was war. I unlocked the door and let the pastor in. I closed and locked it behind him, and took off my head again. He asked me what was wrong. I told him everything.

"They have been horrible, horrible children. They knocked me over and I fell on a bunch of the younger kids. I'm a big dude, Pastor, I can hurt someone. They keep pulling my tail, and they are obsessed with getting my head off and seeing my face. They think I'm someone from the church. Would someone from the church put up with this? Because I'm not going to." Boy, I was fired up!

"Ok, I understand," he said, putting a hand on my shoulder. "You have to understand where these children are coming from."

From hell, I thought to myself.

Pastor Myers continued, "Most of them are orphans."

Great. Just great. Now I feel bad for these little bastards. But aren't orphans supposed to be grateful, well-behaved children? You know, like in *Oliver Twist.*

"Other children here today live with their grandparents and they're the ones who brought them. It's not easy for the elderly to become parents all over again. So they bring them here and just let them go and play to give themselves a break."

Play havoc on Purple Dino Type is what they're doing.

"What can I do to help?" Pastor Myers asked.

I calmed myself down and thought about it for a second. "They can't hear me. I think if they could hear me that might help."

"Ok. We can arrange to get a P.A. system set up for you. It's the one we use for bingo on Wednesday nights. Anything else?"

"I'll go down and talk to them a little bit, then I'm just going to sit and do balloon animals. No more games." I was all business. Am I doing a children's party at a church or selling real estate in Manhattan?

"Thank you very much. The church and Jesus appreciate your understanding."

Ya, ya, ya, understanding, understanding. Where was Jesus when these kids were beating on me? Off to the side laughing?

He continued, "I'll go down and get the system hooked up for you. I'll send someone for you when it's set up. In the meantime, why don't you finish your water? Thank you again."

As he turned to leave, I put my Purple Dino Type head back on just in case there were any stragglers hoping to get a peek at who was in the Purple Dino Type costume. He left and I locked the door behind him. If I said I wasn't thinking about leaving, I would be lying. Oh yeah, I thought about it. The coast was clear; I was already out of costume. I could just leave.

While getting redressed in my sweaty costume, I heard the pastor talking over the P.A. system. "Testing, one, two, three. One, two, three. Can you hear me ok in the back, Ethel? Good."

I hoped his Jedi mind tricks worked on the kids as well as they worked on me. There was a civilized knock on the door.

"Yes?" I replied questionably, in case it was one of the kids trying to trick me with their sneakiness.

"We're ready for you now."

The voice sounded friendly. I put my head on and opened the door slowly and cautiously. There was a nice lady standing there.

"Are you ready?" she asked.

In my Purple Dino Type voice I enthusiastically said, "I sure am. Can Barney ask you for a favor?"

"Sure," she said as she took my hand.

"Can you stay with Barney while he makes balloon animals and keep an eye out for kids trying to pull my tail?"

She laughed, "Of course I can."

I liked her. She helped me get down the stairs and led me back into the gymnasium where all the kids were sitting on the floor in front of the eight-foot folding table on which the P.A. system was now sitting.

"Let's hear it for Barney, kids," Pastor Myers said over the P.A. system as if introducing the host of a game show.

He handed me the microphone and a five-dollar bill. I put the microphone up to the Purple Dino Type mouth and started to talk.

"Hey, kids! Do you know why we're here today? Because it's Jacob's birthday! On the count of three let's all sing *Happy Birthday* to Jacob."

After we sang, I told the kids I was going to make balloon animals and everyone was going to get just one, but they needed to line up and be well behaved. I played Purple Dino Type music though my boom box and put the microphone by the speaker so it could be heard in the whole gymnasium.

I did as I said. I just made balloon animals. After a while the line became nonexistent and they were swarming me again. At least this time I had my helper and she kept the wolves at bay. I did have kids coming up and asking me for another balloon.

"I already made you a balloon."

"That one was for my baby brother. I want a sword."

For the love of God!

Whatever.

There were so many kids I ended up staying a half-hour extra. I was at the party for an hour-and-a-half, and spent an hour on just balloon animals alone. It was like they were now busing kids in just for balloon animals.

I couldn't believe I was done. I didn't even say goodbye; I just picked up my stuff, waved, and left. One of the kids followed me to my truck. I put my bag inside, turned around, and addressed him using my normal voice.

"What?"

"Nothin'," he said with a little bit of attitude.

"Will you leave me alone so I can go home?"

He just smiled and slowly backed up. I was waiting for him to retreat completely so he wouldn't be able to see me with the head off. He stopped and just stood there.

I waited.

He smiled.

I waited.

He smiled.

FUCK THIS!

I jumped into my truck as Purple Dino Type, head and all. I put my face as close to the opening of the mouth on the head to have the best view. I was crammed in my truck, but I was in there. I drove away very slowly and carefully. I was basically driving blind. I drove out of the parking lot and pulled over to the side of the road behind a tree line. I got out and quickly took off the Purple Dino Type head and body. Still in my sweaty clothes, I snuck a peek around the corner of the trees and saw the kid had left. He never saw what I looked like under the Purple Dino Type head. None of them ever saw me.

HA! I WIN! I may not have had fun at the party but I WON. SUCK IT, ORPHANS!

I returned home to a message on my answering machine from Sara. She had thought about what we talked about but couldn't relocate her whole life to L.A. She couldn't get over how much she still loves me but she just couldn't do it. If she didn't have her son she said she would pack and be out in a heartbeat. But she is a mom, a good mom, and must do what's best for him.

I'm offically back in the Los Angeles dating pool. I fucking hate the pretentious dating scene in this town! It was nice sharing feelings of love while Sara was here. This day only confirms what I learned as a child; if there is a God, he really does hate me!

Chapter 4

Worst Party Ever

I'm a grown man and I love cartoons, there I said it. Here it is the mid-1990s and it isn't *cool* to admit you like to watch cartoons as an adult. I feel like I'm part of some secret society that has to watch my cartoons behind a shroud of shame. My trifecta of Saturday morning entertainment included the deadly 90-minute lineup of *Spider-Man*, *The Tick* and *The X-Men*. My cartoon viewing helped me with research for my interactions with kids. It's just one of the perks of the job; who knew my pleasure in watching cartoons would ever come in handy? Not all performers share my enthusiasm for knowledge of the latest trends in children's entertainment. There are people doing parties that never do any research on the characters they portray every weekend.

"Did you watch the movie, JJ?" my boss, Rachel, would ask before we did a gig together.

"Ah, yah. Twice."

"You're so good that way. I was going to but things just got too *crazyyyyyyzeee* at the office last night."

Let me guess, one of your mooching friends came over with some senseless self-made drama you had to discuss over many cigarettes and a few bottles of wine.

"Brookie came over just as I was putting the movie in…"

Can I call it or what? When she finished telling me all the nonsense she'd ask me, "So give me the cliff-note summary of my character."

I enjoy learning all the info on the characters I'm playing or going to be working with, it's just my way. And yes, I have watched the Purple Dino's show, in case you were wondering. I liked it. Believe me, there is much worse kids' programming out there.

I was slightly distracted this morning because I had a "date." My friend Jessie was joining me in my Saturday morning cartoon-viewing ritual. It wasn't a real date; everyone just felt the need to pick on us about watching cartoons together. Unbeknownst to all our friends, we had kissed one night but she decided a few days later our friendship was worth too much to her to lose if things didn't work out.

"We can just have sex if you want?" I told her.

She laughed. "I'm still a virgin, silly boy. I'm waiting until I get married. Don't tell anyone."

"Yah, I think it's best we just be friends. Let me know how that whole 'waiting until I get married' thing works out for you." She's a nice girl but not nice enough for that type of commitment, and I'm not one to buy a car without taking it for a test-drive first.

She came over with donuts, bagels, and croissants. Yum! She made sure to bring enough for my four roommates as well. That was nice of her. I had warned her there was to be no talking during the shows but we could chat all we wanted during the commercials. To her credit, she was well behaved.

I lost track of time and was in a hurry to get out the door and off to work. I had two parties that day, first a Purple Dino Type, and then a Sovereign Lion Type. Another fun-filled day in the blazing July sun of Southern California.

"Fuck!"

I looked all over and it was nowhere to be found.

"I can't believe I forgot my radio. Damn distracting cartoons and virgin!"

I hate forgetting my radio. It's like forgetting to wear pants to a corporate meeting. I love entering a party to music. In my opinion, there is no other way to enter a kids' birthday party. It helps set the tone of my time at the party. "Well, this is going to suck." I picked my head up the best I could and went to the party.

As soon as I entered the party, a boy around eight or nine years old became my assistant, and helped me for the whole party. Both the kids and the adults were into it and everyone was very nice.

I got a plate of food, a beer, and a $10 tip, and I didn't even have my secret weapon with me—my music. I left the party and needed to find a place to eat. It was between eating in the parking lot of a high school or church. I chose the high school. I had two hours to kill until my next party.

The first party went well without music; there is no reason why the second one can't go the same way, right?

I did my usual: found the house where the party was and parked a mile or so away to change into my costume and to prepare, both mentally and physically. I changed into the Sovereign Lion Type costume, arranged the stuff in my bag, and waited until the time grew near to start the party.

The house with the party was on the very end of the cul-de-sac and I had to park in a weird way, parallel to the end of the street. *I hope I don't get blocked in. I'm only here for an hour. I'm sure I'll be fine.*

From the cab of my truck I could see a few older kids running around behind the chain-link fence that surrounded the front yard. I waited for them to run down the driveway toward the backyard before I made my move from weird guy sitting in a truck in a brown fur suit to full-on Sovereign Lion Type, entertainer extraordinaire. When my moment came, I opened the door to my truck, ducked down behind it, and slipped the Sovereign Lion Type head on. I popped my now-hooded head up to see whether anyone had noticed me.

Nope. Excellent!

I grabbed my bag from the back of my truck, sans radio, and headed toward the front gate. I could hear loud rap music coming from the backyard. *Guess it's ok I didn't bring The Lion King* soundtrack to enter to. Nothing says, "It's a two-year-old's birthday party" quite like Snoop Doggy Dogg's Gin and Juice.

One of the "adults" noticed me first. I say, "adults" because no one I could see looked to be older than 21.

"Hey, louk, evry'body, Simba's 'ere!" Her enthusiasm sank slightly as she continued. "I think it's suppose-ta be Simba?"

The kids came a runnin' the moment they saw me. I was still in the paved driveway sandwiched between the white house with paint chipping off it and a cinder block wall that looked to go back and surround the property. The kids surrounded me and I could feel their little fingers poking me, as if testing to see whether I was real.

"Are we gonna get presents?" one little boy asked.

"He's not Santa, stupid!" another boy, around eight years old, said. Then, to get his point across, he smacked the other boy upside the head.

"It's not nice to hit," I said, in an attempt to discipline the youngster.

"Fuck you, Simba! You're lucky I don't hit you."

What was that?

I was shocked. That was not a response I was expecting, especially from an eight-year-old boy. I looked around to see whether any of the "adults" heard what I just heard. Nope, everyone was distracted by me, "Simba." I was led down the driveway, by the girl who greeted me, to meet the birthday boy. As I rounded the corner I could see they also had a moonbounce and a DJ in the corner spinning the tunes.

Is that N.W.A.'s Fuck tha Police I hear now? The two-year-old birthday boy must be into classic rap. Oh, boy! The parents all looked to be between the ages of sixteen and twenty-four, were drinking, and not one of them could give two shits about me. I liked to see parents actually be a little more involved with their child's birthday, especially when it was for a baby. Maybe I should've hung a fifth of Jack Daniel's around my neck to get their attention?

The situation does not look good for this Sovereign Lion Type. As always I'm keeping an open mind and not going to "judge a book by its cover." I'm not knocking teenage parenthood; I know a lot of people who became parents as teenagers. I call some of those people family. The only reason I think it's worth mentioning is because their "life" inexperience was really shining through, to me at least. It was kids making decisions for kids.

The meeting with the birthday boy was very uneventful. He had no interest in me whatsoever. If he could've worked one up, I'm sure he would've puked on me. From my quick observation, he was only one among a handful of children that were two years old and under at the party. My best guess was that most of the kids at this party were from four to ten years old, and there were also a few older kids. Oh wait, those are the parents! My bad. The older kids and the young parents kind of blended together. The only way I could tell them apart was that the "kids" were sneaking beers and the "parents" were drinking freely in the open.

After my brief, non-eventful meeting with the birthday boy, I asked the boy's teenage mother where I should play with the children.

"Ummmmm?"

She was so confused; you would think I had just asked her a question regarding quantum physics. Lucky for her, one of the older and wiser mothers answered for her.

"Isn't it your job to figure that out, man?! What we paying you fo'? Just keeps them outs of our way! Shieeeeet, fuckin' Simba."

"Thank you. I'll do that. It's the least I could do for all the kindness you've shown me."

"Wha' you say?"

"How about over there?" It was more of a rhetorical question for the polite interpreter to the birthday boy's mom. *I can already tell this is going to be a long hour. Hopefully I can distance myself from the idiocy of the parents and only deal with the children without children.*

I had no idea where I was going to do my show; I just needed to get away from the "adults." I looked around the property and saw the gray cinder block wall did indeed go around the entire property. Between the cinder block wall and the chain-link fence in the front it gave the house a cozy prison feel. I found a nice shaded area, under a tree next to the moonbounce. While I knelt down to get something out of my bag, this four-year-old boy grabbed the Simba mouth of my costume, put his dirty little hand in it, and began to hit me in the face. I thought about biting him, but then again, I had no idea where that little hand had been. So, I politely asked him to stop. He just laughed and continued to hit me. One of the older boys finally spoke up.

"Leave Simba alone, Ramon. He can't play games with you sticking your hand in his mouth."

The hand was removed from the mouth of my costume. I decided this was an opportunity for me to recruit some help.

"Thank you, young man, for that act of kindness. I'm going to reward you with a surprise when I leave. I need some help today, would you like to be my assistant?"

The boy was instantly nicer to me while the other kids became instantly worse, worse with jealousy. My idea had backfired. It was all the older kids, the ones who were eight to fourteen years old, that came over to play games. The younger ones were afraid of me and stayed away. I thought I could get them over to me with the parachute. This is a good ploy because that way they can be with me playing but don't have to be next to me. The older kids were not into helping me in any way, shape, or form and expressed their opinions very openly about it.

"Simba, this sucks! YOU SUCK!"

I politely told them they didn't have to play if they didn't want to.

One boy's reply was, "You're a cunt!"

Another kid added, "A cunt's a part of a female that you fuck, fucker!"

Where were the parents?

Oh yes, drinking. And now I know why they were off getting hammered.

Who was this party for, the kids or the underage adults drinking?

58

I didn't give up on trying to restore order to this party and to the children. Normally, with younger kids I put fun little colorful balls in the parachute and bounce them around, simple, yet very fun. Since the only kids playing with me were older boys I figured I would try something they may like, basketballs. I asked, to no one in particular, to get me the two basketballs I saw lying on the ground next to the moonbounce.

They were wedged between the moonbounce and the ground like someone kicked them at the moonbounce expecting them to bounce but had unexpected results and were too lazy to retrieve them, and moved on to other mischief. To my pleasant surprise, all five of the boys holding the parachute let go of it and ran to fulfill my request. In true boy fashion they made it a game, a very rough game that included hitting, swearing, and kicking one another.

"Hey, hey, hey! Don't do that." I let go of the parachute myself and ran over to the boys. I was too late. One little boy around five years old, the youngest playing with us, was crying and worse, bleeding.

"What happened?" I asked him. My question only made him more upset and he cried even louder. I turned and asked a boy that looked very suspicious, "Do you know what happened?"

"Why the fuck would I know what happened? Are you saying I hit him?"

"Are you saying you hit him?"

"I didn't do nothin'. He ran into me."

The boy crying paused long enough to say to the boy with one of the balls, "I HATE YOU! I'M TELLING MOM!" and ran off toward the house.

"IF YOU DO I'LL KILL YOU!"

Wow, all this because I asked them to get me two basketballs. And I lost my youngest player. I rallied the other four boys that were playing and returned to the parachute. They fought over "who" was going to carry the balls the whole way. I tried putting the two basketballs in the parachute to bounce around, but they were heavy and hard to get to bounce that high. Very anti-climatic for all the trouble it was just getting the fucking balls.

"If one of those basketballs hits me I'm going to sue you, Simba," said a six-year-old boy.

I paid him no attention.

A few younger kids finally came over and I tried a few other parachute games but the older kids kept informing me they were bored.

"Simba, this is stupid. I'm bored."

"We have to play nice so the younger kids also want to play. It would be great if you older kids could help me out with that."

"Ok."

They lied. They were playing so rough with the parachute the younger kids would leave me and go back into the bounce. I decided it was time to try something else to get the younger kids back over to play; I pulled out a play tunnel for children.

"Hey, kids," I yelled over to the bounce. "Why don't you come over and play in the tunnel? It'll be fun."

They were not impressed.

I told the older kids they couldn't go through it. This did not make them happy.

"I'll tell you what," I told the older boy I had assigned to be my assistant, "If you help me get some of the younger kids over here to play, I'll let you guys play in the tunnel all you want. Ok?"

"Sure, Simba." And off he ran.

I watched in disbelief as he literally reached in the bounce and started yanking the younger kids out by the collars of their shirts. Although his method was a bit unorthodox, he did do as I asked; he got a few younger kids over to me.

I tried to get the younger kids to go through the tunnel but they refused until someone else went in first.

"We're scared," one told me.

This whole party is like pulling teeth! I am earning my money today, no doubt about it.

The six-year-old boy who had threatened to sue me earlier went in and wouldn't come out. In fact, he screamed to scare the younger kids so they wouldn't want to go into the tunnel. *This party just keeps going from bad to worse.*

I desperately wanted to leave. Why didn't I? I'm a dedicated employee no matter what job I'm doing, that's why. So I stay in torment. I took a few deep breaths then addressed the child in the tunnel.

"Excuse me, can you *please* come out?"

"I'm a monster, aarrrrggh!"

"Monsters go through the tunnel. They don't stop in the middle of it."

"I'm stuck."

For the love of God! Really? This kid is killing me. I think this was my official breaking point. Enter Man Strength.

I said nothing as I put my hand in the tunnel, grabbed him by the hand and yanked him out. I looked down at the boy while he lay on the ground looking up at me with fear in his eyes. I think he finally realized I *was* serious and I was a real person under this costume. A strong person to boot. All the other kids started laughing and pointing at him, even some of the kids in the bounce.

With a quiver in his voice he said, "I'm going to fucking sue you! You hear me…you FUCK!"

I replied, "I'm King of the Jungle. All you're gonna get from me is a tree. Anything special in mind? Maybe a nice birch." I realize birch trees don't exist in jungles but it was the first tree that came to mind. Thanks Robert Frost.

Now, not only was he scared, he was also confused. I could tell he wanted to cry, but was holding it in so the other kids wouldn't have more of a reason to laugh at him. He got up and tried to act cool in front of everyone.

"I didn't want to play stupid games anyways."

Good. Leave, I thought to myself.

He stomped off, most likely to cry alone in some dark corner.

"Can I try the tunnel?" a little boy around four or so asked.

"Sure."

"Can you pull me out like you did George?"

Is he serious?

"Please." He asked nicely, verging on sweet.

He is serious. Who knew yanking that kid out of the tunnel would make me more appealing to play with to this particular group of future inmates? If I had known this, I would've grabbed him as I entered the party and dragged him around a little bit. A few other kids wanted to play the same "game" of me pulling them out of the tunnel. Whatever, I didn't care. I needed to burn minutes before I could leave. They lost interest rather quickly, more quickly than I was hoping for.

It sucks not having my radio. There are some games I could've played to music; the hokey pokey, limbo or yank the kid out of the tunnel some more.

"Simba, why didn't Nala come with you?"

Excellent, the first little girl to come within ten feet of me. How exciting. If I can get her to play something maybe other little girls will join in?

"Well, Nala was not feeling well today. But she told me to tell you she says hello. Ok?"

"She's pretty."

"Yup, she sure is." Suddenly, I felt a sharp pain in my side, like I had been hit with something.

Something hard.

I turned and saw a baseball bat on the ground.

"I didn't do it, he did it," one boy said, pointing to another boy.

I felt another pain, different from the first pain sensation, this time on my other side. I swung around to see a basketball on the ground. I was pissed off. Once again, I wanted to leave. Now I was getting assaulted and the little girl I was talking to ran off screaming.

Calmly, I walked over to my bag, put the tunnel away, and looked at the time. *Shit. I still have 35 more minutes to go. Shit, shit, shit. And SHIT!*

After a deep sigh I decided to just make balloon animals for the rest of the party. With these brats, I hoped it would be the one thing I could do to get them to stop driving me nuts. I took all my things and moved to a table closer to the parents, hoping they would see how their kids were misbehaving and discipline them. Boy was I ever wrong! They were too busy playing drinking games to pay any attention to what the kids were doing. I just kept making balloons and giving them out while listening to the older kids whine, bitch, and complain.

"I want another balloon. Mine popped."

"I don't like this balloon. I want a different one."

"My cousin wants a balloon."

All the usual stuff I'm used to hearing.

"Why can't I have a balloon?" George asked, back from his secret cry.

"You're wasting yours and my time. I don't make balloons for kids who are mean to me."

"Fuck you, Simba! I didn't want a fucking balloon anyways." And he put his point home with a kick to my shins.

Little fucker. I wanted to kick him so hard in the ass he would fly over the bounce and into the neighbor's yard.

I turned my attention back to the good kids who were going to get balloons.

"What would you like? A doggie?"

"Ok." Pause. "A red one."

I went to grab a red balloon and my bag of balloons was missing. *They stole my bag of balloons. Will this party ever end?* I decided to pit the kids against one another and see how that worked out.

"To all the good kids waiting patiently for a balloon I want to say I'm sorry. I'm sorry I can't make any more balloons if my balloons are all gone."

In unison now, "Awwwww."

"If you help me get them back I'll be able to make them for you again. So the game is to find the balloons. Whoever does I'll give them TWO balloons."

"He did it!" a girl around ten spoke up very quickly, pointing to the thief. She wanted that yellow butterfly/green sword combo and she wanted it bad.

Well, well, look who took my balloons. The young man who I yanked out of the tunnel. No surprise there.

"Excuse me, little girl," I said to our whistleblower.

"It's Sally. And I'm not little. I'm ten."

"Very well then. Young lady, can I get you to go get my balloons from George?"

"Ok." She walked over to George, grabbed him by the shirt, and raised her fist. "Where did you put em', George? If you don't tell me I'm going to break your nose."

Once again getting a scared look in his eyes, he pulled the bag of balloons from under the back of his shirt and presented them to Sally. She took them and gave George a little shove to remind him who was bigger. Sally walked back over to me with my bag of balloons in hand.

"Here you go. I want a yellow butterfly and a green sword."

She was all business.

"Thank you, Sally. It'll be my pleasure to make you what you want because you were nice." Then I addressed all the kids that had gathered around me, "See what happens when you're nice?"

"Hey, Simba!"

I looked around to see who was yelling to me.

"Simba, I'm over here!"

I found him. One of the eight-year-old troublemakers who had been making my day at the office so difficult. He had the baseball bat that was used to hit me earlier in one hand and my bubble machine from my bag in the other.

"Simba, watch this!"

He threw my bubble machine up in the air, grabbed the bat firmly with both hands, and took a huge swing at it upon its descent.

SMASH!!

I watched as tiny pieces of my bubble machine went flying across the yard. A blue chunk of the body went one way, a yellow part of the nozzle went another, and the rest just rained down all over the place.

I yelled over to him, "Thank you, I was going to do that myself later on. You saved me the trouble. Thanks!" Without hesitation

I coolly went back to making balloons. I didn't want to give that little bastard the satisfaction of knowing he *really* pissed me off. What I wanted to do was go over, take the bat from him, throw him up in the air, and see how many pieces I could smash him into. I opted to make balloon animals instead.

When most performers make balloon animals they make the kids say some magic word to turn their gloved hands into people hands. Not me. I prefer to keep it magical, I'm the real deal to the children at all costs, even if it means doing balloon animals with gloves on. I became a pro and had many compliments from other performers for my commitment to the character, must be the method actor in me. Well, the tan gloves I had on my hands didn't fit me that well and part of my skin was showing. One of the older kids noticed this and made a point of announcing it to everyone.

"Hey look, it's not the real Simba. He's some white guy."

Because if there were a "real" Simba, he would be at this party. This kid used this against me. While I was making balloons for the younger kids he would tell them I wasn't the real Simba, I was just some white guy in a suit. A very hot suit, I might add.

While I was twisting a balloon into whatever, a kid stole my balloon pump. I looked at the time and saw it was finally time for me to depart. With this knowledge, I packed up my stuff and started to leave without saying anything to anyone about what I was doing. I figured it was worth it to get out of there and cut my losses. I could always buy another balloon pump and bubble machine.

"Where are you going, Simba?" a little girl asked.

"I'm all done. I'm leaving." I didn't even attempt to make it sound sweet in any way. Normally, if I was in a good mood and not on the verge of insanity, I would have made up some crap about how "Nala misses me" and "I have to get back to Zazu." Kids love that shit. It makes you—the character—seem more real to them, even if they saw your "white skin" from the small gloves your boss gave you, because your boss buys gloves that fit his feminine hands not the hands of a real man. I was not in a good mood. I knew it wasn't this little girl's fault, but I had just had it. I was DONE! What sucked even more was that I was still owed a balance on this party.

I went up to an "adult" and asked to see the mother.

"Aren't you goin' to play mo' games? I didn't see you play any games."

I was not in any type of mood to play around. I stuck to business.

"I'm sorry, but my hour is up. Plus—"

I didn't get a chance to finish my sentence before my balloons and pump were returned to me with requests like, "...So and so didn't get a balloon. Can you make us stuff now?"

"Too bad, my hour's up," I said, taking my pump and balloons and putting them in my bag without a thank you or anything. Like I said, I was DONE.

The mother came out. I showed her and told her what was owed and she went back inside the house to get the money. No matter how much it was, it wouldn't ever be enough for all I had been put through.

"You can't leave without your keys, Simba," one kid said with a guilty smile on his face.

I politely went over to him, put my hand on his shoulder, gave him a little *squeeze*, bent over next to his ear, and said in a very deep, formidable voice, "By the time she gets back out here I better have my keys."

I let him go and calmly stood next to the back door, to wait for my money.

She hadn't even come back yet when my keys mysteriously reappeared. The boy sent a little girl over to me to give me back my keys because as the girl put it, "He's afraid you'll bite him."

Not a bad idea.

The mom came out of the house with my money; no words were exchanged between us. Just cash.

Thank God this party is over! I thought to myself as I walked to my truck. A few kids followed me. I'm guessing so they could see what I looked like under the costume. I got to my truck, only to discover I was blocked in and couldn't leave. I tried to get the attention of a guy who was leaning against the chain-link fence of the house and drinking a forty-ounce bottle of Budweiser out of a brown paper bag.

"Excuse me, but do you know whose cars those are? I have to go and I'm blocked in." He paid no attention to me and took another sip from his forty. I repeated myself but louder. This time he noticed me.

"Chill the fuck out, man, I don't know whose cars these are! Jesus Christ."

I.

Just.

Want.

To.

Leave.

Was this really happening? I mean, really? Am I on some hidden camera show? Am I going to win "fabulous" prizes?

I sat in my truck, still in costume, with the AC blasting, waiting for people to move their cars. Everyone on the cul-de-sac had to wait while the birthday boy's father and his friends unloaded three kegs from the trunk of one of the cars that was blocking me in. Now I knew who the party was really for. It took them forever to move the cars. I could've taken off my hood at any time, but there was a large crowd of kids around the fence. I didn't want to give anyone the satisfaction of seeing my face. They could all go fuck themselves. I kept the hood on while I worked my way around, and finally out, of this abortion of a parking situation. And that was no easy feat. I flew out of there and drove away pissed off and in total disbelief. Some parenting styles really baffle me!

Honestly, I felt lucky to get out of there alive. Maybe if I had my *Lion King* music it might have gone better?

Chapter 5

Why Characters Don't Go To Compton

It's noon and I'm just waking up.

I had been up until 3:30am rehearsing with one of my sketch comedy groups for an upcoming show at the Comedy Store. Well, to be perfectly honest, we rehearsed until 11pm or so and then a few of us went to a bar (because nothing opens the creative mind better than a cold beer) to further discuss our character developments, what whiny bitches we have in the group, and the reunification of Germany in 1989. One of my fellow comedians wanted me to regale them with the story of a recent blind date a "friend" of mine set up.

She was dressed in a sweater an old lady would wear for a night of bingo, and it had a huge brown stain on the front of it. Her hair was like a blond tumbleweed had flown on top of her head, and she looked like someone had just woken her up for our date. My "friend" looked over at me and said, "I'm sorry" but laughing while he said it. I decided to give her the benefit of the doubt since surface appearances do not reflect the inner soul.

I wish I could say she had a bad personality but she would've needed one for me to call it bad. She was so "blah" it was beyond painful. I got out of giving her a goodnight kiss by getting some chewing tobacco from my "friend" and explaining to my date, if we got pulled over I didn't want the police officer to smell the one beer I had on my breath. I swore NEVER to go on a blind date again.

My only party of the day was a Honey Bear Type for a little boy named Pierce, who was turning three. Lucky him. Not so much luck to his parents. Goodbye "terrible twos," hello, "watch me fight even more with you to prove my independence as I feel a need to constantly whine to you, 'Let me do it!'" threes.

My routine on days that I have parties is just that, routine.

Wake up.

Scratch balls (on occasion this can lead to masturbation. Who am I kidding? It ALWAYS leads to the five-knuckle shuffle on the ol' piss pump).

Pee.

Make coffee.

Make breakfast (which is usually one of two things, toast or cereal, and sometimes both depending on how hungry I am).

Eat breakfast, drink coffee, and go over my paperwork for my party while watching cartoons.

This is what I do.

The paperwork I have says the party is in L.A. Before I read any further, I know this location is suspect. After looking up the address, I find my suspicions were correct—the party is really in Compton. Compton *is* in Los Angeles. Los Angeles County, that is, not in the city of L.A. as Just Jumps, the company my bosses subcontracted the party through, want me to believe. Unfortunately, this is common practice among many small party companies here in L.A. to ensure they can get the party covered.

Many kids' party companies will put down that a party is in "L.A." rather than be honest and specify it is in Compton, Watts, or any other area that seems a little questionable. Some companies that subcontract will not accept parties in these areas. So the person booking the party just goes with the safe answer.

"It's in L.A."

To me that's more of a red flag than anything. Personally, I don't have a problem going to any of these places. I do have a problem being lied to. It's funny they never say a party in Beverly Hills, Brentwood, or Malibu is in "Los Angeles" because those are more desirable places to perform, and the chances of getting a bigger tip or any tips at all for that matter, are better in those places. Plus, you may end up at some celebrity's house where you could be discovered, given a lucrative career, and never have to do parties ever again. That's the party I'm patiently waiting for.

Before I leave to go to work I always make sure to squeeze out a healthy shit. Nothing is worse than making balloon animals or cutting cake and having to take a dump while TRAPPED in a costume. Trust me, unless you've done it you don't understand. Standing there turtlenecking while everyone is crescendoing to *Happy Birthday*, and you've got your own crescendo happening, not fun.

Before my ass gets to its paperwork I have time to look over mine regarding the day's job some more. "You did Barney for them last year" is written on the bottom of the work order and highlighted in yellow. This is another common strategic move on the part of Just Jumps to make my bosses not question the location of the party. That way my bosses would think, *It can't be in a bad area if our little JJ did a party here last year. La, la, la.*

Oh, the lies. Whoever knew kids' parties were so political.

The paperwork said to look for the house with the moonbounce in the front yard. This always makes me laugh. People never think anyone else around them is going to have a party on the same day and most of the time they are safe in assuming so, but I have been on streets where there were a few parties going on at the same time. Hell, I personally know people here in L.A. who own their own moonbounce and set it up on a regular basis, "just because."

Once in Compton…I mean *Los Angeles*, I drove down the street my paperwork said the party was on, looking at the numbers along the sidewalk and for a house with a moonbounce in the front yard.

This is a really nice street, I thought to myself, *I would've never guessed I was in the middle of Compton. I've been down shadier-looking streets in Beverly Hills.*

Halfway up the street I no longer needed to look at numbers because there it was—a house with a moonbounce in the front yard, as promised. I drove by the house, slowing down to take a real good look. *I don't remember doing a party here last year. I knew those fuckers lied just to get me to come to Compton to do a party. That will teach me for having faith in the honesty of others. How do they live with themselves? Bastards!*

Oh well, I still have a job to do.

I found a place to park on the street about a hundred yards from the house to change into my costume. During my little reconnaissance drive-by, I noticed there were kids out front in the yard playing as well as in the bounce. I had to park far enough away to be able to change without being seen by young, un-jaded eyes.

Once I became Honey Bear, I walked down the street toward the party playing the music associated with my character. I like to think the familiarity of the music helps kids not be so petrified when a six-foot "live" version of their favorite character shows up at their house.

As I got closer to the house, the older kids pointed me out to the birthday boy, Pierce. Pierce's eyes lit up and he ran to meet me. He gave me a big hug and seemed very excited to see me, which is my favorite reaction from kids, especially from the birthday child. It's even better when the parents are looking and they realize their hard-earned money is being well spent. The luck o' the Irish was with me; Yolanda, his mom, was there to witness the whole thing and said, "See, baby, I told you Pooh was coming to your party. Are you happy?"

"I love him so much, Mommy," he said to her, squeezing me as hard as he could. Luckily, I'm a sturdy guy and can handle the bear hug of a three-year-old. Please don't try this at home people—I am a professional after all.

Yolanda was so happy Pierce was happy I thought she was going to cry. It wouldn't have been the first time I saw a parent cry over the happiness I brought to their child. Yolanda gently caressed Pierce's head while holding back tears and wiping her eyes with her other hand.

"Do you want to take Pooh to the backyard and see if he wants to play?" Yolanda asked Pierce.

Pierce took my big Honey Bear head in his tiny, three-year-old birthday boy hands, looked me straight in my mesh-covered eyeholes, and asked, "Do you want to play with me, Pooh?"

A tiny noise came out of his mom, Yolanda. She was fighting back tears again. From that moment, I made it my personal mission to get this woman to break down and cry before I left.

"I would love to, Pierce," I said in my best Honey Bear Type voice.

Pierce turned around, addressing his guests, who had now encircled us, and said, "Let's go play with Pooh." And with that, he led me through the house and into the backyard.

I tried to play parachute games with them but they weren't listening to me so I brought that to an end. I had them sing a couple of songs, do the hokey pokey, I gave out stickers, and finished by making balloon animals. From inside my head I could hear the constant sound of shutters going off.

"Click, click, click."

They took a ton of photos, and when all was said and done, it probably cost them more to develop the photos from this party than it did to pay for my guest appearance.

After the party was over, Yolanda escorted me out.

"Pooh, you did such a great job! Youda' bomb! That means you did good."

"I know what that means. I'm a hip Winnie-the-Pooh. Thank you. You know…the paperwork said that I did your party last year and I don't remember doing your party last year. I don't think I'm the one who did it."

Yolanda put her hand on my shoulder, "I didn't think that was you. You were much better than Barney was. Our Barney last year sucked ass. I knew you weren't him because this year everyone loved you, including me and especially Pierce."

"And that's what matters most," I said adding,"You keep giving me all these compliments my head's going to swell up so much I won't be able to get my hood off."

"You crazy, Pooh! Thank you so much for making Pierce's party so special. He was all like into you and shit. It was great."

The party was already paid for in full, so there was no balance to pick up. That's always nice. Yolanda told me she did it that way so I wouldn't have to carry cash on me in this neighborhood and added, "Don't get me wrong, Pooh, this is a great street, but we's in da hood. Know what I'm sayin'?"

Halfway to my truck, Yolanda realized she didn't feed me at the party and offered to go back and set me up with a plate to go.

"I'd love that, I'm starving. I'm going to change. The green Ford Ranger is mine, you can't miss it. Plus it'll have the head of Honey Bear in the passenger seat."

"You crazy, Pooh. I'll be right back."

She ran back to her place and I continued down the street, still playing my music. I always play music on the way back to my truck just in case I'm seen by non-party-going childlike eyes and it was a good thing I did.

"Hey, Pooh!"

Through the tiny mesh eyeholes I could see three little kids standing at the edge of the curb, kitty-corner to my truck, staring at me as I strolled down the sidewalk. From what I could make out, it looked like a little girl around three, a boy that looked to be five, and an older girl about ten or so.

The ten-year-old yelled over to me, "Hi, Pooh!"

Great, I can't get out of this costume until these kids leave!

I waved to them and focused straight ahead of me, noticing two teenagers way down the street walking in my direction. As I got to the front of my truck I could see the three kids still waving at me. I waved. They waved back and just stood there. I went around to the driver's side and put my bag in the bed of the truck. As I searched through my bag for my keys, I could hear the kids, who were now screaming to me.

"POOH! POOH! POOH!"

Man, they really want me to go over and say hi to them.

As I found my keys in my bag I heard another voice. A deeper voice than that of a ten-year-old girl.

"Hey, Pooh."

That wasn't the voice of a child. With the Winnie-the-Pooh head still on, I turned around.

What I saw next will stay with me for the rest of my life. One of the teenage boys, who had been walking down the street toward me, was now standing in front of me pointing a gun at my head.

I was frozen.

I don't think I could've moved even if I wanted to. Strangely, I wasn't scared. There was nothing I could do. I was standing there in a Honey Bear costume with this big head on, zero peripheral vision, and helpless. I was, in terms easy to understand, at a complete disadvantage.

I had a ton of thoughts racing through my head, the first one being, *These poor children across the street are going to see Honey Bea...FUCK IT! They are going to see Winnie-the-Pooh, one of their favorite Disney characters, get murdered in front of them. The years of therapy they are going to need. I can't even imagine.* From my view, each eyehole in the Honey Bear costume had its own and very different scene. Out of the left eye, I could see this fourteen- or fifteen-year-old child holding a nine-millimeter beretta handgun to my face. I had a really close view of the gun and could tell it was not a toy. I shot one similar to it many times in my youth when my family butchered animals on the farm, when I was only a few years younger than this poor, confused child.

Out of the right eyehole, I could see the three children kitty-corner to us, standing there in complete shock, just waiting for Winnie-the-Pooh to get his head blown off and drop lifeless to the ground. They were no longer yelling, they were silently standing there awaiting my execution. They couldn't turn away.

I couldn't turn away.

They couldn't run.

I couldn't run.

Silently I screamed to myself, *I CAN'T BELIEVE I'M GOING TO DIE THIS WAY! IN A FUCKING WINNIE-THE-POOH COSTUME!* The scream died down to utter disappointment. *Why me? What did I ever do to deserve this? I survived getting hit by lightning as a child, catching on fire twice and being held a political prisoner in Yugoslavia and I was going out like this? There is so much I still want to do with my life. I realized I DO want to fall in love, get married, and most surprisingly, have children. All gone because a confused teenager wants bragging rights that he killed Winnie-the-Pooh in front of three little children, raping them of their wide-eyed innocence. Gone. All of it gone with one single bullet motivated by the raging, misdirected hormones of a perplexed teenager. If there is a God, here's his chance to prove it to me and meet me at the pearly gates.*

When people say their lives flash before their eyes before a life-threatening accident, I can now agree that yes, it indeed does. You have so many thoughts running through your head at the same time that they become a rapid hodgepodge of various meaningful and meaningless images. There were things coming to my mind I hadn't thought about for years, such as the girl I had a crush on in junior high. *I wonder if Tanya is happy.* It made no sense to me as to why, in my final moments, those thoughts were making a guest appearance among more explainable things such as, *I'll never again taste my mom's home-cooked roast beef with potatoes, carrots, and gravy, finished off with a strawberry shortcake for dessert. I want to see London and Santorini again.*

At this moment I had zero control over my thoughts, I welcomed them all, then said goodbye to them forever. It's strange how time seems to slow down almost to a standstill, and seconds can seem like a lifetime. In actuality, the whole exchange, up to that point, was all of five or ten seconds.

"Don't!! He's my guest!" I heard Yolanda yell, as she ran down the street with my plate of food.

"I'm just kiddin'," the boy told her. "Right, Pooh? We cool."

He mouthed the word "Boom", laughed as he lowered his gun, moved in close to me and quietly said, "You got lucky."

I closed my eyes, lowered my head, and exhaled my fear.

"That's wrong! That's just plain wrong!" Yolanda yelled, waving my plate of food around. "I'm going to talk to your grandfather, and don't think I'm not going to."

"Don't freak out," he told her, calm, cool, and collected as if he did this on a regular basis. As if it was his job. "It's not even real," he said, putting the gun away, smirking, knowing he was lying and expecting to get away with it.

Yolanda didn't think to ask him to see it or even hand it over to her for that matter. We had all seen it enough.

Yolanda, the three kids on the corner and I, watched as the two boys walked down the street, continuing on their original path and laughing as they left.

Laughing, laughing, laughing, without a care in the world.

Oh, to laugh, I wonder when I'll be able to do that again. Thanks for stealing that from me, boys. I hope you catch chlamydia one day.

Yolanda put the plate of food on the hood of my truck and grabbed me by the shoulders, "Are you ok? I'm so sorry."

It looked as if she was going to cry.

"I'm more concerned about the kids across the street witnessing the whole thing," I told her.

"I'm so sorry. So, so very sorry," she said, as if she said it enough times it'd make the whole event disappear.

"I want to take off my head but not while the kids are watching."

Without skipping a beat, she yelled to the kids across the street, "Pooh is very tired and he needs to rest. You can go home now." They walked away and I was finally able to take my hood off. The boy with the gun came back to apologize, but Yolanda was set on telling his grandfather. After yelling at the boy again, she turned back to me.

"He lives with his grandfather and I know he's had a rough life but there's no excuse for this. I'm so sorry, so, so very sorry. It's things like this that make you guys not want to come here."

She started to cry. Mission accomplished. I knew I could get her to cry before I left. I wished it could've been done in a different way though.

"You know how many companies I had to call to finally get someone to come here last year? I thought this year would be different. I'm so sorry, so, so very sorry." She paused to wipe away some tears and continued, "I am so embarrassed. I have to save for so long to give this to my son and this happens. All those kids hardly ever get a chance to see a character come to a party. It's so special for them and means so much. I know we get charged more because no one wants to come here."

She gave me a hug and asked me a question.

"Is it ok to take a picture of you without the Pooh head on?"

"Um, sure." What was I supposed to say?

What an odd request at a time like this. She took the photo and I'm sure it looked like a mugshot. You know, that blank stare people give when they've just been busted. Except that mine was more of a "deer caught in the headlights" gaze. But the same void expression, nonetheless.

While driving away I got to thinking about what could've happened if that kid, not even out of high school, had pulled the trigger. I didn't want to die in a costume. I was still very much in shock. As I drove, the reality of it all finally caught up to me. *I could have died. Is this job really worth my life? Maybe I should look into becoming a waiter like most actors.*

My hands started to shake uncontrollably. I had to pull over along the side of the road and calm down. Unfortunately, this was not a new feeling for me. I've had to pull over to the side of the road a few times in my life—when I saw a woman throw herself off the 101 underpass at Barham Boulevard and land in front of me, when my roommate committed suicide, and when my nephew passed away. It's not a good feeling. You feel so out of control and helpless. I hate it.

Lucky for me Yolanda was there, otherwise it could've been more disastrous. I can hear that phone call to my mom and dad: "Mr. and Mrs. Lassen, your son, Jason, was shot in the head in the middle of a street in Compton. He's dead and he was dressed as Winnie-the-Pooh. Reports say he had a balloon animal shoved up his ass."

I may question the existence of a God but after today I really believe in angels. And today mine were watching over me.

What doesn't kill us only makes us stronger. Literally.

I had some new emotions to deal with—it was the first time since my nephew's death I realized I wanted children. And I needed to love someone first. *Maybe I need to start with finding the love for myself?*

Chapter 6

I'll Entertain Your Kids While You Entertain The World: Part One

"Hey, Jay, are you available to do a party with us today? I'm sure you can use the money. It's for the Spielbergs."

It had been two years since I heard those words and I always knew there was a possibility I would hear them again. I had the opportunity to work on a fishing boat in Alaska and turned it down because Nick had given me the heads up a few months ago they may need me to do this party.

"Sure, I can do it."

"Great. There's just one thing I need you to do."

I should've known there was going to be a catch. "What?"

"You have to pick up a Fred Flintstone costume from another company. Let me give you his address. His name's Caden, you'll like him and I KNOW he'll like you." He chuckled.

While driving to pick up the costume, I didn't allow myself to get too excited. I knew my bosses a little better now. Anything could change from the time I picked up the costume until I met them at their house/office. Hell, I could show up at their house and they could have left to do the party already! It had happened before and I was sure it could and would happen again at some point. Gotta love self-absorbed actors with delusions of grandeur!

Nick had told me Caden from Big Joy Parties was expecting me and to just walk in when I arrived. I still knocked before entering. I'm crazy conventional that way.

"Hello? It's Jason from Fun Entertainment," I announced, opening the door and poking my head in.

The door opened to a small foyer off of a large living room with very high ceilings.

Somebody's a neat freak, I thought to myself. I was impressed the living room was very neat and tidy, especially since it was a bachelor pad.

At the far end of the room was a set of stairs leading up to an area overlooking the living room, hence the very high ceilings. I love this type of layout. You can stand against the rail of the raised area and look down at your kingdom like an omnipotent, medieval overlord. To pretend to be a kind king is so boring and overdone.

The king of this kingdom, an in-shape shirtless man wearing extremely short cut-off jeans, walked over to the edge of the area up the stairs and waved me to come upstairs. Once at the top of the stairs it was clear to me this was Caden's home office area and that the cleanliness ceased at the top of the stairs. It was like every other home I had seen with a kids' party business being run out of it. It looked like the Disney characters' dry cleaners exploded. There were costumes all over the place. Some were hung up, others draped over chairs or strewn about on the floor.

Caden was on the phone and without wavering he grabbed a chair hidden under a pile of costumes, tipped it over, so that more costumes were now on the floor, and motioned for me to have a seat. So I did.

"So you want a Dalmatian for an hour? You know, you could have two Dalmatians and I'll give you a price break for the second one." Caden rolled his eyes, pointed at the phone receiver, and replicated a mouth talking with his free hand. He nodded his head while listening to whoever was on the other end rattle on and on.

"Yes, I understand what you're saying but I'm telling you from experience—" Caden's sales pitch was interrupted by the other phone on his desk ringing. "Listen, sweetie, my other line's ringing. I'll tell you what, you think about that second Dalmatian while I answer it. I'll be right back, ok? Thank you."

He picked up the other phone, which was pink by the way.

"BJ Productions, how can I help you? Yes, this is Magnum. Anal? Sure, I've got some real studs that both give and receive. I even got one hottie that's a squirter, not a blobber and can squirt a gallon…and on command to boot. Give me your info and I'll call you back with all the juicy info. Thanks, bye." Without skipping a beat he went back to his first call. "So have you given any thought to having two Dalmatians at your daughter's fourth birthday party?"

What the fuck just happened?

"Good choice. Two performers are always better than one. Ok, let me get your info."

Caden stood with the phone receiver pinched between his shoulder and head, took down the info with one hand, while his free hand played with the fringe of threads that were a product of him making his jeans into short shorts.

"Thanks, baby, you won't regret it. Bye now and thanks for calling Big Joy." Caden hung up the phone and turned his attention to me. "Sorry about that, it's just been so crazy lately. So, let me *finally* introduce myself, I'm Caden."

"I'm Jason from Fun Entertainment."

"Yes, that means you need head."

"Excuse me?"

"The head of Fred Flintstone, silly. Nick didn't tell me he was going to send over a dirty, dirty boy."

Caden rummaged through a stack of bulging brown grocery bags in a corner of the room.

"Here it is. Let me check to make sure it's all here."

"Please do. I'd hate to get to the party and not have Fred's signature leopard print toga on. Then it would turn into a totally different type of party."

"And I can book that type of party if that's what they're into."

I bet you could.

I left Caden's apartment with both my costume and anal virginity in tow.

When I arrived at Rachel and Nick's, Nick was outside loading up their van. As soon as he saw me he got a big shit-eating grin on his face.

"How'd you like Caden?"

"Interesting fella' that one. Nice guy. And very interesting."

"You know he's a working actor. Did you recognize him?"

"He didn't look familiar."

"He was in *Cocks and Robbers 3* and *The Horneymooners*."

"Sad to say, I haven't seen 'em."

"You know he's gay, right?"

"I kinda got that impression."

"He's big in gay porn, if you know what I mean. You know how he met his boyfriend?"

"I'm sure you're going to tell me."

"Caden went from acting in gay porn to producing and directing them as well. So he directed this one film and one of the actors in it won 'Best New Cummer' that year at the Porn Awards in Las Vegas and that's who he hooked up with. Caden said they would take turns holding the award while they fucked."

Please stop. I've heard enough. I tried to change the subject to business.

"So here's the Fred costume."

"Do you think they jerked off on the award?"

Normally Nick has adult ADD and it's easy to distract him, unless of course he's thinking and talking about sex. You'd never guess by looking at him, he looks very sweet and innocent. He could pass for the twin of actor Peter Scolari from *Bosom Buddies*. You know, the one that's *not* Tom Hanks. I helped Nick finish loading up the van while listening to more anal sex talk. He was going on about some dancer friend of his from high school and college that's not gay, even though he's a dancer.

"I'm telling you, Jay, that guy scores with all the horny chicks he dances with."

Normally, I don't mind sex talk but when Nick does it he acts like a twelve-year-old boy being bad, constantly looking over his shoulder to see if his parents can hear him.

Personally, I couldn't get over the fact that, not only did this guy run a gay porn business out of his house, but he was also booking children's parties in the same space. Now that's multitasking! I'm so glad I was there to witness it because I would've never believed it if I hadn't. Could you imagine if he ever got the phone calls mixed up?

"Double anal is a little more expensive but it is *sooooo* worth it."

"My son's turning five, mister!!!"

"You're right. Double anal may be a bit much. What do ya think about a donkey show?"

Nick finally stopped talking about sex while driving to the Spielberg's house and that's only because Rachel was with us. If she wasn't, I'm sure he would've talked about it for the rest of the day. Rachel took advantage of our time in the car to brief me on how the party was going to go. This was quite standard protocol for any show they did that was more of a performance than the standard games, face painting, and balloons. This was a party at the Spielberg's, after all. Rachel filled me in on the kids' idiosyncrasies and what I should expect from them.

"And don't ask Steven for an autograph either," Nick randomly interjected.

"Nick! Jay Jay knows better than that. He's very professional when it comes to all our celebrity clientele," Rachel scolded him from the backseat while he drove.

Nick looked back at Rachel in the rearview mirror and quickly finished his story, "One of his maids once asked him for his autograph and she was fired immediately."

"Nick!"

It was time for me to inject my opinion. "I don't blame him for having her fired. It's one thing if he's out and about but his home is his home. I would've had her dragged outside and shot via firing squad. After she was flogged of course."

Humor. The best way to smooth over any uncomfortable situation. And with these two, there were a lot of them.

We arrived at a very modest, unassuming gate, nothing like what I expected. I wanted to see guard towers complete with Navy

Seal-trained snipers and a moat filled with piranhas, sharks, and man-eating starfish. It's very well hidden without being really hidden at all. Nicely done.

"Hello, how can I help you?" the box at the side of the driveway said to us.

Being the control freak she is, Rachel leaned across Nick to answer the polite box. "Hey, it's Rachel and Nick from Fun Entertainment. We're here for Sawyer's special day."

The box sat silent as the gate responded to our arrival by parting like the Red Sea for Moses.

Once again, the house was nothing like I expected. It was really nice but much smaller than I imagined. We were running slightly behind schedule, another common trait of my bosses. But if we were on time there would be no drama and drama was their main motivation for getting out of bed every morning. We rounded the circular driveway and parked in front of a humble non-twenty-car garage. Now I was impressed.

I don't think the van came to a full stop before Rachel opened the side door and leaped out. "I'm going to run and let Kate and Steven know we're here." And with that she was gone. I'm sure the voice from the box out at the front gave Kate and Steven the exciting news of our arrival.

Nick and I unloaded the van, took all the games we were going to play with the kids, and went to set up everything for the party. Nick led the way and I awkwardly followed with my hands full of fun, fun, fun. You know a house is big when you start to lose your bearings. Now my expectations were being met. When we finally re-emerged from the house we were under a veranda and facing the back of the house. WOW! That's the only word that comes to mind. Mother Fucking WOW!

"Pretty sweet, isn't it, Jay?"

I could hear in Nick's voice that all of his visits to the Spielberg's didn't hinder how impressed he was with the compound. And I understand why. We were standing at the top of what seemed to be several levels, each more impressive than the next. One level had a tennis and basketball court and I think I saw a football stadium behind some trees. The bottom level at the tree line was a swimming pool that was bigger than the Lebanon community swimming pool I swam in back in New Hampshire in my youth. To the right of the pool was a four-bedroom, three-bathroom home Nick referred to as the pool house.

"They own all the land around as far as you can see. The woods behind the pool and pool house have a bunch of paths and trails that seem to go on for miles. But you can't get lost. If you look closely you'll see cameras everywhere. Big brother's always watching you."

I can understand why they have the grounds under heavy surveillance, being who they are and with all the wackos in the world, but as a kid, it has to suck having your every move videotaped, only to be reviewed for the courtroom that is Mom and Dad later.

"Did you push your little brother?"

"I didn't push anyone."

"Really? Are you sure? Let's go to the tape, shall we?"

That would suck.

Nick and I had a few more things to get from the van. As we gathered the last of our things, the Spielberg kids showed up from school with some of their friends.

Sawyer, the birthday boy, ran over to Nick as soon as he saw him, "Hey, Nick, who's that?"

"That's a friend of mine. He's helping me out."

"Do you guys want to play soccer?"

Nick looked over at me as if waiting for me to tell him what we should do.

"If we have time, why not?"

Nick shrugged his shoulders, "Sure, Sawyer, why not?"

"YES!" Sawyer yelled with a fist pump.

The kids started to pick teams, set boundaries, and argue. I see the rituals of playing haven't changed since I was a kid. Of course, when I was younger someone would've already been hit, hurt, or hurt from being hit by now. Nick knew we didn't have time to waste, so he made it simple for all of us.

"Ok, listen up! It's all of you kids…versus the two of us."

"Ok, Nick, but we're going to kick your and your friend's butts!"

We were having a lot of fun, but Nick and I couldn't keep up with the kids. Damn them with all that energy and youth. Luckily Rachel saved Nick and I from having heart attacks by coming out and announcing it was time to start the party. Rachel led the kids inside while Nick and I sneaked off and changed into our costumes. Nick was Barney Rubble and I was Fred Flintstone. We had the voices down pat; like me, Nick's very good at doing voices.

Being able to do a believable voice that sounds like the character you're playing helps add to the authenticity of the characters, especially for kids. They see right through performers who can't do voices that well, and call them on it. Our friend Mark is a great children's performer, but he can't do voices for shit. He's the first one to admit that he does the worst Purple Dino Type voice. If he does a party as a purple dino, he just won't speak. He told me when the kids ask him what's wrong with him and why he can't speak, he just shrugs his shoulders and laughs. So consider yourself lucky if you have a character at your kid's party and he sounds remotely like the character he's portraying.

Once Nick and I were fully dressed I couldn't help but laugh. We made the perfect Fred and Barney. Nick's shorter and skinnier than I am and visually it was a great juxtaposition. Now we were just waiting for our cue from Rachel to make our grand entrance into the party.

Rachel had the kids gather outside under the veranda where Nick and I had put all of the games. She made the kids do and say some silly things to get us to come out. Nick, still with his Barney Rubble head propped up on his forehead, looked over at me, "It's showtime! Just follow my lead." He put the head down and out we went.

I like doing parties with Nick. He takes control and does almost everything. I just get to sit back, support where needed, and enjoy the ride. It's always a bonus when you're doing a hooded character that you can easily see out of. Fred and Barney are easy to see out of because they are made of lightweight foam and have big eyeholes. I could clearly see all the kids and behind them, way in the back, were Rachel, Kate, and behind a video camera wearing a baseball cap was Steven.

I was doing as Nick instructed and just followed his lead. Occasionally, I would catch myself looking over at Steven and geeking out.

That's fucking Steven Spielberg! And he's videotaping me entertaining his kids!

I grew up watching his movies. Hell, some of his movies helped inspire me to want to get into films. And there I was. And there he was. And we were both at his HOME. I couldn't believe it no matter how many times I said it to myself.

"Isn't that right, Fred?" Nick's voice would break my trance.

"That's right, Barney."

Everything was going well…until…Nick and I started doing this bit with the boom box radio we had brought along to play music. Nick picked up the radio and I went to grab it from him.

"Barney, give me that radio."

I pulled the radio toward me and pushed it back toward him as if he wasn't going to give it to me. Nick picked up on this instantly; he knew exactly where I was going with the bit.

"Gee, Fred, I really want the radio."

"I said give it to me, Barney!"

Every time we moved the radio back and forth between us the kids would laugh. So we just kept doing it. Neither Nick nor I mind milking a gag for all it's worth. We work together in a sketch comedy group so we're good with coming up with stuff on the spot. So between performing together in sketch comedy as well as kids' parties, we knew how to work well together without stepping on each other's toes or killing a joke prematurely. I guess I still had more to learn because without warning Nick finally let go of the radio.

"Ok, Fred, you can have it."

I don't remember whether I wasn't ready for him to give it to me, or my adrenaline was running high, but I pulled with all my might. Pulling hard was my cue to Nick to let go and let me have the radio. We must've been on the same wavelength because he let go the same moment I pulled hard.

Radio in hand and with a hell of a lot of momentum, I fell backwards toward the spackled wall. My hands were full with the radio so I didn't use them to break my fall. I guess I could've let go of the radio but oddly, that thought never came to mind. My right shoulder slammed into the wall and, since I was off balance, I hit hard and slid down the sandpaper-type outer wall coating. The song *Free Falling* by Tom Petty would've been very appropriate to have been playing on the radio at that moment.

*And I'm free...free falling...*down a wall slicing into my skin at the Spielberg's house.

The whole way down I could feel the little rocks breaking off the wall and either cutting into my skin or imbedding themselves in it. I hit the ground hard.

Very hard.

I'm a two-hundred-plus-pound guy, and that's a lot of weight to come crashing down.

Among the children and Nick laughing I heard a few noticeable gasps. I lay there a few moments, stunned. From the eyeholes in the Fred head I could see Rachel and Kate covering their mouths in shock. Steven looked away from the viewfinder of his video camera, looked at me, turned to Rachel, and asked, "Is he ok?"

With that I bounced up and said, "Barney! Why you!"

Nick was still laughing. I couldn't <u>see</u> him laughing, but I could clearly <u>hear</u> him.

"Gee, Fred," he said with a chuckle, "Sorry about that."

Rachel jumped in, "Ok, kids, now let's go down to the swimming pool with Barney and Fred. Barney will lead the way. Right, Barney? Ok, kids, let's go down to the pool. Fred and I will be right behind you."

She came over to me and examined my shredded, bleeding shoulder. She covered her mouth again.

"JJ, are you ok? That looks bad."

"I'm alright. Let's go to the pool."

I don't know what hurt more: grating my shoulder on the spackled wall, or busting my shit in front of all the kids and the Spielbergs. I was hoping to make my performance a memorable one for the Spielbergs, but throwing my body against a coarse stone wall wasn't what I had in mind.

Once down by the pool, we pulled out the parachute and played some parachute games. My shoulder was on fire and I could feel blood oozing from my wound and down the small of my back. Some relief came when we had Batman, another character, show up. We laid the parachute down, had all the kids sit on it, and waited to see what Batman was going to do. He pulled out a deck of cards from his utility belt and did some card tricks for the kids. I never knew Batman knew how to do card tricks. Is there anything Batman can't do? After a few tricks, Batman disappeared as quickly as he had arrived. That was short and sweet. And a little odd.

"Mom and Dad, can I have Fred and Barney at my birthday party? Oh, yeah, I also want Batman to show up for twelve-and-a-half minutes, do some card tricks, be lame, and take off."

"Sure, anything for you, Sawyer. We'll even have Fred heave himself against a wall for you. Would you like that?"

"That'd be AWESOME!!!!"

After our sense-of-humorless Batman relieved us of his company, we had all the kids go into the pool for a nice, tiring swim. I took over the duties of cleaning up while Nick got the kids into the pool. I was packing up the parachute and saw Rachel and Kate talking. When they finished, Rachel came over to me.

"Hey, Fred, Kate told me to tell you to take a break and go clean up a little bit."

"Is it that bad?" I asked.

"It looks like it really hurts. I can see pebbles and stuff in it. Pebbles, get it? You're Fred, and Pebbles is your daughter."

"That's a good one, Rachel. Where should I clean up?"

Rachel pointed me to a changing room I could go into after the boys changed into their swim trunks. The time came and I went in and got a good look at my handiwork. *Wow, it does look as bad as it feels.* The mark ran from the top of my shoulder all the way down the back of my arm to my elbow. Part of the costume was shredded a little bit; I hope Caden doesn't want me to pay him back for ripping his costume. I'm sure his "payback" methods are very creative. I cleaned up and went back out to play with the kids. Nick and I ran around the pool with super soakers trying to squirt the kids. It was like shooting fish in a barrel or kids in a pool.

After we sang *Happy Birthday* to Sawyer in the "pool house," we led all the kids back up to the house to the screening room to watch a movie. It's Steven Spielberg; of course he has a screening room in his house. I told you this house was big.

We loaded up the van and drove to Nick and Rachel's house. The entire way home the three of us kept laughing about me falling down. I think Nick summed it up the best for me though.

"Just think, Jay, how many people can say they made an impression on Steven Spielberg? And you also left an impression, as well as some skin, on his house."

I was disappointed I didn't get a chance to meet Steven or Kate. I'm sure they would not soon forget me. For all I knew, they were at home replaying the footage of me falling over and over, laughing, and saying, "Who is that masked man?" and "I wonder if he's got a resume and headshot?"

Why yes, yes I do!

Chapter 7

Dear *Penthouse* Forum, I Can't Believe This Happened To Me...

"Thanks for coming, Santa and South Pole."

It really bothers me that Nick helps himself to ALL my characters' names. Sleepi the Clown, Captain Aarrrrgh! the Pirate, and now he's raped me of South Pole the Elf. I know somewhere out there, some other dude dressed up like an elf has given himself the name of South Pole. But I'm the only South Pole the Elf that works at Fun Entertainment. South Pole is the elf name I gave myself right from the get-go of doing Christmas parties as an elf for Nick's company.

Nick is very creative in his own right but it's not unlike him to "cheat" whenever possible. Especially when he likes other people's ideas more than his own. South Pole the Elf is one of those that fit in the category of "I like, I take." I believe his compulsive cheating stems from his overwhelming competitiveness with any and all things in life. The man will bet on *anything* and then do *anything* to make sure he'll win that bet. Including cheating. Nobody's perfect. Let's just say I learned not to play games with him. Usually, I consider it a compliment when someone as creative as him "steals" one of my ideas and tries to sell it as his own. But not when it comes to my character names. I'm funny that way.

"Thanks for having us. Merry Christmas!" I said, hurrying to the car to be able to get out of the Santa outfit that much sooner before our next party.

This party was my third of the day and I still had one more to go. I started my day off being Santa at a company party I go to every year per their request. They gave me a twenty-five dollar tip and two plates of food to show their gratitude for, as they put it, "Yet another year as Santa well done." Then I did a South Pole the Elf at a tennis club in Rolling Hills Estates and received a fifteen-dollar tip for my efforts in putting up with the children of uppity, stuck-up, high-class suburbanites.

"Hey, Jay, they gave us a seventy-five dollar tip," Nick informed me while jumping in the car.

Add another thirty-seven fifty to the mix and so far the day had been pretty good in tips alone, and we still had one more party to do. December is by far the busiest month of the year for parties and the best month of the year for tips. And it's a good thing too—in January and February things slow down tremendously in the children's entertainment business. Probably due to all the parents blowing their bank accounts on Christmas, Hanukkah or in some households, both.

"That was a fun party. Don't you think that was a fun party, Jay? I think it was a fun party."

While Nick talked, I cooled down. This fucking Santa suit gets hot. No one ever thinks about Santa's real needs. And Santa really needs it not to be so hot inside people's homes. I would so like to be able to go home right now and kick back with a beer or twelve. I can't believe it's 8:45pm and we have one more party to go to. Oh, the things one goes through for their art…and a paycheck!

Nick and I had roughly half an hour to prep for the next party. We were scheduled to get there and start at 9pm but in true Nick form we ran late at our last party so we'd have to enter this next party late and stay late as well. It's Nick's regular M.O., not mine. Now I'll be lucky to get home by midnight for that beer…or twelve.

Let me enlighten you on what was requested of us for that last party that made it so fun. They had contacted Jackson over at Joyful Parties and asked him whether it was possible to get a more "adult" or "dirty" Santa and elf.

"You know what I mean right, Jackson? Someone we could have a little more fun with," the lady asked (and I bet a part of her felt dirty for asking).

Jackson being who he is said, "No problem. I've got just the guys for you."

Jackson's motto, for as long as I've known him, has always been, "Whatever you want, I can get for you. Nothing is too outrageous." And he means it. You want a bisexual little person dressed in ass-less leather chaps to ride into your party on the back of a shaved sheep? He can get it. He's very well known for getting anything you can dream up. Anything. Let's just say, I've used him a few times for bachelor parties and my people were very impressed with what showed up. The more odd the request, the more pleased he is to deliver it to you. Jackson was extremely happy to get another call for the same night also for a risqué Santa. And that was the party we were headed to next.

"You know with this last party how there were kids running around and we had to be a little sneaky in our perversions?" Nick was getting that look in his eyes.

A look he gets whenever he starts to talk about sex or anything related to sex. I know I can be a little perverted but I can keep my comments under control, however Nick seems to have no control. And it's worse when he's given permission to let his freak flag fly. Tonight, his flag was at full staff and blowing in the wind.

Nick continued with the enthusiasm of a twelve-year-old boy talking about watching a porn tape he swiped from his father's secret porn stash in the garage. "Jackson told me this next party we are going to specifically asked for a 'Naughty' Santa, with blue eyes, and one of his 'Perverted' Elves. He said to follow their lead and match their raunchiness. The dirtier they get the dirtier we can get. How awesome is that?"

I knew that was a rhetorical question so I didn't bother to answer. I was enjoying being out from behind that friggin' Santa wig and beard, even if only for a short time. Nick must have taken my silence as agreement and continued on with his excitement.

"And you want to know the best part?"

Once again, a rhetorical question.

"This woman who's having the party is supposed to be some big-shot producer or casting director or something. I wonder who she is."

"What does it say her name is on the paperwork for the party?" I couldn't believe I had to spell it out for him. He's been doing this so much longer than I have, stuff like that should be common sense.

"Funny. I don't remember."

"Where's the paperwork?" I figured I would take the initiative and remind him how to find a name on a piece of paper.

"It's in the back with all the other stuff."

"If it's back there, how are you able to remember the address, yet you don't remember the client's name?"

"The address is important now. Her name's not."

Good point.

"Plus I had Rachel's crazy-ass assistant, Lauren, map out all the routes to and from each party for me." Brief pause while the wheels turned in his head. "Hey, Jay, did you have sex with Lauren?"

"No."

"You wanted to though, right? She's cute."

"Yah, she's cute alright. Crazy as a shithouse rat though. You know, the only thing worse than an actress is an actress with daddy issues. Or is that redundant?"

"Did you see her naked?"

Wow, he really was prepping mentally for this party. I thought he was going to pull his dick out and start jacking off.

What I said next, I knew was only throwing gas on a fire but what the fuck, from here on out we were the 'Naughty' Santa and his 'Perverted' Elf. "Yah, I saw her naked. Big fucking cock tease if you ask me. I'll tell you one thing though, her pussy sure did stink."

"Did it really?"

That sure got his attention.

"I'm sure if you really want to get a whiff of your own you can just smell the crotch of any costume she wore over the weekend."

Knowing how sick Nick can be I'm sure he did just that one time or another. Doesn't make him a bad guy. We all got needs.

The rest of the ride to our last gig consisted of me trying to stop sweating and scrubbing the old spirit gum from my face to make it smooth for its last coat of the day, while Nick went on and on about how dirty he was going to get at this next party. I changed into a dry tee shirt and reapplied spirit gum to my face to don the Santa wig, mustache, and beard for one last time that night. By the time we reached our destination I was ready to go and so was Nick.

"OH MY GOD! Look who's here, my husband and one of his elves."

We were greeted at the door by our hostess, who was dressed as a sexy Mrs. Claus. She was wearing a very tight, revealing red bustier with a matching short white fur-lined skirt. A pair of knee-high black leather boots, also lined with white fur, and a Santa's hat accentuating it all. I think I literally saw Nick's jaw drop to the ground.

"So…" Nick paused to look up her name on the invoice.

"It's Mrs. Claus," she replied, watching him struggle to find the contact name. "Do 'cum' in."

He didn't find a name on the paper, what he did find he showed to me as we entered the house. Written in big, bold letters at the bottom of the invoice, "**CLIENT WANTS TO BE REFERRED TO AS 'MRS. CLAUS' FOR THE EVENING. SANTA MUST HAVE BLUE EYES! VERY IMPORTANT! THANKS, JACKSON.**"

Besides the ol' mantra, "the customer's always right" there wasn't any other name on the paper, so we had to oblige. And it turned out we weren't the only ones who had to respect her wishes. She even had her guests refer to her as Mrs. Claus and they seemed to be getting off on it as much as she was.

Mrs. Claus had us follow her into the living room to "Get this party started." There were five couples and two other female friends over for the festivities. It was a much smaller party than the one we had just come from, which easily had sixty people. And a lot of them were children. I could tell this party was going to be very different. Firstly, all the guests seemed to be three sheets to the wind already. *What time did this party start? Noon?* And they showed no signs of slowing down. Good for them. I'll be there myself as soon as I get home tonight. Except unlike them, I'll be drowning my sorrows of loneliness and depression.

What's worse than an out-of-work actor? An out-of-work actor who dresses up like Santa for a month for Hollywood power players and is reminded he's a lonely, depressed, out-of-work actor dressing up in costumes all year round for Hollywood power players who, out in the real world, wouldn't piss on him if he was on fire. They might have one of their servants do it if they felt generous.

Hell, I'm not asking for them to make me a star in their next movie, but how about a line or two to help me pay the rent, get free food at craft service, and feel like a working actor for at least one fucking day before I have to get back in a goddamn Purple Dino costume? Fuck, now I need a drink! Gotta love the holidays.

Mrs. Claus's guests were enjoying the holidays in the form of drink and lots of them. I hope they all brought their sleeping bags; I would hate to see any of these people behind the wheel of a car. Shit, some of them were having a hard enough time coordinating themselves to the bathroom.

Come to think of it, there were only two cars in the driveway. I remember asking Nick while walking to the front door if he thought we had the correct address. It's weird; usually it's hard finding a parking space near a house having a party. Yet we parked in the driveway behind one of two very expensive cars. One of Mrs. Claus's guests let it slip that she had a car service pick them up from their homes and it was going to take them home when the party was over. Ahhh, the perks of having cash. Speaking of which, I've got to earn mine now.

The guests were very vocal right from the get-go. For us it started right at introductions.

"Ladies and Gentlemen, and I use the term lightly." Laugh, laugh, laugh. Mrs. Claus continued, "I give you my husband and lov-ver, the Naughty Santa Claus. And his perverted little elf…" She realized she didn't know Nick's elf name. "Introduce yourself, Mr. Perverted Elf."

"My name is South Pole the Elf," Nick answered proudly. He should too; it's a great elf name.

"Isn't that the bigger of the two poles?" a male guest asked, laughing at his own innuendo.

"And thicker too," Nick added and got laughs all around, which only egged him to continue, "Want to see?" and he reached down his green tights, made a fist, and projected it out in front of him in his crotch region. Once again, the laughter only made him get closer and closer to the line. "Stand back, people. I don't know how big this thing's going to get!"

This time a female guest commented. "It looks circumcised. Santa, I didn't know you hired Jewish elves."

The roar of laughter that followed made it official—we were 'Naughty' Santa and his 'Perverted' Elf and *this* was going to be a very interesting party.

My Perverted Elf got a few things set up to play the first game. I had my doubts about whether or not these drunkards were going to be in a game-playing mood. To my surprise everyone seemed to be ready and rearing to play. It gave them something to do while they drank.

"Hey, South Pole, are you setting up a game or playing with yourself?" a male guest yelled.

With his back to the group, Nick started mock "jerking off" and making moaning noises.

"Not on the game, South Pole. Try to aim it at the tree," I said, looking at the guest. "Damn elf can't keep his hands off of his candy cane."

"Is it striped like a candy cane?" a female guest inquired.

"Striped black and blue from playing with it all the time," I added, to much laughter.

The first game we played was a basic memory game. We set up a bunch of Christmas-related items on a platter, showed it to them for one minute, and then they had to write down on a piece of paper as many of the items as they could remember. Whoever remembered the most items won, simple. Their alcohol-soaked brains were doing so poorly we were forced to put them into two-person teams.

"I swear I saw a dildo on that platter," a woman proclaimed.

"I think that's more wishful thinking than actual reality, sweetheart," her game partner and husband added.

"Well, if I was being properly taken care of, I wouldn't have to have wishful thinking. Right, *sweetheart*?"

"She got you, Tom," another wife said.

"She'll get me later, don't you worry," Tom trumped.

I trumped his trump. "Keep pounding the drinks, Tom, and the only thing she'll get is broken promises wrapped in a whiskey dick."

"You're good, Santa," Tom said, not heeding my warning and tossing back yet another big drink.

"I'm just saying you can't play pool with a piece of rope, Tom ol' buddy." I was on fire and in my element.

"I told you I get nothing but the best, and we got the best," Mrs. Claus said to her guests, driving her point home by grabbing my ass. "Mmmmm, I want that under my tree." Her grasp lingered along with the laughter.

"Or in your mouth. Santa's not the only one who's naughty is he, Mrs. Claus?" Tom's wife laughed at her own half-joke.

I felt like I was at open mic night at the Comedy Store on the Sunset Strip. The jokes were nonstop. Everything out of everyone's mouth was one innuendo after another. And everyone was trying to "outdo" the previous comment or add to it. It was your standard joke format—setup, punch, setup, punch, punch, punch, punch.

The memory game was still going poorly. We ended up breaking everyone up into two groups, men against women. The women won.

"What do we win?" a female guest inquired.

Another winner voiced her opinion, "I hope it's a one-way trip to Santa's lap, Kristy."

Up to the mic next, Tom's wife, "If we're lucky, maybe the next game can be, we get to sit on Santa's face and let him guess our weight."

"Lisa!" Kristy squealed. "Great idea, I love it."

And the winner is Santa with, "Let me clear a spot for you, ladies." While wiping down his face and beard with his right hand.

"Ladies, ladies, ladies, keep your hands off my man. I am Mrs. Santa Claus after all," Mrs. Claus said, interlocking arms with me while pulling me toward her. "Mmmmm, somebody's been working out." Mrs. Claus gave my bicep a quick squeeze while finishing her drink.

"How about we have you guys try and guess Santa's weight?" Nick proposed.

"As long as he doesn't have to sit on my face," a male guest said.

"I do take requests," I said.

"Yah, well I request that Santa and his elf take a fucking shot already!" a drunken, deep voice from the back commanded.

I looked over at Nick to see what he was going to say. Personally, I wasn't driving for hours and I'm a big boy so one shot or two would have no effect on me. Nick looked back as if waiting for me to decide what to do. Luckily, it was decided for us.

"Tony's right, boys." It was our hostess, Mrs. Claus. "I'm the one in charge here tonight. Right, gang?" She addressed her guests who responded approvingly with hooting and hollering. "See, boys, tonight I'm the boss and whatever I say goes. I'm the one calling the shots and right now I'm calling for two, one for each of you. Tom and Lisa, set these boys up with some Jack Daniel's."

"I guess we can't say no can we, Santa?" Nick asked, waiting for his shot to be poured.

"No, South Pole, my perverted little elf, no we can't." And Jack just happens to be my poison of choice in the whiskey department.

Nick and I downed our shots. Nick isn't the seasoned pro at hard liquor that I am and it showed. He choked a little, coughed, caught his breath, and said, "Smooooooth." Everyone laughed. "I think we need two more, don't you, Santa?"

"Fuck, yah I do" is what I wanted to say. And to my shock, I said it. This might've been the first time I actually ever said exactly what was on my mind at a party. I downed my shot, and damn it was good. I exhaled loudly with a few stray drops of Jack dripping from my faux mustache and said, "HO, HO, HO, NOW THAT'S WHAT I CALL CHRISTMAS SPIRIT!!"

The rest of the party followed suit and took a sip from whatever they were drinking. Now this party was on fire.

"Ok, people, it's time to focus," Nick said, getting everyone's attention, "and to guess Santa's weight."

I've never seen so many adults so eager to play something so silly. Nick handed out pieces of paper for everyone to write their guest-a-ma-tions on.

"I don't know about anyone else here but I can't make a guess until I feel up Santa to be able to tell how much of that is real. And how much of it is fake," Lisa said, getting up from her spot on the arm of the couch.

"Go easy on him, honey," Tom said, sitting back and taking a drink.

Once again, the guests were going crazy with catcalls and cheering Lisa on. Lisa, who was wearing a short, black dress and was very easy on the eyes to boot, came up to me as if I were her prey. I think she even growled at me as she put her hand on my shoulder.

She looked over to Nick and made a request, "Chair please."

"'Cumming' right up." One of the other guests got up from their chair and handed it to Nick to give to Lisa.

Lisa grabbed the chair and made me have a seat. She then proceeded to circle me and run her finger along my back and arms. Once in front of me she started to dance like a stripper.

"Do it, baby, do it!" Tom yelled encouragingly while refilling his glass.

She looked up at him; what kind of look she shot him I have no idea. I was too busy enjoying the view of a nicely heart-shaped ass going from side to side in front of my face. She got up, dropped down on her knees, and flung her head and long, blonde hair back into my lap.

"Do it, Lisa, you sexy bitch!" Kristy yelled from the back of the room.

The more they cheered her on the more she got into it.

"Come on, people, this girl needs encouragement. Give her some," I said, knowing if I wanted more, she needed more first.

Everyone started yelling and going crazy. A few people even came up to her and threw down $100 bills. Not $1s but $100s. I saw at least seven of those bad boys get tossed. She shoved them in the top of her dress in between her sparkling cleavage. She massaged my legs and flung her hair on my face and down to my crotch. Her grand finale came in the form of her putting one hand on my right shoulder, while placing one foot between my legs and flinging the other up on to my left shoulder. *Black lace panties aren't very Christmassy*, I thought to myself while enjoying the show. She raised her right hand in the air as if she just conquered Mount Santa. And let me tell you, like most climbers, once they reach their peak, she too raised a flag. Mine.

Holy fucking shit, I'm as hard as AP Calculus!

Everyone clapped while Lisa dismounted me with the aid of a few of the other girls. I felt like I was in seventh grade again, sitting there, afraid if I stood up to go to the chalkboard everyone in the class would see my ginormous boner.

"Thank you, Lisa, for the show. I think it's time for Santa and South Pole to take a break." It was Mrs. Claus from behind me.

Now? You want me to get up now? Shit. I need to think of something to get this redwood down. Dead puppies, dead puppies. Nope. Granny panties, granny panties. Almost. Dead puppies wearing granny panties, Dead puppies wearing granny panties. There we go.

"So entertain yourselves for a moment while our boys take a break."

I started to get up but Mrs. Claus came around to my front, sat down, and straddled my right leg. She put her hand on my face and moved in close to my ear. She inhaled, got closer to my ear, and whispered, "I'm not wearing any panties." Then she gyrated ever so slightly on my leg and stood up.

I wasn't sure what I was supposed to do with that information but I liked it. I guess it could go in the ol' spank bank to be withdrawn at a later date. Mrs. Claus took me by the hand and led me out of the living room and into the kitchen. South Pole was right behind us.

I didn't think Mrs. Claus had anyone working the party but there were two ladies dressed all in red and white prepping stuff and cleaning up as we entered.

"Hola, Mrs. Claus," one of them said.

This lady really was serious about the Mrs. Claus role. She made everyone refer to her as Mrs. Claus and they were doing it, happily. I didn't get the sense that people were doing it because she was filthy rich and the boss. They seemed to be doing it to play along in, "one of her crazy, fun games that she does." There was something about her I couldn't put my finger on. She was like a woman who didn't have a care in the world.

"Do you guys need anything special to eat or drink?" Mrs. Claus asked.

"Water's fine," I replied.

"Actually, I could use a bathroom," Nick said.

An odd-looking smile came across the face of Mrs. Claus. Did she just have the bathroom redone and was happy she was going to be able to show it off?

"Of course, South Pole. Take your time. I want to pass out some gifts before you two take off tonight. I'm going to take Santa with me to get the bag of gifts for my guests and go over a few things with him, so just take your time and relax until we get back. Maria, can you show South Pole to the restroom, please?"

"Si, Mrs. Claus. This way, Mr. South Pole."

"Santa," Mrs. Claus said, extending her hand to me.

I took her hand in mine.

"Come with me," she said, leading the way out of the kitchen and up a set of stairs.

We went to her bedroom, which had a big red bag filled with gifts, at the foot of the bed.

"Is that the bag you were talking about?" I asked.

I heard the door close behind me. I turned to see Mrs. Claus locking it. *She really doesn't want anyone to see what they're getting from her this year.* She walked toward me with an air of confidence like a woman on a mission. My palms started to sweat. I was already hot and sweaty from being in the costume, but my palms were sweaty for a whole other reason. I was getting excited and blood was beginning to rush to my naughty bits. How appropriate for a "Naughty Santa."

Saying nothing, Mrs. Claus book-ended my face with her hands and kissed me. I don't know how pleasant it was for her— she got a mouthful of fake hair and a lot less actual lips. She pulled back and stared at me as if I was dinner.

"I fucking love the color of your eyes."

"Thank you."

I went to remove my fake facial hair, the better to kiss her with but she stopped me and kissed me again, only harder this time. The harder she kissed the harder I got. This was a first for me. I've never had a hard-on at a party before (and if I had I would've sought help IMMEDIATELY) and the first time I do, I get two. She guided my hands around her waist. I gave her a squeeze and she let out a sigh and started biting my lip, and I felt her fingernails actually dig into my face a little bit. It didn't seem to phase her that she was hurting me and I didn't say anything—I was just happy to be kissed and to have a hard-on. Christmas can be a lonely time. For us both obviously.

Mrs. Claus gave a slight moan that was a wee bit loud and cut short by her realization that it was a wee bit loud. She became very primal and rough, grabbing my arms, chest, and ass while grunting the whole time. I think she was having fun trying to control her noises while making me her bitch. Personally, it all didn't seem real to me and was happening so fast. Normally, I'm just happy to get a break and a glass of water. This was much better. I was expecting it to stop at any moment, so I just enjoyed it while it lasted.

"I um—"

I went to speak but was immediately stopped by Mrs. Claus. She put a finger up to my lips and said, "Shhhhhh." And put her finger in my mouth moving it in and out slowly.

Removing her finger, she started to kiss me again very roughly, one of her arms wrapped around my neck while her other hand went downtown. Not my downtown, hers. That's right she was taking care of herself and flicking the bean using the same finger she had "shhhhed" me with. Once again the moaning started; luckily I had a lip for her to bite into and a back for her to scratch to help her control herself. It's the least I could do for all the kindness she was showing me.

She let out a loud grunt and let go of me and herself and went for the tie string on my Santa pants. Not with her hands but with her teeth. In record time she had my big red Santa pants and underwear down around my knees. She stood up and pushed... no wait... shoved me down onto the bed. There I was a half-naked Santa lying on her bed all sweaty with a big stiffy doing my best impersonation of a sundial. And it was high noon.

Mrs. Claus gave a little giggle as if saying to herself, *Oh my god, what am I doing? I need to stop. Does this make me a whore? Whatever it is, I like it.* Like I said before, I was expecting all this to stop at any moment, so I continued to enjoy every moment because the next one may be the last.

Mrs. Claus's giggle turned into a hunger. She went for it. I lay there with her mouth wrapped around me and felt like I needed to go home and pen a letter. And that letter would start with the sentence, "Dear *Penthouse* forum, I can't believe this happened to me..." A part of me felt bad she was down there in regions that had been hot and fermenting in sweat all day and probably had a little bit of an odor, or at this point was more like an "OH-DEAR." She didn't seem to mind so I got over being self-conscious real quick.

Like I said, I was expecting it all to stop at any moment. It didn't. She was also taking care of herself at the same time, talented woman.

Mrs. Claus was going at it like it was her job. With the amount of dedication she was giving it one would think she was on payroll. You know how sometimes when a person puts it all the way in their mouth, they start to tear up—let me tell you, she didn't cry or nothin'.

This is a woman who knows what she wants. I can respect that. I could tell this was one job she'd done before and *really* enjoyed her work. She wasn't stopping or showing any signs of slowing down. I believed she was going to follow through with her actions and finish what she started. I think I actually felt the sheets being sucked up through my ass.

Holy shit!

She did it.

I did it.

I don't know how but she got us both across the finish line at exactly the same time. Like I said before, talented woman. Wow, did this really happen? I need a sandwich and a nap. I didn't realize Mrs. Claus was such a ho, ho, ho!

I lay there basking in the glow of my post-ejaculatory bliss while I could hear Mrs. Claus brushing her teeth in the bathroom. She came out and as if nothing happened said, "When you're rested, don't forget to bring the bag of gifts with you." And she walked out of the room and headed back downstairs to entertain in a more traditional sense.

I got up and pulled up my pants. *That was weird,* I thought to myself, as so many other thoughts ran through my head.

Did that just happen?

Why did that happen?

Why do I feel like I should take her out for dinner and a movie?

Why am I analyzing the shit out of this?

I feel used.

I like it.

I grabbed the red sack, walked back down the stairs and entered the living room with everyone's gifts from our most generous and very giving hostess, Mrs. Claus.

"Hey, look who's back? Santa!" somebody said. It could've been a male or female, I wasn't paying much attention. I wanted to lie down.

"What's in the sack, Santa?" a man from somewhere asked.

I'll tell you what's not in a sack. I was back to my old self thinking something and not verbalizing it. I felt like everyone at the party knew what we had done. It was odd. I felt naughty. I looked over at Mrs. Claus who hid the whole affair very well.

"Well it seems like Santa brought you all presents. Isn't that right, Santa?" Mrs. Claus asked.

"That's right," I said, still not believing that a few short minutes earlier my baldheaded mouse was in her mouth.

"Why don't we have Santa sit down and you can all take turns sitting on his lap and telling him what you want for Christmas?" Nick suggested.

"That's a great idea, South Pole, I'm first," one of the female guests said, putting down her drink and coming over to sit on my lap. She plopped herself down and started to talk in a little girl voice. "My name is Samantha, and I've been a bad girl."

And Santa's been a bad boy but you don't see me advertising.

Samantha continued, "I think I need a spanking. Does anyone else think I need a spanking?"

The crowd went nuts and yelled to me to spank her. She assumed the position on my lap and said, "Hold on, Santa. Bart, get the camera." Her husband, Bart, got the camera and got front-row center. Samantha looked up to me and said, "Now I'm ready."

What can I say? I spanked her. At first it was gentle but she and Bart kept saying, "Harder, Santa, harder!" So I spanked harder.

"Don't make Santa take off his belt, little girl."

"Don't tease me. Do I get a gift now?" she asked, cramming my face in between her breasts.

South Pole found the gift from the bag with the name "SAMANTHA" on it and passed it to her.

"Did you get that, Bart?"

"You getting your gift? Yes."

"No, me with Santa's face in my boobs."

"I missed it. Do it again."

"Oh, Santa, I love my gift." She once again put my face in her cleavage and held it there while I listened to the sound of a camera shutter in the darkness of her womanhood.

"Click, click, click, click."

"Got it, Sam."

Sam started to stand up.

"Where are you going?" Mrs. Claus asked, "You need to open it."

"Oh," Samantha said, tearing open her gift.

"What is it? What is it?" Bart asked with the camera ready.

"It's for us both, darlin,'" she said, holding it up for all to see.

It was a strap-on dildo. Everyone laughed and of course made all sorts of off-color comments.

I looked over to Mrs. Claus. I wish I could say I looked with no hidden agenda but I'd be lying. I looked over to make eye contact and see whether she would shoot me a "I remember what we did" look. Nothing. Did it not mean anything to her? Was she trying to hide it from everyone? Yah, that's it, she was not letting anyone else in on our little secret.

My gaze over to Mrs. Claus was interrupted by Samantha putting her hand on my face and saying, "It's too bad you only 'cum' once a year, Santa."

"He's not the only one," Bart said, in an attempt to be funny.

"And it'll stay that way if you don't watch it, Mr. Man," Samantha shot back.

Samantha returned to her seat and then everyone at one time or another came up and sat on my lap and told me what they wanted for Christmas. All the woman sat on my lap, but only one or two of the men did while giving me their "wish list."

"I want a Porsche."

"I want more furs."

"I want more blowjobs."

Speaking of blowjobs, if you peeps only knew just how dirty and naughty your hostess is!

After everyone came up and got their gifts, Mrs. Claus, my very good friend, addressed the group.

"I want to thank you all for coming tonight."

Does that include me?

"As you all know, I've been in the middle of going through a divorce."

A few sympathy comments were said.

"And I got the best Christmas gift of all today. My divorce became official."

Her announcement was met by applause.

"South Pole, can you hand me the last gift in the bag, please?"

Nick reached in and pulled out the last present from the bag and handed it to Mrs. Claus. It looked like a picture frame.

"Thank you, South Pole." She unwrapped it and showed it to everyone. "My little gift to myself, I had my divorce papers framed."

Everyone laughed and came up and gave her hugs.

"Now you need to go out and get fucked," Tom said once everyone was sitting back down.

Mrs. Claus shot me a knowing glance before addressing her guests once again, "Sounds like a plan."

South Pole made an announcement that we had to get back to the North Pole to warm up some elves. Everyone said goodbye to us, gave us hugs, and pats on the back.

"Great job, guys. You're fun," Kristy said while hugging me.

"Bet you don't do many parties like this," Lisa added, waiting for her turn to hug me.

"Hope you guys had as much fun as we did," Tom said, shaking my hand.

"I can't speak for South Pole here, but I can personally say I had quite an amazing time like no other before," I replied happily, holding onto my naughty little secret.

Mrs. Claus did the good hostess thing once again, and walked us to the door. I looked at her and became sad. I honestly thought if you had a shit-load of money finding love was easy. It's probably harder. You can't tell if a person likes you for you or your bank account. I need to hurry and find someone before I hit it big.

"Thank you so much, guys. This is for you." She handed us each a very expensive bottle of wine and a wad of cash. "Everyone pooled in some money to give you guys an extra tip."

"Thank you so much," Nick said, taking the wad.

"No, no, no. Thank you guys for making tonight really special," Mrs. Claus said, reaching for my arm and giving it a rub up and down before continuing, "I really needed it."

Me too, I thought to myself before saying, "I mean this when I say, thank you for everything, Mrs. Claus."

"I know. Drive safe." She closed the door and I knew I'd never see her ever again.

"Now that was a FUN party!" Nick said having no idea just how "fun" it was.

"Ditto."

A part of me did wonder if I'd ever run into her professionally at an acting audition. I would walk into the room ready to audition and there she would be sitting as some big-shot producer or casting director. She never saw me without my fake beard, mustache and red hat, she'd never know it was me, her special "Santa."

I never got her real name but I'm sure I'd remember her face if I ever saw her again. If I did, I'd thank her for making me feel attractive again. She didn't have to do what she did and who knows if she'd have done it regardless of who was playing Santa at her party. I'd like to think she wouldn't have and her attraction to me was for me and my personality, since she never saw my face.

I really needed the confidence boost. And the blowjob didn't hurt either.

Chapter 8

Stop! That's My No-No Place

I arrived at my bosses' house to pick up my stuff for a last-minute party I agreed to do, only to find they were not there. I was greeted at the door by their friend Ryan.

Ryan's a friend of Nick and Rachel's who had just moved to Los Angeles from Germany. They met him while performing *Little Shop of Horrors* for the summer in Hamburg. Ryan played the giant, man-eating plant and they couldn't rave enough about how "*Ahhhhh-maaaaze-zzzzzzing*" he was.

Having never seen the play or movie, I had no idea what the part entails, or how Ryan's 6'4" lanky frame was beneficial to the role. I just knew his chiseled, weathered face was covered up by a big, awkward costume, and that part of it I *could* relate to. Ryan moved to L.A. for the same reason so many others do—an attempt at fame and fortune as an actor. While waiting for his "big break," he was learning how to perform at kids' parties for money. An all-too-familiar story.

Ryan informed me he was going to assist me at my party tonight because Nick wanted him to "learn from the best." I looked over the paperwork; it said it was for an Armenian christening starting at 8:30pm. How odd for a kids party to start so late? I asked Ryan whether Nick had said anything about the party since I had no idea what an "Armenian christening" is exactly.

"Well, he said to think of it as the Armenian financial equivalent of a Sweet 16, Bar/Bat Mitzvah, or a Quinceañera. Except that the guest of honor is usually around two years old and will never remember the party. This is the event to show everyone how much money you have, and the more you spend equals how much you love your kid. He said we'll have fun and he's done a whole bunch of these."

Sounds different. I like different. I love experiencing different cultures' traditions and ways of life. One of the little perks to this job is I get an inside view into a lot of different cultures on many economic levels. It's very facinating to me. I even tried dog once. And by "tried" I mean I ate some cooked dog meat. It did NOT taste like chicken. New experiences are like a drug for me and give me a "high" unlike anything else. That's why I love traveling. You can read about the Greek island of Santorini, believed to be one of the possible locations of the lost city of Atlantis, but there is no better way to learn about it than to experience it for yourself. The smells, the food, the people – I love it all! I'm excited for my first-ever Armenian christening.

We arrived at the restaurant where the party was taking place a half-hour before we were scheduled to start.

"Why are we here so early, Jay?" Ryan asked.

"I like to get to my gigs early because I don't like being rushed. You never know how traffic's going to be, and all it takes is one fuck-o to forget to gas up and you're late. I hate that. I'm going to go and make sure this is our party."

I got out of my truck and could hear the music coming from inside the establishment over the street traffic—that's some loud music! Gathered around the front door was a group of men in their thirties and forties standing in suits smoking. It looked like a scene out of a mobster movie, not a kid's birthday party.

I walked over to the group of men that were outside, yet were somehow still surrounded by a cloud of smoke.

"Excuse me, is this the Armenian christening for—?"

"Yes. Who you, my friend?" the man interrupted me. He had a very thick Russian-type accent. It was the kind of accent I've come to expect to hear in one of the many bad acting classes I've taken out here in Los Angeles.

"I'm Barney. The kids' entertainment."

"Ah, yes. The Barney." He took a long drag on his cigarette that could barely be seen behind his large, sausage-like, ring-covered fingers.

"Do you know where I can find Joe, the father of the child being christened?"

"Ah, yes. The Joe." He exhaled the smoke from his lungs.

It amazed me the smoke seemed to stay around him and not float away. It was something out of a cartoon. I can honestly say I was kind of mesmerized by it, but continued my conversation with "The Smoking Man" anyway.

"Is he here?"

"You do birthday parties, my friend?"

"Yes, I do."

He took another long drag on his cancer stick and inhaled it deeply.

"So. You do birthday parties, my friend. This is different. This is Armenian christening. Party will go until four in the morning. This is different than birthday party, my friend. You will see. Different, yes."

I was waiting for him to exhale, but it didn't happen.

"Ok. So do you know where I can find Joe?"

He took a long drag on his cigarette, still without exhaling his last drag. "Yes, my friend. The Joe is by the back door. That is where you find The Joe."

Wait for it.

Wait for it.

Wait for it.

Nothing. I know this man exhales, I saw him do it earlier. I was fascinated and slightly creeped out at the same time. I might even have been staring a little bit.

"What is it, my friend?" The Smoking Man said to me, breaking my trance.

"Oh, um, thanks, thanks for the info."

I started to walk away when he yelled back at me.

"Remember, The Barney. Is different."

I waved back to him in acknowledgement I had heard him. He still didn't exhale. In fact he took another drag before I got around the corner. I'd hate to see what his lungs looked like.

I went to the back door, as instructed, and asked for Joe.

"I'm the Joe," a rather large man in a black suit said. And yes, he too was smoking, but he was actually exhaling. "What you do?"

"I'm your Barney for the evening."

Joe pulled out a huge wad of cash from the front right pocket of the trousers that were two sizes too large for him.

"How much?" he asked, unclipping his money clip and flipping through what looked like 30 or so $100 bills.

"I'm sorry, I left the paperwork in my truck and didn't see what your balance due is."

"Is ok. I pay you later." He stuffed the money back in his pocket. "Now you eat."

"Thanks, but I can't eat before I do a party. I don't want to throw up on the kids," I told him, patting my stomach.

"You are funny, the Barney." He took a long drag on his cigarette, finishing it.

"I like you." He threw his still-smoking cigarette butt on the ground in front of him. "You eat after. Where you park, my friend?"

"On the street."

He lit up another cigarette, "Is no good. You must park back here, my friend. Go get car and park back here. Is good, yes?"

"Thank you. I'll be right back and ready to start at eight."

Joe took the first drag of his newly lit cig-a-butt, nodded, and waved me off with the back of his hand as if to say, "Is good, my friend, of the friend. Go get your truck, my friend." Or at least that's what I imagined he would've said if he had spoken. Joe was too busy to speak; he had some serious smoking to attend to.

I did as I was instructed. I got my truck, parked in the back, and changed into my costume.

"Jay, Nick tells me you're dating a girl who was a child actress."

Ah, yes. That. Nick loves to name-drop even if the name is not his to do so. Sara was a child actress who couldn't find work as an adult, and resorted to working in an office at a music publishing company and doing kids' parties on the weekends. I explained to Ryan that Sara and I are just friends. I wanted to be more but she flat-out told me, "Why should I date you when I could find someone like you with money?" How typical in this town! Once I understood it wasn't going to work, due to her mind swimming in the shallow end of the pool, I stopped pursuing her.

I recently came to the realization I'm getting older and everyone I date from here on out is a potential life partner. I'm tired of wasting time and the moment I feel it's not going to work I end it. So far it's been working great for me. I still hang out with Sara but she's a cock tease and needs A LOT of attention all the time. Way too much work to make it worth it if you ask me. I'd rather spend my efforts on the two sketch groups and two bands I'm involved with, they are much more rewarding.

Once fully dressed, Ryan took me by the arm and led me to the front door. As we passed by the group of smoking men, my Smoking Man friend felt compelled to grab me by the arm as I passed him and said, "Remember, The Barney, is different. Not birthday party. Is different." Was that a warning? *Should I be scared?*

We opened the door and were hit by a wall of sound fueled by a thundering bass beat. The music was so loud I thought my ears were going to explode. The huge Purple Dino head I'm wearing vibrated with every beat, muffling the sound, yet it was still painfully loud. Now I'm a huge heavy metal and rock music fan so I don't mind my music loud but even I couldn't handle the decibels of this music.

Ryan looked at me and commented, "Wow, that music sure is loud!"

"Yeah, it is."

"What?"

Ryan was standing two feet in front of me and couldn't hear me talking through the Purple Dino head. This is not good for the lines of communication required during this party. I grabbed his arm and pulled him toward the mesh screen that was over the mouth of the hood.

"Can you hear me now?" I yelled.

"Yeah!"

"This is going to make it very hard for me to talk to the children!"

"What?"

Is it me, or did the music just get louder? "This is going to make it very hard for me to talk to the children!"

"Oh, yeah!"

The hall was long and narrow, and we were at one end and a stage with a band was at the other end about a hundred feet away. The vestibule area we were in was about twenty feet long by forty feet wide with a nine-foot ceiling. It was decorated with an abundance of red and gold carpeting and drapery. I could see into the main hall where the band was playing. That room was much bigger.

Ryan led me to the doorway to the main hall when all of a sudden we were spotted. A little girl around five years old stopped dead in her tracks and screamed.

"IS BARNEY!!!"

She came running over to me at full speed, jumping up and wrapping herself around me. Her legs flailed as she tried to climb up my body.

This was all it took for everyone to know I had arrived. The kids went insane and started coming out of the woodwork. They seemed to pop out from everywhere—a side door, the dance floor, under the carpet; it was scary, like zombies coming out of every nook and cranny for my brains. The paperwork said the party was for twenty-five kids, but there had to be at least twice that amount, maybe four times that amount. It was crazy. The room was jam-packed with kids, adults holding kids, kids holding kids and I was in the epicenter of it all. There were so many little hands grabbing me while everyone was screaming and yelling out my name,

"BARNEY! BARNEY! BARNEY!" Ryan had allowed himself to be pushed out of the way by the mob, and was now on the outskirts of the crowd, demoted from "helper" to "onlooker." Amateur.

A familiar face came into the room and the crowd parted like the Red Sea. It was The Joe, the man throwing the party.

"Out of way, out of way, let me through. I am paying for party, let me through." Joe made his way to me and took me by the hand. "You come with me, The Barney. You come with me now. We dance, is good."

The Joe led me through the ocean of children and into the main hall. I thought the other room was cheesy, this room had it beat. Big cream-colored pillars placed about every twenty feet along the edge of the high-ceilinged room were so big it would take two adults holding hands to cover the circumference. The pillars were decorated with red boas, gold ribbons, and what looked to be flashing Christmas lights. Not the small white twinkle ones, either. I'm talking about the big, multicolored ones. The kind that was popular in the 70's. A humongous chandelier hung from the center of the ceiling with four smaller ones hung from each corner of the room.

The Joe led me down the center of the room, which was split by round, twelve-person tables on either side. The tables were decked out as if it were a wedding; very fancy everything—tablecloths, silverware, and centerpieces that rotated on a mirrored lazy Susan with various photos of the family posing with the christening child.

The Joe was in front of me the whole time yelling at people; my guess was he was telling them to get out of his way (he was paying for ALL this, after all!). I couldn't tell exactly what he told them because it became harder and harder to hear him the closer and closer we got to the band. Once on the dance floor I noticed it was lighting up "disco style" in bright primary colors, and changed in sync with the beat of the music. I got a glimpse behind me and saw the kids had followed me and The Joe to the dance floor.

The Joe held up his hands and started yelling…Oh wait, he was singing. Once again I started to slowly become encircled by the children. I had been on the dance floor for all of a minute and the music was already killing my ears; it was louder than a Poison concert I went to in 1988.

The Joe kept bringing random people over to dance with me. I think I danced with his son, who was the guest of honor, his mother, and some crazy grandparent that could hardly move much less dance. Ryan, my "helper," was nowhere to be seen. There were a ton of kids, and their numbers seemed to get larger with every passing minute.

While dancing, one of the adults snuck up from behind me and thought it would be funny to try and pull my head off.

Great example to set for the kids, you fuck-tard! Lucky for me my hands were already up in the air, a la The Joe, and I was able to put the kibosh on the pulling off of the Barney head.

The older kids motioned for me to bend down so they could talk to me. I did as they asked, but was careful in case it was another trick to try and take my head off, since it seemed the "in" thing to do, thanks to one drunk adult. I held onto my head and bent down. I had a very hard time understanding what they were saying.

"Barney, you have to take off your head. You are scaring all the little kids."

I tried to answer them, but they couldn't hear me because of the obscenely loud music raping my ears. That, and the fact that I had on a big Purple Dino head didn't help things out, either. I did my best Marcel Marceau to get the point across that I was not going to be taking my head off anytime soon.

I couldn't get over how loud the music was. Some of the younger kids were covering their ears out on the dance floor. I couldn't figure out why no one was saying anything and why they weren't turning it down. What were they waiting for? Blood to start coming out of the kids' ears while they lay on the floor writhing in pain, begging to be put out of their misery?

During my dance-a-thon, I noticed two men on the dance floor with video cameras. Having done some professional camera work in my time, I could tell these were not your run-of-the-mill consumer video cameras. The Joe was serious about capturing video footage of this event for the family archives. Each camera had a blinding light mounted on it, and when the two cameramen stood next to one another it looked like a Mack truck was heading toward you. I noticed people would act up in front of the camera while looking up at the band.

There were two giant video screens on either side of the band, the action captured by the cameras was being "broadcast" on these screens. I watched for a little bit as people would see themselves on the screen and act like they were on *American Bandstand* being broadcast nationwide. Everyone in this town wishes they were an entertainer. Not only could I see the two different camera shots from the dance floor, but I could also see shots from other places around the party. How many cameras were there here? Was that a shot from the kitchen? I looked around and noticed a small video village tucked away to the left of the stage behind a curtain; a big, gaudy red curtain, of course.

To add to the insanity, The Joe tossed a handful of cash up into the air and I watched as everyone, from children to adults, went batshit pushing one another out of the way to grab as much green as they could. From what I could tell, it looked mostly like one dollar bills but I do think I saw a five-spot or two in the hands of a few people.

The Joe was spending more on this party than the U.S. government spends on defense. I couldn't fathom how much this whole event was costing. One thing for certain—it was much more than I make in a decade.

I knew dance time was over when The Joe approached me and said, "You go play with little childrens now."

I must have danced nonstop for the first half-hour or forty-five minutes of my time; it was hard to tell since the music NEVER stopped. It was one long, painful eight-hour song written especially for christenings.

I was exhausted and drenched in sweat from dancing in a big, furry costume for so long. I didn't have to say or do anything to get the kids to follow me, they just did. I could've walked out the door and into a magical land, and they would've followed me the whole way, no questions asked. Ah, the power.

I FINALLY saw my assistant, Ryan, sitting arms crossed with a big smile on his face. I motioned for him to follow me into the vestibule area.

We pulled out the parachute to play some games. It was not pretty. The parachute was way too small for a party with this many children. They were fighting for spots to hold onto, and the ones that did have a hold of it shook it really hard and pulled on it viciously. Not exactly what I call playing. I couldn't be heard, therefore I couldn't get control of the kids or the game.

Ryan wasn't helping. He just stood there, not even trying to communicate with me to find out what to do. He didn't make a very good assistant. I know he had never seen any parachute games, so he didn't know how to take control of the activity. I suppose it doesn't help that he's a wallflower. You'd never guess he was an actor. Usually we actors are outgoing, extroverted people and don't need prompting to "come out of our shell." Not Ryan. He is the actor equivalent of Eeyore. Maybe it would've helped him if I sang *Suddenly Seymour*? I was screaming instructions to him from inside my purple-headed prison. Nothing. The kids were beating on me, trying to take off my head, and he was not saying or doing anything about it. I couldn't see whether he was even trying.

As my frustration grew, I tried to collect my thoughts to figure out what to do next. I knew it would have to be something that didn't require too much communication with the kids. A rather large man in an ugly brown suit with a cigar decided my next step for me. As he came around the children, he had a look in his eyes of a man on a mission. He reminded me of a mobster straight out of *The Godfather* on his way to "deliver a message."

He took my hand, pulled me away from the kids and the parachute, and started rambling on in Armenian to me as if I could understand him. I could hardly *hear* him much less *understand* him. I decided to follow him; hell, he was doing me a favor by taking me away from the pig-fuck this party was turning into. At this point my best plan of action is to be eye-candy and to be seen as much as possible so The Joe believes he's getting his money's worth. Cigar Man led me to a chair back in the main room with the band and wanted me to sit. At least that's what I think he wanted. I sat at the table next to an old man. Cigar Man took my arm and put it around the old man.

Oh, I get it. He wants me to pose with the old man for a photo. Why didn't he say so? Actually, he might have, and I just couldn't understand him. I needed more than an assistant at this party—I needed an interpreter and a megaphone. While waiting for Cigar Man to take the photo, the old man put his hand on my leg, rather high up my leg, I may add, and asked, "Is Barney boy or girl?"

Not waiting for me to answer, he decided to find out for himself. He proceeded to go all the way up my leg and put his hand on my crotch. He took it a step further and started to fondle me and roll my cock in his hand as if rolling a cigar.

"Ah, Barney is boy! Ha, ha, ha!" he announced to no one in particular.

Still curious, he moved his hand from my crotch and started to touch my breast. I couldn't believe I was being molested, and in plain sight of everyone. I think the cameraman was there documenting the whole thing and it was being broadcast nationwide.

"It's got a beat you can dance to, but I'm going to give it a seven out of ten, Mr. Clark. Or can I call you Dick?"

I pushed the old man's hands off me and stood up. He wasn't going to let me go that easy. He proceeded to grab and squeeze my ass. This old man was going to town on my ass as if kneading bread, and for an elderly gentleman he had very strong hands. I'd have to check later to see whether he left any marks. I turned to him and waved my finger at him as if to say, "No!!" I turned away from him and tried walking away. This time it was Cigar Man who wasn't letting me leave. The old man must have thought "no" actually meant "yes" because he came up behind me and grabbed my dick. Again! And this time he was full-on jerking me off. I had to turn around, yet again, and push him away from me. Hard. Man Strength was not enough in this dire situation; I had to resort to Man Strength Plus.

Man Strength Plus refers to 1) the amount of force a performer must use when his normal "Man Strength" isn't enough to get him out of a character hood-wearing situation, and 2) the force required to convey the fact that he's now serious. And I was now officially serious about getting out of this situation.

He stumbled a bit, but he just laughed and kept coming at me.

Do I need to push this man even harder to get him to stop violating me? I thought to myself, trying to escape.

Purple Dino Type decided enough was enough. I pushed everyone out of my way. I was not being gentle. When I pushed Cigar Man he just laughed, put his hands up, and started dancing. The old man had one of the kids help him grab his walker and he started making a beeline for me. A few thoughts came to mind at that point: *What is wrong with this old man? Does he have some sort of Purple Dino fetish? Where the fuck is my so-called assistant during all this? Can no one see I'm being desecrated?* After this party I would need therapy, and you'd better believe I would make Nick pay for it. He knew what I was getting into.

As I was making my getaway, a woman came up to me and demanded, "You play with children now! Make balloon. Make balloon. My baby very sad. Want balloon now." She had to yell over the music and it was still hard to hear her. I wanted to tell her to go take a flying fuck, but she actually had a good idea. For the moment I ignored her and made my way back to Ryan and the children.

I could see the kids fighting over the parachute and Ryan standing off to the side, unmoving and doing nothing. Still functioning on Man Strength, I grabbed the parachute from the children and put it in my bag. It was easy since they weren't expecting Purple Dino to pull out Man Strength. It's a tool of last resort.

Without a word, I put the parachute back in my bag and motioned to Ryan to follow me. I needed to find a place with a high visibility factor. I walked back into the main hall, took an immediate left and set up base camp in the rear left corner behind one of the round tables.

I situated myself with my back to the wall and pulled Ryan over to me. I put my mouth right on the eyehole of the hood and yelled as loud as I could—and trust me, I can yell. He pointed to his ears and shrugged his shoulders as if to tell me he couldn't hear me. I was frustrated to the point where I wanted to hit something. I restrained myself, reached into my bag, pulled out the balloons and pump, and handed them to Ryan. He nodded and finally understood what I wanted him to do. Frustration level dropping only slightly, but dropping nonetheless, I planted my desecrated ass in a chair in the corner and got out my face paints.

What a nightmare! The kids couldn't hear me ask them what they wanted me to paint on their faces. They just kept yelling and repeating themselves, over and over. Ryan never stopped making balloons. He would make as many as they wanted. And since hearing was such a challenge in the costume, the older kids and adults started resorting to hitting me on the Purple Dino head to get my attention. I would wave my finger back and forth at them, trying to make them understand that "You DO NOT hit me in the head!" They just kept on doing it. The adults were actually worse than the kids. And then, there he was—the dirty old man that felt me up. He was on the outskirts of the children and I could tell he was trying to make his way toward me. The kids were like a human blockade he could not penetrate, thank goodness. I waved to him. Not so much to say "Hello," but more to say, "Fuck you!"

I reached in my bag and pulled out the gift bags I was supposed to hand out to the kids. Because the paperwork said there were 25 kids, I only had around 28 gift bags. Clearly there was a shortage. As soon as the kids noticed I was handing out FREE stuff, they swarmed me like locusts and literally started to climb over the table as well as one another to try and get a goodie bag. Actually, at that point they didn't care about each other so much as they cared about the free loot. The older kids were pushing the younger kids out of the way, and a few pushed hard enough to make some younger kids fall to the floor.

I was trying to tell the older kids the younger kids got the gift bags first. No one could hear me, and even if they could've I don't think they would've cared; they just wanted FREE stuff. I could see the mothers of some of the younger kids pick up their respective children and hold them up to me so I could "see" their child. If they thought I hadn't seen their kid they would push the other kids, young and old, out of the way to get to me. They would always start yelling something to me in their native language first, then they would move on to English.

"YOU GIVE MY CHILD, NOW! NOW, I SAY! YOU GIVE!"

These mothers had no consideration for anyone. By this time Purple Dino had major attitude. I started turning away from these mothers. What were they going to do, hit me on the head? They couldn't—they had their hands full of children.

I looked at the green pager in my bag that served as my timepiece—10:20pm.

"Party's over!" For me, at least. I had been scheduled for two hours, from eight to ten. Now I needed to get out. Desperate times called for desperate measures. If these people were going to act like animals, that's how I was going to treat them. I grabbed a huge handful of lollipops and threw them out into the pack of children. You want to talk about pandemonium? They went berserk! Why hadn't I thought of this earlier? Watching them relentlessly push, shove and hit one another over candy was the first time I'd had fun at this party. I think I even saw a few kids biting one another. This was my chance to escape. I grabbed my bag and left the comforts of my corner. I left poor Ryan to fend for himself. I wanted—no, let me rephrase that, I NEEDED—to get out of there.

I ran into the foyer and started heading for the front door. A security guard waved me over to a door to the left of the room.

In a thick Southern accent he said, "Over here. The kids won't find ya' in here."

It was like an angel had been sent to help me. I was so relieved. This whole thing was finally almost over. To say I was happy would be an understatement.

Once inside the room the guard closed the door behind me.

"I used to play Chuck E. Cheese," he said, a big wad of chewing tobacco in his mouth. He spit into a clear Coca Cola bottle and continued. "It's safe for you to take that off if you want. I feel for you, man."

I took off my head and thanked my guardian angel from heaven.

"Man, o' man, you ar' a sweatin'."

I asked my savior whether he could tell Ryan where I was. "He's the really tall guy with—"

"I know who he is. He's the only other white guy here other than us two," he said, making his way out the door.

Since I was alone, I took the opportunity to take off my costume, which was now about fifteen pounds heavier from all the sweat.

Ryan and the security guard came into the room.

I looked up at Ryan before he got too comfortable, "Hey, is it possible for you to find Joe and get the rest of the money from him? Here's the paperwork that shows his balance due. Feel free to show it to him so there's no question about how much he really owes."

"Ok," he said, taking the paperwork and heading back out the door.

The security guard kindly gave me a bottle of water.

"Thanks, I can really use this."

"No prob-lame-o. I got me one of them there mother-in-laws that only speak Spanish." Then it got weird as he continued with his tale. "But she knows not to give me shit or I'll beat her spic ass. I came home drunk one night, and my ol' lady gave me shit and I booted her *and* her mother out, telling them to leave the boy. Hell, they lucky I didn't beat 'em. I want to fuck the secretary at my other job anyways. Chuck E. Cheese is a great place to meet single moms who want to fuck. I just bring my boy and tell 'em I'm a

124

single parent. My boy's bilingual and he's only seven and curses at his teachers in Spanish. One teacher knew Spanish and he got in trouble. I didn't cuss out the teachers until I was in sixth or seventh grade. I told them they touch my boy, I'd kick they fucking teeth in. Those Armenian fucks out there are loaded, huh? It costs ten grand to rent this place. They're just as bad as those fucking Jews or the Russians."

I sat there, slack-jawed in disbelief. What made this bigot think I was remotely interested or agreeing with a single word he said? I couldn't believe the ignorance and hatred spewing from this man's mouth. Even I knew this party was in no way, shape or form representative of how all Armenians act; it would be like saying all us Irish are nothing but drunk brawlers. Maybe that's not a good comparison? Bigot Boy continued on with his diatribe.

"I want to put the cuffs on these little camel jockeys and tell them I lost the key. I hate working these fucking gigs! Man, these fuckers got money and they pay. At least this time no one gave me shit for dippin'. They just told me I can't bring my spit bottle with me. I bet they thought that shit would keep me from having a dip. Stupid fuckers, I just give them a big 'fuck you' by not spitting it. I just swalla' it."

Ryan returned, thank GOD!

"Here it is. And Joe insisted we get something to eat. He almost wasn't going to pay us until we ate. I promised him we would. He said there was a place for us to eat next to the kitchen that had a door to the back parking lot so we could just leave when we are done."

"I know where that room is," the guard said as he spit into his bottle, which apparently he didn't need.

We followed the guard to the room off the kitchen in question, sat, and plates of food were brought to us as if they were expecting us. "That Joe, such a giver."

While we ate Ryan told me we got a fifty-dollar tip. "Joe pulled out a huge wad of $100 bills from his pocket and had to sift through the wad to find a $50 bill."

Ryan's story was interrupted by another voice.

"See. Told you, is different." I turned around to see The Smoking Man.

"Hey, how are you?" I asked him as if we were old friends.

"Is different, my friend, no?"

"You could say that." I had to restrain myself from letting him know just *how* different this experience truly was.

"This for you, my friend. For you." He put a bottle of brandy on the table in front of me, patted me on the back, and walked out of the room saying, "Is different. Is different."

I never saw him again.

We finished eating and made our way out a back door that led to the parking area. It was around 11pm when we were leaving, and the party was just getting started. There were so many people now it was even crazier than when we first arrived. As we drove out of the parking lot I had my window down for some air. I stopped at the end of the driveway to wait for oncoming traffic to die down so I could merge.

Ryan looked at me and said, "That wasn't that bad."

The next day I called my Armenian friend to tell him about my experience last night. He laughed and told me not all Armenian christenings are like that one. He's originally from Chicago and was also amazed by how "out of control" the christenings get here in L.A. "It's like they all feed into the whole Hollywood scene and think they are celebrities. It's crazy the amount of pressure the culture here puts on us. I wanted to do a small christening for my son and my in-laws are freaking out about it. They want me to go into debt over it. We're not all like that."

I reassured him our friendship alone should prove I judge people on an individual basis and not as a collective. I have no problem doing another Armenian christening to have something to compare this experience to. I thanked him for his words of wisdom on the subject, offered to perform at his son's christening and took another shower. I can't seem to get the stench of smoke and rape out of my skin.

Chapter 9

Star Wars: The Party
(Or Let's Party Like We're Rich!)

A Long Time Ago…

In A Galaxy Far, Far Away…

Words that swept away and inspired a generation. Words that to this day, every time I see them send chills up my spine while instantly transporting me back to being a seven-year-old boy at the drive-in.

I feel compelled to explain the concept of a drive-in movie theater because it has sadly fallen the way of the dinosaur. Basically, you drive into this giant open field riddled with posts evenly spread apart into columns and slightly elevated rows. You park your car next to one of the posts, which has two speakers on it. While facing the screen you take the speaker that's closest to you and rest it on the window inside of the car. If you were lucky, and I'm talking luck O' the Irish, rabbits foot, four-leaf clover, scoring-a-date-with-the-prettiest-girl-in-school-and-getting-to-second-base lucky, and no one parked next to you, the backseat people could acquire the other speaker and have their very own audiosource.

As a frequent backseat sitter I can personally attest that this was heaven. There were runs, not figurative but literal runs, to the concession stand for popcorn, candy, and *so-der*. There was a playground area in front of the ginormous, larger-than-life screen where us kids could play and run around until the glimmer of light shot out of the projection house signaling the start of the evening's entertainment.

I treasured every trip to the drive-in even if I wasn't going to attend as an actual paying moviegoer. No, I'm not talking about being smuggled in the trunk of a car or jumping any fences. My mother used to work the late shift as a waitress at a local truck stop, The Tally House, which was across the street from the drive-in. I always begged my father to take me with him when he went to pick my Mom up from work.

He would go into The Tally House, sit, have a cup of coffee, and sometimes get a bite to eat, while waiting for my mother to finish her shift. Meanwhile, I would sit in the truck, which he would always park facing the drive-in movie screen so I could watch the movie that was playing. There was no audio but I didn't care. To me I was "at the movies." When this ritual began, my father would, from time to time, get up from his post at my mom's counter and come out and check on me. He would go back in to finish his meal and coffee and report to my mother.

"Nope, he hasn't budged one bit."

And I never did. I was in another world, one I wanted so desperately to be a part of. I could not see this movie enough. Back in those days when a movie was in the theatres it may take years for it to get shown on television or at least it seemed that way to my seven-year-old *Star Wars*-drenched brain. Once a movie stopped playing in theaters, that was it, it stopped playing. This was a time before commercial VCRs, DVD players, and—dare I say it—the Internet. So if you liked a movie and wanted to see it you needed to get out and go before it was gone. I even went as far as to find out from friends whether their parents were going to take them to see *Star Wars* so I could conveniently go over and spend the night. Yes, I was obsessed.

It was after many, and I mean many, viewings of *Star Wars* that I realized what I wanted to do with my life.

The night of my epiphany I can remember as if it happened minutes ago. I was watching *Star Wars* while sitting on the duct-taped seats of my dad's 1967 weathered red Chevy pickup truck at The Tally House parking lot. I had rolled down the windows so if

I listened really carefully I could slightly hear the audio emanating from all the tiny little speakers across the road at the drive-in. It must have been late in the summer because this particular night it was so cold I remember my father making a comment about it.

The movie came to the part where Luke is going through the trench of the death star on his way to destroy it.

"Use the force, Luke," I could hear Obi-Wan Kenobi say.

Then it came to me. *That's what I want to do!* No, not use the force, but fly in space on a faraway adventure where the good guys always win. I knew for damn sure I didn't want to join the air force and be pigeonholed into just one fun-filled, adrenaline-fueled career. I wanted to do many fun and exciting jobs and have tons of exciting adventures. I wanted to be an actor. But not only an actor, I also wanted to create and write these stories of adventure. What other profession would allow me to be whatever I wanted—a cowboy, an animated character, or a superhero with super-powers? Little did I know the tiny seed planted by George Lucas's celluloid classic would eventually land me in Hollywood…doing kids' birthday parties.

"JJ, JJ? Are you ok? You kinda spaced out there for a second when I said we're doing a full-on *Star War* party."

"Sorry, what were you saying?"

In true Rachel fashion she name-dropped to help ensure I couldn't say no to whatever she was going to propose, telling me it was for the eight-year-old daughter of the head of MTV.

"Isn't it weird for a little girl to be so into *Star War*?" she asked.

Not if she's a wicked, awesome eight-year-old girl. Like I said, the very mention of *Star Wars* transported me to my seven-year-old New England self, including my verbal vernacular. What Rachel said next floored me, but didn't surprise me.

"And the silly part of all this, JJ, I've never even seen any of the *Star War* movies."

It's not Star War; it's Star Wars. That's like saying Star Trak instead of Star Trek. Big difference, people, big difference. I can't believe she's always so proud of her ignorance and wears it like a badge of honor. It's her fucking job to know this stuff! She also proudly admits she's never seen half of the Disney characters she plays at parties. Her and Nick never "act" like any of the characters they play, they always play themselves dressed up. If kids can get past the fact that Snow White and Prince Charming are in their mid-thirties and look weathered, I guess they can get past the fact that these characters act nothing like they do in the movies. Rachel continued with the verbal massacre.

"I have no idea who some of the characters the client requested are. It's a good thing I've got boys like you in my stable to help me out."

Please stop. You're killing me. I so want to punch you in the face, strap you in a chair, pry your eyes open a la Malcolm McDowell's character, Alex, in A Clockwork Orange, force you to watch ALL the— as you put it—Star War movies, and then finish by punching you in the face again!

I kept all that inside and retorted, "Are you kidding? It sounds like a blast. Who do I get to be?"

When I was young, I used to always want to be Han Solo but usually ended up being Luke, because I had blonde hair and my cousin had black hair. Every once in a while, when I played with my friend and fellow *Star Wars* fanatic Jeff, he'd let me be Han Solo. Jeff was awesome when it came to playing *Star Wars*.

I knew Nick would be Luke because he physically resembles the character, complete with semi-bowl haircut. The scary part is he didn't cut it especially for the party—that's how he always looks. I was hoping now was my time to be Han and a lifelong childhood dream would finally be fulfilled.

"So if you don't mind…"

This doesn't sound promising.

"I would like it if you did Yoda."

FUCK!!!!! Is what I was thinking but it came out more like, "Great." I can honestly say I was disappointed but what the hell, it was going to be fun and it is a *Star Wars* party after all.

Rachel informed me she was thinking about hiring the girl I'm seeing, who is the daughter of a daytime soap star and an actress herself, to be one of the game booth operators. I told her I broke it off with Clair. She's also dating a married man with two kids who's the lead in a play she's doing, as well as an up-and-coming baseball player who would rather get drunk and ignore her. She was home alone one night and saw on the news a rapist was loose in her neighborhood. She called me to come over and make her feel safe. I asked her if she called either of the two other guys she's seeing and she said "no" because she knew they wouldn't do it. When I asked Clair about us dating exclusively, she told me I was making it "too easy" and I'm "too nice" for her to date me romantically. I left the next morning and haven't talked to her since. What is it with the women in this town? Why are they all so insane?

Rachel assured me she'd get someone else to run the game booth. To Rachel's credit, she can be sensitive to the needs of others when the mood strikes.

I spent the rest of the week practicing my "Yoda" voice in my cave-like apartment on Vineland Avenue in West Toluca Lake. Ahhhhh, the solitude of absolute darkness. My apartment was on the bottom floor and got very little, if any, light. It was very easy for me to get consumed by depression, comforted only by the sweetness of drink. "Hello, Jack Daniel's, would you like to dance in the dark with me?"

Before I knew it the big day had arrived. I awoke overflowing with excitement that could hardly be contained in my husky 5'8" frame. On that day, I was a beacon of light like a Maine lighthouse that lit up my life as well as my apartment. Yes, I was that excited. What can I say—I'm a big, fucking geek!

After my morning coffee and slightly burnt toast, I went to the office to load up my truck with the game booth pieces and supplies for the party. As usual, my bosses were running around like chickens with their heads chopped off. Hearing Rachel verbally castrate Nick was not uncommon, especially when she was stressed about something party related. I guess in her brain all her emasculating of her husband throughout the year was forgiven during the hour-long "I'm thankful for my beautiful, amazingly creative husband" speech she always gave at Thanksgiving. At times, it amazes me how they even run a successful business. In between verbal onslaughts she composed herself enough to put on a big smile and a happy-go-lucky attitude to address moi.

"JJ, don't forget to take the Yoga costume with you since—" She stopped talking, put her right hand over her eyes, tilted her head down, put her left hand on my shoulder, and started to chuckle.

She let out a snort, and continued speaking, "Did I just say 'Yoga' costume?" She took her right hand off her eyes and looked at me. "I did, didn't I?" It was a rhetorical question. "That's just how *crayyyyzeeeey* it is this morning, JJ. I meant to say, don't forget your Yoda costume."

"It's already loaded. Along with all the stuff I need for my other parties today."

In true actress form she kept it all about her. "I can't believe where my head's at this morning. Yoga costume. Now that would be an interesting party!"

Once my truck was loaded I couldn't get out of there fast enough. I knew I needed to leave the office with enough time to get to Beverly Hills, drop off the stuff for the *Star Wars* party, and haul ass to my first party. My bosses love to be "fashionably late" to EVERYTHING. It doesn't matter whether it's their personal life or business life (and in my personal opinion the line between the two was starting to blur and blend together).

Luckily for me, my first party was in Beverly Hills but if I was late to it I would've had to stay late, which would've translated into less time at the *Star Wars* party. And that was NOT going to happen. It was bad enough I already knew I had to leave the *Star Wars* party before it ended, because Rachel had scheduled me to do a Tasmanian Devil in West Covina later in the day, and it was going to take me an hour-and-a-half to get to it and get dressed. At times it makes me wonder whether they do any of this stuff on purpose. Nah. That's giving them waaaaay too much credit. I don't really think they give anything that much forethought, unless it has to do directly with them or their image. "Ohhh, look at us, we're so kooky and creative we can't keep track of time. *Laaaaaaaaaaaaaa aaaaaaaaaaaaaaaaaaa!*"

I dropped the stuff off at the *Star Wars* party location in Beverly Hills, bolted to my "Cowboy Barney" gig, and then hauled ass back to the *Star Wars* party.

As I pulled up to the house I saw my friend Erik dressed up as Chewbacca waving and welcoming people at the front gate.

I slowed down and stopped in front of him. "Hey, Chewie, looking good."

He responded with grunts and groans from afar and then came running across the road over to my driver's side window. "Hey, Jay, I saved you a parking spot right there," he said, pointing to my immediate right.

"Rock star parking for Yoda, awesome. Thanks, man. How's it going?"

"Great, I got to get back to my post." He slapped the top of my truck cab with his big, furry mitts and ran cautiously across the road.

I pulled over, parked, and got into my Yoda costume. I love Erik. Not only because he scored me with some sweet-ass parking, but when he gets into character, he really gets into character and he *never* breaks away from it. He transforms himself into every character he does, from baby alien to pirates, by adopting their personalities, speech patterns, and voice, as well as their physical quirks. He is truly a joy to watch and a pleasure to work with.

The Yoda costume Nick gave me to wear was basically a long burlap sack that would cover my feet while on my knees and an old string to tie around my waist so it wouldn't drag. I threw it on and looked like a homeless man standing outside the mansion of a Hollywood mogul television executive. Knowing I was going to be on my knees for the party, I put on a pair of kneepads, a little costume piece my boss, Nick, neglected to give me. I honestly think he likes suffering during parties. He once mentioned the first time he ever did Yoda at a party, five minutes into it his knees were killing him and he broke character and stood up. I was mortified. He said he told the kids he used "The Force" to be able to stand up. Lame.

I put black clown makeup around my eyes and mouth, a standard for anytime I wear a mask like the Yoda mask. It helps with the overall illusion by hiding my very fair Irish skin tone. The eyes of the Yoda mask were not cut out, they were just tiny holes slightly larger than pinholes and it didn't fit snug to my face so I'm sure I didn't need the black makeup around them but yes, I am that dedicated. I was also missing another crucial accoutrement of Yoda's, his cane. Fucking Nick! Sometimes I swear that man's head is up his ass. You can't blame him though, I'm sure it's quieter listening to his wife screaming with his head up there. *Ahhhh, the sound of silence.*

I was still a Yoda in need of a cane. Luckily for me trees lined the road and I was parked right next to the perfect candidate for a cane. I broke me off a piece of that bad boy, adjusted it to my "Yoda" size, and I was ready to go. I put on the mask and like a chick on a porn set, went down on my knees for the next two hours.

Like Erik, I'm a purist; I always want to be in character so if any kids coming to the party, or even just driving by, saw me, the fantasy wouldn't be ruined for them. For me, this began the moment I donned the mask and became Yoda. I was getting ready to cross the road on my knees when Erik ran across the road to escort me so I wouldn't get run over before even getting to the party. I could hear it now, "Sorry, kids, the all-powerful Jedi Master Yoda, who fought off evil for 900 years, just got hit by a Toyota Corolla while crossing the road. Guess he didn't look both ways. Don't cry, Yoda's not real, just like the Easter Bunny and Santa's not real either. Enjoy your cake."

A few cars drove by and the people yelled out some hellos and waved. I'm sure Erik and I were quite a sight—he was a six-foot-plus Chewbacca and I was easily half his size as Yoda while on my knees. I chatted with Erik for a few minutes in between guests arriving.

"Have you seen this place? It's huge!"

"No, not yet. I just dropped off the game booths this morning here at the gate."

"Wow. That's all I got to say is wow. This is going to be a great party. Very hot but fun."

"I just put my costume on and I'm already sweating, I can't imagine how you must feel wearing all that fur."

"Make sure to drink lots of water…here come some kids, hold on."

Erik switched into Chewie mode, for what looked to be two different families approaching us. There were two sets of parents, one with a little girl around seven years old, and the other with a boy and a girl, who looked to be eight and five respectively.

"Look, you guys, it's Chewbacca and Yoda."

"AAAAAARRRRRRRHHHH!" Erik bellowed.

"Yes is Yoda, come, come, come," I added, welcoming them to the party.

The dad of the seven-year-old girl walked over to us and said, "Say hi, honey."

"Hi," she said to neither one of us in particular.

The other dad, not to be one-upped, said, "Hey, son, why don't you give them high fives?"

"Daaaaaad," he said, slightly embarrassed.

"Yoda can only give low five, yes, yes, yes. Low, low, low," I said, holding up my hand that did not have a cane in it.

The boy held up his hand and I had to do all the work, as if I wasn't working hard enough already.

"Now it is Chewbacca's turn, yes, yes, yes," I said, knowing Erik would know what to do next and he didn't disappoint.

Erik held his arm up as high as he could, towering over all of us.

"I can't reach that high," the boy said, this time a little more playfully.

His five-year-old sister didn't hesitate to jump in, "I can reach it," she said, trying to jump up to slap hands with Erik. After a few attempts, she requested the aid of her father. "Daddy, pick me up so I can reach." He did and once she slapped Erik's hand, he let out a big growl, "AAAAAAARRRRRRRRRRGGG!"

Not to be outdone by his sister, the boy wanted to do the same thing. There were cheers all around.

"Thanks, you guys," the parents said, walking away with their kids to go into the party.

In my normal voice I told Erik I was going to head in as well.

"I'll be in shortly. I'm only out here for another half-hour or so," Erik said, peeling back his arm fur to check out the time on his watch.

On my knees, I walked very slowly to the front door and went inside. The outside of the house was very deceptive. It literally looked like a small home hidden behind a forest of trees and bushes. Then you go in the front door and it's like this whole other world with a big, spacious entrance hall and enough foot traffic to rival any airport. I absorbed as much as I could as quickly as I could through the tiny eyeholes of my mask. In a matter of seconds I was met by someone who, like myself, was working the party.

"Oh, hello," she said with a giggle. "Can I help you?"

"Hello, yes, yes, yes. Can you show Yoda way to the party?"

"It's this way," she said, heading off to the right.

Man, she was moving fast. She stopped at what looked like a large metal industrial door. I heard a "ding" and the door opened. *Son-of-a-bitch. It's an elevator. How fucking big IS this house?* I thought to myself. My guide must be a regular here because she seemed unfazed by the enormity of it all.

We got into the elevator and I asked sarcastically, "Which floor is Yoda going? Yes, yes, yes." Thinking there would only be two levels.

"We're going to the lower third level."

What's on the first two lower levels?

She continued. "Everyone is meeting in the racquetball court."

Once again, I thought, *How fucking big IS this house?* I was waiting for the muzak to start playing and for shoppers from the compound's mall to hop in the elevator. To my slight disappointment, it only happened in my head.

"DING."

"Lower third floor. The racquetball court is this way." My guide started to lead the way and quickly I may add.

"Yoda must go slow. Slow, slow, slow."

She turned around. "Sorry, Mr. Yoda," she said, waiting for me to catch up.

It was so hard for me to "walk" because I was literally walking on my knees with a cane while dragging a long burlap sack. We made our way down the hall to the racquetball court. I said it to myself over and over and still couldn't believe it, *Racquetball court, racquetball court, racquetball court. Nope, don't believe it. Then again, this is Beverly Hills so anything is possible.* The day was still young.

We arrived at the racquetball court and it was filled with children being transformed into their favorite characters from the *Star Wars* movies. There were four big mobile wardrobe boxes, about six feet tall and two feet wide that opened up and were filled with all sorts of costumes, complete with toy guns and lightsabers. It was truly a sight to see.

They had every costume you could think of from the movies. From the basic ones like Luke Skywalker, Princess Leia, Han Solo, and Lando Calrissian, to ones you would never guess they would have like Darth Vader, Chewbacca, Boba Fett, C3P0, and Stormtroopers. That's right, they had Stormtroopers costumes! I have wanted my own Stormtroopers costume ever since I first saw *Star Wars.* One day I will have one, trust me I will.

Why I didn't do this party theme as a child is a mystery to me. I did have my eighth birthday party at our local Burger King on the Miracle Mile in Lebanon. One of the gifts from my parents was a Stormtroopers gun and I posed with it just like Luke did from the Red Card series for a few photos. I know all you *Star Wars* geeks will know what I'm talking about. For the rest of you, trust me, it was a cool pose. Yah, I was a big geek. Who am I kidding? I'm still a big geek. A side note: I did have ALL of the cards in the original first series of blue cards but sadly, I accidentally left them on the school bus. As soon as I realized this I ran after the school bus, hitting the side of it trying to get the bus driver to stop. To my surprise he stopped and let me back on to look for my cards.

They were gone.

Forever.

The really sad part is, of the 15 kids that got off the bus at my stop, eight of them were related to me. They all knew what a fan of *Star Wars* I was and about my card collection (because I always had them with me and talked about them all the time). To this day I hope it was one of the other seven kids that STOLE my cards before one of my sisters or cousins saw them lying there defenseless and vulnerable. And I just want to say to the person who took them, you can go fuck yourself! My seven-year-old heart is still broken over it.

"Yoda!" one of the many girls dressed like Princess Leia in the middle of the room yelled over to me.

I waved.

She waved back.

I looked around the room as best I could through the tiny pinholes and realized the ONLY choice of female characters from the *Star Wars* movies is Princess Leia. Who else do they have to choose from really, Aunt Bee? They should've had Leia's different wardrobe choices, except for the slave outfit she wore in *Return of the Jedi*. That costume is for big girls and boys. It sucks that the basic white costume is the girls' only choice. I did notice one brave girl who dressed up like a Stormtrooper. Love her! You go with your bad self!

The girls seemed to care I was there more than the boys did. When my name was yelled out, the boys turned for a second, then went back to getting dressed up. Most of the girls dropped what they were doing and came over and surrounded me.

"Yoda, you're so cute," one girl said.

"I love your ears," another added.

"Here come in. I'll show you the way." She reached down, grabbed my hand, and pulled me like I was a toy. She almost pulled me off balance, but lucky for me I'm a pro and I saw it coming from a mile away.

"Yes, yes, Yoda will come. Heh, heh, heh. Yoda move slow. Yes, yes, yes."

I was dragged to the girls' wardrobe section.

"Yoda, my name's Denise and I'm six. Do you like my necklace? You need a necklace like mine so you can be pretty just like me."

"Oh, that would be nice. Nice, nice, nice. Yes, indeed."

"I like your voice."

Denise proceeded to make me a necklace and put it on me. I was now pretty, just like her.

I didn't see any of my other co-workers in the room with me. I decided to ask my jewelry maker.

"Have you seen Luke Skywalker or Han Solo? Heh, heh, heh."

Not looking up from her next project, a bracelet I believe, Denise said, "They're all on the basketball court with the other kids."

Basketball court? To tell you the truth, by this point *nothing* would surprise me.

"How do Yoda get there?"

"Just go up the stairs."

I don't fucking think so!

"Yoda use elevator. Heh, heh, heh."

I made my way through the kids who were modeling their newly acquired costumes and accessories and got back on the elevator. "What button to push?" Looking at the floor buttons I realized the floor I was on—third lower level—was not the highest number down. There was yet a fourth lower level. *I didn't have this many problems navigating the Spielberg's home, so I can navigate this dude's digs. Fuck it, I'll start going up floor by floor until I find the rest of the party! Lower second floor, here I come. With my luck, watch it be the only thing on the lower fourth floor.* I took advantage of the few seconds I had alone in the elevator and stood up. "Ahhhhhhh, relief."

"DING!"

Like a Pavlovian dog, I reacted and was back on my knees before the door opened. And it's a good thing too—there were two eight-year-old boys, both dressed like Luke Skywalker, right in front of the elevator. One was dressed in white, like Luke from Episode IV, and the other was dressed in black like Luke circa Episode VI.

"Yoda. Cool," Episode VI Luke said.

"Cool, yes, yes, yes. Yoda cool, heh, heh, heh," I said, making my way out of the elevator.

"I like that he's shorter than us," Episode IV Luke said to Episode VI Luke.

"Basketball court, do you know where is?" I asked, awaiting an answer from either-era Luke.

Episode IV Luke jumped in with, "That's where we're going. Come with us."

We walked down this narrow, forest green carpeted hall where off to our left were plexi glass windows that looked down into the racquetball court. Where the plexi glass ended a set of steps began. There were only five steps but there might as well have been five hundred.

Shit.

Steps. Why'd it have to be steps?

The two Lukes just jumped down the steps and turned around as if waiting for me to do the same.

"Come on, Yoda!" Episode IV Luke said, climbing the stairs, only to leap down them again.

Showoff!

"Yoda coming, slow, yes, slow."

I put my right hand on the handrail and with my left I lifted up my burlap robe, readying myself. Pointing my feet behind me, I formed a straight line from my knees to my toes and edged myself to the first step. Using the kneepads, I was able to pull off a controlled slide down the steps.

"That was awesome!" said a familiar voice behind me that didn't belong to a boy.

I turned to see my friends Mark and Kevin, otherwise known as Darth Vader and Han Solo respectively. *Fucking lucky Kevin with*

140

his good looks being Han Solo! Exactly how good-looking is Kevin? Let's just say if kids want a real-life Ken and Barbie to come to their party, EVERYONE in town calls Kevin and his wife, Kendra, to do the party. Disgusting, I know. They are both actors of course, but most children's entertainers here in Los Angeles are. Mark's no slouch either; he normally dons his face for Prince Charming parties. Thanks to our boss, Nick, looking a lot like Mark Hamill and being the boss, Mark's pretty face was covered up that day by a mask. But can true inner beauty really be hidden by a mask?

"I'm impressed, Yoda," Kevin sai…I mean Han Solo said.

"Do you need help?" Mark 'Darth Vader' asked in his normal voice, while leaning down to me, "Who is this?" he asked almost giddily.

Knowing the two Lukes were still in earshot, I used the costumed character code to answer his question. "Yoda is good friends with Mr. Jason. Yes, yes, yes."

Both Mark and Kevin started to laugh.

"I love it. I absolutely love it!" Mark said, once again in his normal voice.

I love Mark to death, he's a great performer and fun to work with but he can't do voices for shit. Luckily he knows it. I felt a need to remind him to try to do the Darth Vader voice, or at least the heavy breathing.

"Darth sound like normal person, you do. You no breathe funny."

"Oh right," he said, switching to his best Vader voice. "Let us help you get to the party, Yoda."

The two Lukes ran on ahead of us, good thing too because we came across another set of steps.

Still using my Yoda voice, I asked, "Any kids around, heh, heh, heh?"

They both looked around and the one without the mask on answered my question, "Nah, you're good."

"Thank God!" I stood up and walked down the stairs. "Much easier. Periscope down." And I reclaimed my Yoda-sized self.

Mark and Kevin laughed.

Mark added, "I thought I had it rough wearing a mask and being all in black, but I believe you do have me beat."

We walked until there was no more hall and it became two big glass doors that opened to the basketball court, which had been transformed into a carnival midway, sans rides. There was several game booths set up and all were being run by familiar faces, but the *coup de grâce* had to be the laser tag maze that had been set up. *Wow, all this for a girl's eighth birthday party!*

"Hill-loooooooooooooooooow, boys! Laaaaaaaaaaa!" Our boss, Rachel, who was dressed like Princess Leia with a Polaroid camera hanging from her neck, came walking over to us. "You boys look fabulooooooooous!"

Must she always sing her vowels?

Rachel had the other two guys go out and mingle with the children while she escorted me around the makeshift midway a bit to do the same. The basketball court was built in such a way that the wall opposite the house and the one off to the right were giant cement retaining walls holding back the hillside. The left side of the court was a small mound of nicely manicured grass, flowers, and trees that had a staircase running through the middle of it that led to and from the b-ball court. I had to ask.

"Princess Leia?"

"Yes, Yoda."

Pointing with my cane I asked, "Where do the stairs lead?"

"Well, my dear Yoda, those lead to many things. One being a movie screening room, where the children will be watching one of the *Star War* movies later."

It's Star Wars not Star War and of course there's a screening room— when you're this rich there is always a screening room!

"And you're not going to believe this part, it has a concession stand and everything. 'I'll have a large popcorn please. How much? Free? Great.' How crazy is that?" she said rhetorically with a snort. "Snort! I can't believe I just snorted. Laaaaaaaaaaaaaaaaaa!"

It sucks I have to leave early to go do a party somewhere else! And unless it's at George Lucas's Skywalker Ranch or an actual set from any of the movies, I doubt it will be more interesting than this one. To subject myself to any further disappointment I decided to not ask any more about what else was at this house. My poor little heart couldn't handle it. Luckily we had a lot of distractions in the form of little children.

"Can I have a photo taken with you and Princess Leia?" a cute little Princess Leia asked.

"Of course you can," Rachel said, "Just let me find someone to take it for us."

Although Yoda and Princess Leia had never met in any of the movies yet, none of the kids questioned us hanging out together and taking pictures with them. I had an answer for any child if they did ask. I was going to tell them we met through our mutual friend, Luke.

We had a few more photos taken and I said "hello" to all my friends running the game booths before I had to rest.

"How are the knees, Yoda?" Rachel asked, honestly concerned.

"Yoda thinks it'll be fine if he not move for a bit."

We found a nice semi-shady spot in the corner where the house and concrete retaining wall met, where I could make base camp and let the kids come to me. From my spot I could see some of the seven- and eight-year-old boys being difficult pains in the ass. Overall though, I would have to say the kids seemed to be enjoying themselves. How could they not? It was a fucking *Star Wars* party on steroids! It always helps when the birthday child is having fun and she looked to be having a blast. I was happy to see she appreciated everything.

From the moment I established my base camp I had a constant flow of girls around me. I wasn't nearly as fun as the other characters, probably due to my lack of being able to run around or do anything besides talk funny and look cute. The boys were more into taunting Chewbacca, and to Erik's credit he ran around playing with them even though he was in a huge carpet suit. And it was a very hot day.

The mask I was wearing had one air hole for the mouth and two tiny pinholes for the eyes. I was sweating so much that sweat would either pour down the back of my neck or worse, out of the mouth of the Yoda mask. When I leaned my head forward, all the sweat from the mask flowed down my face along the contours of my jaw and collected in the chin of the Yoda mask. There was so much sweat it would overflow from gathering in the chin of the mask and come out of the tiny mouth slit Nick had cut out for me, making me look like I was drooling. I'm not talking about a drop here and there; it was full-on *A River Runs Through It*. If I stood in one place in my corner for too long a puddle would form around me. I'm sure it looked like I was melting or pissing on myself.

One little girl, Christy, and her friend Bobbie hung out with me for a while chatting about all sorts of stuff. Christy kept telling me over and over that she was four- and-a-half, that her name was Christy, and that she loved me.

It was time to empty my mask again. I leaned my head back, felt the water pour down the small of my back and continue down my ass crack, then I leaned it forward and a steady stream of saltwater of my creation flowed out of my mouth. Next show in ten minutes folks!

Christy got a concerned look on her face and asked me about my condition. "Yoda, are you drooling because you want a piece of birthday cake?"

"That's ok, Yoda not hungry," I told her.

"I can get you one." She ran off with Bobbie in tow and returned with a piece of birthday cake for me. "I can feed you if you want." And with that she started putting cake in my cake hole. I had cake all over me, except in my mouth.

Great. Now, not only was I soaking wet but I was also covered in birthday cake!

"Isn't it yummy, Yoda?" Bobbie asked.

What a mess I must look like. Peering through the eyeholes I saw Chewbacca/Erik making his way over to me.

He leaned over to my ear and asked, "Hey, Yoda, why don't you come inside where it's air conditioned for a minute and get a drink?"

"Yes, yes, idea Yoda like, yes, yes."

Sweat was starting to get in my eyes and I couldn't see shit. I asked Christy and Bobbie if they wouldn't mind helping me follow Chewbacca inside. I thought we were going to go inside through the glass doors I came out of earlier, but we went a different way. I didn't know what the fuck was going on and I didn't care—I just wanted to cool down for a minute. I followed Chewie and the two girls, no questions asked. We went in through these big French doors and into a nice air-conditioned room that I believe was off of the basketball court. Chewie got me a bottle of water with a straw in it so I could drink without taking off my mask. I was determined to stay in character even if only for the benefit of the few kids in the room. The room we were in was very loud and had a familiar sound to it. I pushed the mask to my face to get a really good look and peered out of one of the tiny pinholes I had for eyes.

Ok, now keep in mind I told you this place was big. Remember how I said nothing would surprise me? Well I spoke too soon. Anyone in Beverly Hills can have a basketball court. Screening rooms, a dime a dozen. What I saw truly impressed me. There was a sign on the wall that read, "Lower 4th Level Arcade and Bowling Alley." That's right! They had a fucking bowling alley in their home. There were only two lanes but it was a bowling alley nonetheless. You've got to be kidding me? Does this place ever end? I mean really? How much money do these people have? I'm sure this is only one of many houses they have on top of it all. I wish I was rich.

Chewie and I were relaxing at the bar, drinking our waters from straws and pretending we were filthy rich. Princess Leia/Rachel came into the arcade looking for us.

"You two are definitely a sight to see." She came over and got in between us. "Hey, lovelies, can we get you outside for some last-minute photos before we have to corral the children to the theater for the movie?"

"Arrrrrrgggggh-phft!"

"That mean yes in Wookie. Yes, yes, yes."

Rachel cleared out the room and once outside she made an announcement.

"Helloooooooooooooo, children. Ok, everyone, last chance to have your picture taken with your favorite characters before the movie starts in the screening room."

There was a rush of kids who suddenly realized there were characters at this party and they needed to have their photo taken with each and every one. After the quick last- chance photo op, all the other characters herded the kids to the screening room. No matter how many times I say it I still can't believe it. Screening room, screening room, screening room!

When all the kids were gone from the basketball court Rachel looked at me, held up her hand, and said, "You rock, dude!"

"I know." I wasn't being arrogant; I was quoting Han Solo from *The Empire Strikes Back.* You true fans know what I'm talking about.

"Why don't you go get a quick bite to eat in the kitchen before you fly to your next gig?"

"That sounds great. Where's the kitchen?"

She laughed, knowing how huge this place was. "There's a gate next to the side of the house that leads directly to the kitchen. It's behind some trees by the French doors that lead to the bowling alley. Gotta run, JJ." And she did just that.

Still on my knees, with Erik's help I found my way to the secret door. Once I passed through it and the door was shut behind me I stood up and removed my mask. Wow, my legs were burning and my knees were killing me! At least I had another party to do. I walked up the path to the door of the kitchen. There was a very large security guard standing in front of it.

"Excuse me, sir, who are you here with?"

I was Yoda, I thought to myself. Quickly, I realized that no one, other than my fellow cast mates, knew who I was. I entered the party on my knees, where I remained for the whole party. Now here I was standing in front of this man wearing a burlap sack that was soaking wet and had food all over it. Basically, I looked like a bum.

In my Yoda voice I said, "The all-powerful Yoda, hmm, yes all power am I" and showed him my mask.

A smile slowly grew across his face, "No shit. Man, you sound just like him. That's crazy!"

I took off my burlap sack.

"You've got to be thirsty, Yoda?"

I looked down at myself. The shirt I was wearing was soaked and actually dripping. It looked like I went swimming in it.

In my Yoda voice I answered the man's question. "Ah, why yes, yes I am."

"You don't have to keep doing the Yoda voice; it sounds like it hurts your throat. I'll hook you up with some water." He opened the door behind him and led the way. "Come with me, brother."

I could see Nick, who was dressed like Luke Skywalker, standing in the kitchen as we approached. Was he even at the party? I never saw him the whole time. Granted, my vision was slightly impaired so he could've been there and I would've never noticed unless he came up to me. As the security guard and I entered, Nick made an announcement to everyone in the kitchen.

"Ladies and gentleman, I give you the all-powerful Yoda. Do the voice for them. This is so trippy he sounds just like him. Do it, do it."

Everyone stopped working for a second waiting for me to speak.

"Oh yes, Yoda am I. All powerful, yes, yes. Very thirsty yes, yes."

They all started to laugh and clap for me. The security guard pointed at me and made an announcement of his own.

"Get this man some food and water before he passes out."

I was quickly given water. I thanked the security guard for helping me out before he had to "Get back to his post" as he put it.

Nick and I both got plates of food and something more to drink. Nick looked different. *Had he colored his hair?* I had to ask in between bites, it was killing me.

"Did you do something to your hair?"

Enthusiastically, like a teenage girl who just spent $200 on a new haircut and was waiting for someone to ask because that meant it was noticeable, he replied, "Yah, man, I got highlights. Aren't they cool?"

Sure, if you're seventeen years old and making yourself all spiffy for the junior prom in the hopes you'll get laid, or possibly get a little tug on the ol' baldheaded mouse.

Nick unfortunately continued, "What do ya think?"

I think you don't want to hear my real opinion, which is that you look like a thirty-something-year-old man trying desperately to look like a teenager to go for that "younger" look Hollywood is always after. Granted, Nick did have a very young-looking face in his twenties and could pull off auditioning for teenager parts, but Father Time caught up with him on his thirtieth birthday with a vengeance.

"It looks good," I lied, big-time.

"Did you see the go-cart track at the back of the house?"

I wanted to punch him in the teeth. Now I knew where he had been the whole party. Was he trying to be cruel?

"I was wearing the Yoda mask the whole time. I didn't see shit," I politely reminded him.

"Oh yah. Hey, did you see the Cleveland game the other night?"

Now he's just being stupid. I have told his ADD brain over and over again that I don't like sports. I don't watch them, I don't follow them, and I don't care. I was saved by the kitchen staff who broke up Nick's babbling with compliments for me.

"You did an amazing job. The kids loved you."

"You're very dedicated."

"I saw you when you first got here and not once did you get off your knees."

It's nice being appreciated.

Nick and I finished up. It turned out we both had other gigs to get to, albeit his was off to another famous, wealthy client and I was heading to West Covina. The mother of the birthday girl came into the kitchen and came over to Nick and I.

"Which one of you was Yoda?"

"I was," I answered, covering my mouth because I had it full of my last bite of food.

"I thought you were a midget. Then someone told me they saw you in the kitchen and you were tall and doing the voice for everyone. I just have to tell you how amazing you were. You were great! The kids absolutely loved you! I can't believe you were on your knees the whole time. Now that's dedication. Everyone's doing a great job, but you, you sound just like him. Thank you so much!"

"We hire nothing but the best. I'm Nick, Rachel's husband."

"She was just asking about you. Let me show you to the screening room where she is. Thank you again, Yoda."

"It's Jason."

"Thank you, Jason, you were great."

She and Nick left.

A couple of people from the kitchen staff made me a to-go plate and gave me a few bottles of water as well.

"Thank you so much. You didn't have to." I was touched by their kindness.

"We like you and you seem like a nice person, so why not? Right?"

"Thanks."

I walked back to my truck, doggie bag in hand, and started the hour-plus drive to West Covina.

An hour into the drive I got a page from Rachel. I waited to call until I reached the exit of my party in West Covina. That way I was close to it, and finding a payphone that works in this town is not as easy as one may think.

"Hey, Rachel, it's Jason. What's up?"

"Where are you? Right now, where are you?"

"I'm in West Covina."

"Shit. You're not going to believe this but the birthday girl's mom wanted you to come back to the party."

"Really?"

"Well, the kids were watching the movie and in it I guess Yoda dies."

They were watching *Return of the Jedi*.

Rachel continued, "Some of the girls walked out of the movie bawling after you died. They all went looking for you back on the basketball court. And when you weren't there they got even more freaked out. I was asked if there was any way possible for you to come back and show them you were alive and that you were 'just acting' for the movie."

"I don't know what to tell you, I'm getting ready to do my party here in West Covina."

"I'll think of something. Thanks, JJ. Have a good party. Bye."

I love that a whole new generation of kids is enjoying the *Star Wars* movies as much as I did. I felt bad for those little girls but I had to get my ass in to my next party. Those little girls will have to remember that what happened in the movie, happened...

A Long Time Ago...

In A Galaxy Far, Far Away...

Chapter 10

Demon Wayans

"I'll pay you to do it."

"Emma, you don't have to pay me, it would be my utmost pleasure to help you out." And if it ups the chances of me getting into your pants, all the better.

"No, I have to pay you, it's a big favor."

Emma, my co-worker, and friend without benefits, had recently joined what she described as, "A large group awareness training program" that promised to "help her fulfill all her human potential, capacity to create, generate, invent and design from nothing" as well as teach her skills that will forever change her life. I had heard of this cult…I mean, of this particular program before.

Hannah and June, two of the girls from my sketch comedy troupe, were members and once they joined, they NEVER shut up about how wonderful it was and how much it impacted their lives. The brainwashers at the program told them they needed to be more proactive in their careers and to think outside the emblematic box. I shit you not; those were the *exact* words they were told—I can't make up these gems.

"If you want something to happen, YOU have to take steps to make it happen."

Wow, what insight! That's some deep shit. I'm so glad there are people out there who can enlighten me on such things as, "sitting on your ass doesn't get things done." I could've told them that for a much reduced cost.

I got used to the constant blabbering about how wonderful the program was and the irritating constant hard sell to recruit myself, as well as others in our sketch group to "just enroll in one weekend session that IS guaranteed to change your life!" But, when those crazy, whacked-out bitches came up with the brilliant idea to have a yard sale, "with one catch"—in the program there's always *a catch*—that was all the confirmation I needed to know it was all bullshit.

"While people are at the yard sale looking around, we'll perform stand-up and sketch comedy," June explained with that wide-eyed look people in cults get when they've truly gone over the deep-end, and have been beaten down to blindly hand over truckloads of cash.

I wouldn't consider that thinking out of the box as much as not thinking at all. I've been to yard sales, I like yard sales and the last thing I want is to have my junk-collecting be interrupted by some comedians, and let's be honest, if the only gig they can get is at a yard sale, they can't be *that* funny. The rest of our sketch group was with me while we looked at the girls slack-jawed like they were from another planet.

"They told us you might act this way. Resistance is proof you need help from the program," Hannah added, consoling a sobbing, yet still wide-eyed, June.

Reluctantly, we all caved and told them we were willing to give it a try. It was a ginormous flop and embarrassing to boot; from that day on, Hannah and June were forbidden from mentioning the program to me, or anyone else in the group, period.

Talking to Emma today is the first I've heard about the program since. I can tell she's still new to it; she's not wide-eyed or trying to recruit me to come with her to their weekend retreats. She seems just to be overjoyed I've decided to help her out.

It seems like it'll be a hoot, and I'll be able to help out a friend and fellow actor at the same time. It doesn't get much better than that.

She wanted me to go to Damon Wayans's office and personally drop off her headshot and resume to him.

"I called his secretary, Angela, and ran the whole thing by her. She thought he would really like having you come dressed like his character Homey D Clown and sounded excited about the whole thing. I asked her whether he liked surprises, and she said he does. So I told her not to tell him so it would be a surprise. Pretty cool, right? I asked her the best time for you to go over to their offices and she gave me all the info. I wrote it all down for you right here."

She gave me her packet with her headshot, resume, and a short letter explaining everything. We were at our bosses' office; she had given them a heads up on what she wanted to do, and they told her it was ok for her to make a Homey D Clown costume from various other clown costumes. She had no idea what his costume looked like and was very fortunate that I am a fan of *In Living Color* and Damon. I knew exactly what to wear and how to act. Once I was dressed up, Emma thanked me again. I guess if I was going to ask for sex that would've been a good time. Oh well!

I recently broke up with a girl I had been seeing and was looking for some love. Who am I kidding? I wanted SEX! My ex, Beth, was a Jewish girl from the south with some major daddy issues. Her dad once told her she was not pretty or skinny enough to be an actress, and she was wasting her time moving to Hollywood. Once an actress always an actress. After years of living in La La Land I've finally realized two actors don't mix. From here on out I'm no longer dating actresses; they are way too much work and crazy as shit. I'm sure there are exceptions to the rule but I'm not going to waste my time pursuing a real relationship with them.

While driving to my assignment for Emma, I remembered Damon used to work in the same mailroom at Paramount Studios I worked at when I first moved to L.A. I worked with the guy who had been assigned to train and show Damon the mailroom ropes.

A few hours into the workday Damon told him, "This is not for me," and left after lunch. He never returned. I guess it's a good thing he had an entrepreneurial older brother who could get him into the industry. Ahhhh, nepotism, the best way to quickly succeed in Hollywood.

I arrived at Damon's office building and set off to find him. It was a two-story pea green building in the valley housing a few production offices. I found the directory in the very plain-looking, two-elevator lobby and looked up Damon's office location.

"*413 Hope St.* Second floor. Excellent."

I took the drab-looking elevator to the second floor dressed to the hilt in my Homey D Clown costume, Emma's package in hand. The doors opened and there was a sign posted on the wall in front of me.

"*413 Hope St.*" with an arrow pointing to the right.

As I stepped out of the elevator and turned right, I heard the very distinct voice of my Polish friend Andrzej (pronounced Andre).

"Aaaaaahhhh…Uuuuuuummmm…Dat's right."

He was sitting at a desk, in the offices to the left of the elevator. His back was to me, but I knew it was him. There is NO mistaking that thick Polish accent of his and his quirky, nuanced voice that makes him sound like he's always searching for the English words of what he wants to say. I didn't want to bother him since he was on the phone, so I figured I would catch him on my way out, after I completed my mission.

I continued in the direction the sign in front of the elevator told me to go. A big, gray door was propped open and led to Damon's production offices. I cautiously poked my head in to see if Damon was milling about before I entered. I didn't want to spoil his surprise. It was a big, open space, kind of like a carpeted warehouse, and it was cold. Not so much in temperature as in an overall feeling that overcame me of the space and the people in it. Centered in the expansive room was a maze of cubicles made out of the usual movable five-foot bluish-gray walls synonymous with production worker bees.

I figured Damon, being an executive producer on the show, probably had one of the fancy offices on the perimeter of the room. Now, I needed to find his secretary.

One by one, the worker bees started noticing me as I walked by each cubicle looking for Damon's secretary. I could hear them buzzing to one another.

"Look, look!"

"What'dya think he's gonna do?"

"I don't know, what do *you* think he's gonna do?"

I walked over to a man behind one of the cubicle walls, and he smiled when he looked up at me.

"Excuse me," I said in my Homey D Clown voice. "Do yoos knows wheres I cans finds me an Angela?"

"Sure. She's right there," he said, pointing out her five-foot, bluish-gray luxurious office to me.

"Thank you."

I went over to her cubicle and peeked in. She looked up from her computer.

"Hi, Angela, I'm here," I said, still in character.

"Who are you?" She looked at me blankly not acknowledging I was currently dressed like Homey D Clown.

I switched to my normal voice, "I'm Emma's friend."

Still nothing but a blank stare.

I continued, "She talked to you and you told her that it was ok for me to come in today."

I wanted to say, "Well, I'm dressed like a fucking clown; you had a conversation with a girl named Emma about a clown showing up; use the power of deduction, sweet tits. Or were you expecting some other clown today?"

"I don't know any Emma."

Was I in the right place?

"You are Angela, right?"

"Yes, that's me."

"Emma told me she talked to you about this project she's doing, and you said this was a good day and time for me to show up."

"Why are you here?"

You would think a person working for Damon would remember having a conversation with someone about having a man dressed as his most famous character from TV show up to his office. You would think!

"I'm here to surprise Damon and to give him this," I said, showing her the envelope with Emma's headshot and resume in it.

"What are you going to do?"

This woman was so clueless. How the fuck does she even remember to breathe?

"I'm here to do a telegram for him."

"Oh my God, that's so funny. You should do it."

No shit, Sherlock. That's why I'm here. I couldn't believe she STILL had no recollection about who I was, why I was there, and what I was talking about. Did Damon have two assistants named Angela, and the one Emma spoke to was out sick today?

"He's on the phone right now. As soon as he's done you can go on in. He's gonna love it!"

Funny, that's the same thing you told my friend Emma! Except that in your head that conversation obviously never happened.

By this time, almost everyone was sticking their heads out or above their cubicles waiting to see what I was going to do.

"He's off the phone…You ca—"

But before she could finish, Damon came out of his office toward us.

"What is this?" he said, looking straight at Angela while pointing a finger at me.

Angela, with a slight hesitation in her voice, told him, "He's here to see you."

Without wavering Damon said, "No, *IT'S* not. Get my wife on the phone!"

And with that, he turned around and went back into his office, never once even looking at me.

What a DICK!

Angela looked at me as if Damon was going to beat her later with one of the other employees if she didn't get rid of me. "Sorry about that. You should go. You need to go. Now. Please."

I was so pissed!

156

To him, I wasn't even human—he referred to me as "It."

With a tinge of attitude, I handed the envelope to Angela and walked away. On my way past the cubicles, his employees started asking me questions.

"What are you goin' to do, man?"

"You want to know what I'm *doing*?" I spoke a little loudly, hoping to disrupt the Demon "asshole" Wayans's phone conversation with his wife. "I'm leaving, THAT'S what I'm doin'. And I suggest the rest of you do the same."

They started to laugh in a nervous way. After meeting their boss, I could see why they all looked like beat-down minions.

"No, really, whatcha gonna do? Come on, man, do it!"

"Are you gonna strip?" another asked.

All I needed was a little audience.

At the main door to the office space I turned around, still full of attitude, and addressed them, "I told you already. I'm leaving. You should, too. You want to know why? Because your boss is an asshole!"

I could see them all look in the direction of Damon's office before they broke out into restrained laughter.

I continued, "I'm sorry, he's not an asshole. I meant to say he's a FUCKING asshole!"

More laughter, and it was a little louder this time.

"Before I bid you all adieu, allow me to express my deepest sympathies. I'm so sorry you all work for such a fuck head, and if I were you I would rather be on welfare than work for such a dick. I hope your show fails. Bye!"

They were still laughing when I walked out the door.

On my way out I saw my friend Andrzej looking around the corner from his office entrance.

He started laughing at me. "Hello, Pon Jason." (Pon is the Polish equivent to Mr.)

He could tell I was upset.

"What is wrong?"

"I don't want to talk about it in here. Do you want to go for a quick walk?

"Sure, sure," he said, very concerned, but still smirking. I *was* dressed as a clown after all.

He walked me out to my car and I told him the whole story of why I was there.

In his thick Polish accent he said, "I, I, I...don't understand, I hear them all laughing. And I NEVER hear laughing from his offices. NEVER. I do hear a lot of um...yelling. But never laughter. And then I saw you, dressed like, like, like...this."

I filled him in on the sordid details of what happened while I was in the office, and what Damon said to me, about me, or in my general direction. Take your pick.

"He's a dick," Andrzej said. I think, in some ways, to make me feel better. He could tell I was really upset. "I hear his people um...complaining about him all the time. Don't let it bother you. And everyone who comes to his offices are always um...angry, not nice, and have attitudes. Bad people. Bad show. Bad man. Can you tell I don't like them?"

Andrzej gave me a huge hug and an apple, and went back to work.

I was so devastated. I was pissed at him for being an asshole. It never fails to baffle me when people in this town who have fame, fortune, and a job doing what I am busting my ass to do, don't seem to appreciate it. People are people and they are nice or they are not, regardless of their socio-economic status. I've met all types of people in my travels doing parties and money doesn't change who you really are on the inside. If you're an asshole and poor, you'd be an asshole if you were rich. A sad way to go through life if you ask me.

He ruined me from being able to watch anything with him in it ever again.

EVER.

I loved *In Living Color*. Not anymore.

I loved *The Last Boy Scout* with Bruce Willis. Nope. Thanks for taking that away from me, prick!

I can't believe I watched *Blankman* and defended him to others for it!

Now I won't be able to see him on my TV screen without getting sick to my stomach. If I turn it on and ANYTHING with him comes on, I'm changing the channel. That way, if for some reason, my viewing habits are being recorded, I won't be supporting that man's career in any way, shape or form. Fuck him!

This whole experience left such a sour taste in my mouth, it is time for a change, even if it's just for the summer. I told my bosses I needed to decompress for a bit and got a job at a balloon store in Westwood by UCLA. It was great, I learned a whole new set of skills to add to my acting resume. I jumped into my work making balloon sculptures and bouquets with both feet, absorbing as much information as I could. My boss let me use the company van to run to acting auditions and make deliveries along the way before and after.

I met a whole new group of friends who were not in the entertainment industry, just normal people. One little hottie, Annette, caught my eye. She's a student at UCLA and works in the office answering phones and selling. We became friends immediately and it was nice to finally meet a woman who was both beautiful *and* wicked smart. I thought I could feel some sexual tension between us. I was sexual and she was tense. I found out she's been seeing a guy for almost two years so I kept the flirting to a minimum.

Opportunity knocked again and before I knew it I was on a plane heading to Salem, Massachusetts, to work at a haunted house for my friend Erik during the month of October. Before I left, I promised Annette I would send her a postcard.

A few weeks after I began working in Salem, I heard on the radio Damon's show, *413 Hope St.*, was cancelled.

Boo-Ya!

Karma, fucker!

Chapter 11

Happy Thanksgiving?

Ahh, Thanksgiving.

One of the best and worst holidays all rolled (I love rolls, especially with butter) up into one. I don't know what it is about this festive "let's give thanks" holiday that makes people crazy. I, of course, have a few theories. First of all, if you are within a 500-mile radius of *ANY* family member you just *HAVE* to go to their place for Thanksgiving dinner. It's an unwritten family rule. And if you don't go, the family drama that will ensue will rival that of any soap opera.

"Did you hear John didn't go to Aunt Sally's for Thanksgiving? His parents must be so disappointed in him. He must be adopted."

The demand that family members set aside any and all disagreements for just this one day is like a pressure cooker. Let's face it, folks, some people don't belong in the same room together, period. There is so much anxiety for everything to be perfect that something usually goes wrong. That's when I laugh and make things worse and am forced to apologize to my cousin for making fun of her "twice-baked potatoes." I thought they were misnamed, so I renamed them for exactly what they were—twice-burned potatoes!

The biggest gamble on Thanksgiving has to be the one spent with friends, or worse, strangers. It's a gamble because you never know how it's going to go, and more importantly, if the food is going to be good. Thanksgiving is all about the food. And lots of it. These "orphan dinners" are very popular in Los Angeles. And it makes sense, if you think about it. You have people from all over the United States moving here to pursue their dreams of breaking into show business. All these people have a few choices for any given holiday—go back home, go to a friend's house, or stay home alone and cry. I have experienced all three at one time or another.

Every year for Thanksgiving my bosses host one of these orphan dinners at their home for friends, most of which are their employees. They're great hosts, and always have a nice, big turnout. They are in the business of throwing parties, after all. I would expect nothing less than a good time. But like I said, these gatherings are the biggest gamble of all. Everyone attending is assigned to make their "favorite traditional Thanksgiving dish," and this is where it gets dangerous. I can handle having five different potato dishes served with the warning, "This is how my family used to make it." I figure I'm bound to like at least one of the homemade concoctions.

But there is only one turkey. If this crucial main dish is done wrong, your Turkey Day ends up becoming all about the sides that are a gamble to begin with. It gets worse when you show up and the host says, "We let so-and-so make the turkey their way this year. She's such a good cook I know it's just going to be *ahhhhh-maze-zing!*" And nine times out of 10, it's so not good. I'm all about trying something new, and love surprises to my palate, but Thanksgiving is sacred to me.

"This is not the day to try something new!" I want to shout to all the other orphans, "Just because your family liked the recipe of lathering the turkey in a layer of paste made from mayonnaise, cranberry sauce, and okra does NOT mean strangers are going to 'just love it.'" Ick. And of course everyone tells the maker of this exotic dish, "Wow, that's so good. I must get the recipe." I'm telling you right now, they don't want that fucking disgusting recipe, they're just being nice. If they really liked it, they would ask you to make it again at some point throughout the year.

The absolute WORST thing about these orphan dinners—especially the ones hosted by my bosses—is sitting at a very long Frankenstein-style table put together from any table lying around (card, patio, plastic, etc.) and being forced to go around the table and listening to everyone express what they are thankful for. Barf. I hate this. Being forced to tell everyone what I'm thankful for does not constitute a good time for me. Add to that there are anywhere from twenty to forty people in attendance, and you could end up sitting at that fucking table for FOUR HOURS, which actually happened one year. Our hostess, Rachel, said this was a tradition in her house growing up.

I always kept my thank you speech to a minimum. "I'm thankful for family and friends."

"There must be more you're thankful for, JJ?" Rachel would prod me and anyone else with a short speech to "elaborate."

"No. That's pretty much it."

"Are you sure?"

"Why the FUCK do YOU think I feel the need to pour my guts out to all of you when I only know a fraction of the people here?" is what I wanted to say. It came out a little differently. "Yeah, that's it."

Being that most of the people in the room were out-of-work actors, there usually was no need for prompting. A few people literally stood on their chairs and reenacted what they were thankful for, sang what they were thankful for, or did an interpretive dance to what they were thankful for, complete with music they had prepared ahead of time. The first year, the "thanks" were heartfelt, honest, and simple. After that, year after year it became more of a competition, and made something already annoying into something unbearable.

Annette, the hottie from the balloon store, invited me to Thanksgiving at her family's house and I was tempted to go. She got the postcard I sent her from Salem last month on her birthday, and didn't get anything—not even a phone call—from her boyfriend, so I was looking pretty good to her now. We kept trying to arrange a date but every time we planned it a friend of mine, Erika, who was working on *Sister, Sister*, got me on the show and I could finally get my Screen Actors Guild card.

Annette knew I was an actor and was understanding. She's that awesome! If I went to Annette's for Thanksgiving, it would be our first date and that's way too much pressure! So when the opportunity came up for me to do a party and work on Thanksgiving, I jumped at it.

Rachel told me it was for Tarlton Morton, the now-ex-wife of Hard Rock Cafe co-founder Peter Morton. Well, actually, Tarlton and her family were going over to her friend Kathy's for dinner. As a 'gift,' Tarlton wanted to hire two people to entertain all the children and keep them out of their hair while the adults ate. Nothing says Thanksgiving, a popular family holiday, like an expensive set of babysitters to keep the kids out of your hair. Heaven forbid they cling to your drinking arm!

Rachel promised to charge her the holiday rate and passive-aggressively with a laugh, told her she'd better tip whoever goes *very* generously since it's a holiday and all. My friend and writing partner, Doa, also quickly signed on for the party.

On Thanksgiving Day, the two of us decided to carpool to Kathy's house in Pacific Palisades. Tarlton must have been somewhat sober when she called to book the party because Rachel convinced her not to have us dress up in costumes—we were actually dressed as ourselves, in nice pants and button-up shirts. It really wouldn't have surprised me if she asked us to dress up like a pilgrim and an Indian, or even a turkey and mashed potatoes. With Tarlton, anything was possible and this woman always gets what she wants.

On the car ride Doa explained why he signed up for this gig. He doesn't have family here, so he'd rather make money. "Who cares? Plus, it's always fun seeing whether Tarlton is sober or all strung out on something. I love 'fucked-up Tarlton.' She's such an unpredictable bitch," he said with glee. He agreed with me going around the table giving thanks sucked; we were both happy when last year our friend Ellen spoke up forty five minutes into it and asked, "Can we fucking eat already?"

We arrived at the house at 5pm and were met at the door by Tarlton herself.

"I don't care what you do; just make sure you keep the kids upstairs so they don't bother the adults."

Translation: Keep the kids away from us while we get sloppy drunk and do lines of coke off the turkey.

Kathy's house was a mansion. I joked to Doa they'd better give us a map so we don't get lost. Kathy is a very lovely person and has always been nice to me—her kids, on the other hand, are a different story. They are spoiled rotten, and at times are just plain mean.

Kathy appeared and said gratefully, "Thanks, you guys, for giving up your holiday for us tonight. You are going to be upstairs in Hannah's room, and that'll be your area to work. Hold on a second." She yelled up the stairs, "Guatalita! Guatalita!"

A Hispanic woman in her mid-fifties came running down the stairs, "Si, Miss Kathy?"

"Guatalita, this is Jason and Doa. They are going to be playing with the kids tonight. We NEED you to help them keep the kids upstairs, ok?"

Kathy walked away, and Doa told Guatalita to lead the way. We walked up the long set of stairs to the second floor. The railing went all the way to the top, curved around, lined the edge of the hall, and formed a complete circle around the second floor. It was white with fancy posts and just enough room between each post so a child could sit and dangle their legs between two of the posts while looking down at the vestibule.

Standing at the top of the stairs was Kathy's chubby eight-year-old daughter and resident shit-starter, Pansy. She's always been a handful at parties. She's the type of kid who'll push another, usually smaller, child right in front of you and not only deny having done it, but then claim she was pushed. That girl's got the devil in her. Now we were on her turf. Pansy was staring at us as if sizing up which one of us she was going to push down the stairs first.

"Hi, Pansy," I said in an effort to break the ice.

"Where are you going?" she asked stoically.

Guatalita answered her, "I am taking them to Miss Hannah's room."

"I'll take them."

Guatalita didn't even attempt to fight Pansy, "Ok, Miss Pansy." She turned around and went back down the stairs, leaving us in the hands of the crazy one.

"Come with me."

Doa and I exchanged a slightly concerned look, but followed her anyway. She led us down a hallway and into a room that obviously belonged to a girl. The whole room was draped in pink and cluttered with stuffed animals of all sizes, from ones that were small enough to fit in the palm of your hand, to ones that were six feet tall.

"Where are the other kids, Pansy?" Doa inquired.

"The stupid boys are in the game room, and I'll go get the girls. Wait here." She took off out of the room and down the hall. We heard Pansy yell and then she reappeared, dragging her sister Hannah by the arm and two other little girls in tow.

"I want to stay in my room," Hannah protested, as Pansy was dragging her into the room. Hannah was five years old, and at times could be just as bad as Pansy. The main difference, however, was that Hannah was much cuter than Pansy. And she knew it. I'd seen her pour on the charm on more than one occasion. A wolf in sheep's clothing, if you ask me.

"Pansy, is this Hannah's room?" I hated to ask, already knowing the answer.

"This is my room. My mom told ME she wanted us to play in my room."

"Your mom told US we were to play in Hannah's room. So until she comes up and tells us otherwise, we have to go to Hannah's room." I turned to Hannah and continued, "Hannah, where's your room?"

"This way." She stuck her tongue out at Pansy, and stormed out of the room.

Doa followed Hannah while I waited for Pansy.

"Are you coming, Pansy?"

"No. I want to play in my room!" She turned and jumped onto her canopied California King-size bed, crossing her arms and pouting.

"Ok. We'll be in Hannah's room, so you can join us whenever you want to." I left ol' pouty face and went to Hannah's room.

I walked in and there was Doa amongst seven little girls, sporting a wig.

"We're playing dress up. Wanna play?" he asked with a laugh.

"Ummm, maybe." I saw Tarlton's three-year-old daughter, Bailey, so I knew her five-year-old brother, Randy, had to be around somewhere. "Hey, Hannah, where's Randy?"

"He's playing video games with the other boys."

"Can you show me where they are?"

"Sure. Don't move, Doa. I'll be right back." Hannah got up and went past me and out the door.

"Nice hair, Doa."

Doa mouthed the words, "Fuck you" to me.

"Are you coming?" Hannah asked, as if I was inconveniencing her.

"I'm right behind you."

"No you're not. Let's go."

She was a bossy, little bitch! But she did have an excellent teacher in her older sister, after all. These girls were going to be quite the handful for their parents when they were older. But I guess they turned them into what they are, so they deserve what's coming. I know I'm hardcore, but I call it like I see it.

As we walked along the staircase railing, I could picture Pansy and Hannah sitting with their legs dangling through the posts, trying to spit on guests as they arrived. I'm sure they've done it at one time or another.

We rounded the first corner and Hannah led me to a room in the next corner. The door was open with a sign hanging from it and in big, bold, red childlike writing were the words: "GAME ROOM."

"Here," Hannah said, pointing toward the room and turning to head back to her room.

166

I stuck my head inside and there was Randy with two older boys, playing Nintendo.

"Hey, Randy, how's it going?"

Not looking up from his game, and probably having no idea who I was or why I was bothering him, he replied, "Good."

Randy and the younger of the other two boys were playing against each other while the oldest boy looked on.

"How are you boys doing in here?" I said to no one in particular.

"Good," replied the oldest boy, who looked to be about ten or eleven, intently watching the other two play.

I knew the answer to my next question, but I had to ask for professional reasons.

"Do you boys want to do some arts and crafts?"

"No. We're good."

"If you change your mind let me know. We'll be in Hannah's room, ok?"

No response. Silence is agreement. I went back to join Doa and the girls. There were only ten kids total. I thought there were going to be more. The less kids, the better for Doa and me anyway. To be honest, I didn't care whether there were five dogs, two cats, and a goldfish as long as the check cleared.

I got back to Hannah's room and Doa and all the girls were gathered around a kiddie-sized table making turkeys on paper by tracing the outline of their hands. I wasn't surprised to see that little Miss Pansy decided to join us. I could've commented on her attendance, but why throw gas on a fire? It was Thanksgiving, after all.

"I'm all done. What's next?" Pansy asked, holding up her turkey art.

"The other girls are still working on theirs, can you wait a minute?" Doa asked, curving around his thumb.

"I was talking to Jason."

"Well, excuuuuuuuse me," Doa shot back.

I dove in, "What would you like to do, Pansy?" I asked politely, wanting to put her over my knee and give her a spanking that had been a long time coming.

"I don't know. That's why you're here."

Doa shot me a look as if to say, "Can you believe this kid?"

I took a couple of deep breaths and spoke, "Pansy. Doa and I are not here to tell you what to play. We're here to play anything you want with you."

"Yah, so we don't go downstairs and watch the grownups drink wine."

This time Doa and I gave each other a look, knowing Pansy knew more about what was going on than the adults did. It made me almost like her a little. Almost.

"You want to make a bracelet or a necklace from some beads we brought?"

"Ok. Here you can have this," Pansy said, handing me her artwork.

The arts and crafts were a big hit. The girls would make something and want to make something else right after. We had to keep an eye on the younger girls because in true kid form they kept wanting to put the beads in their mouths.

After Pansy got her fill of making stuff and started to get bored, she wanted to do something else.

Rachel, my boss, had bought a new arts project to play with the kids called blow pens. She had never used them before but told us they "looked fun." They did look fun but they also looked really messy and kind of gross.

"How do you play with that?" Pansy asked in her snotty way.

"I have to read the directions. I guess you blow in one end of the pen and the ink comes out of the other end," along with the blowee's saliva, and splatter on the paper. How is this fun?

"Let me try." Pansy grabbed the pen and started to blow. It was so gross. So that made the other girls want to try it that much more.

"Let me try now!" Hannah demanded.

"I'm not done yet," Pansy barked back.

"You can both use them. Take turns using different colors," I said, handing them each a different color pen.

All the kids were trading them back and forth and making "spit art."

Doa leaned over to me and asked, "Is that sanitary?"

"Sure doesn't look like it. What was Rachel thinking?"

"She was thinking she wouldn't have to be here for this."

"I hear ya."

After a while the older girls got bored of using paper and decided it would be more fun to splatter the ink from the pens on the backs of Doa, myself, and the other kids. Good times.

"Ok we're done with these," I said, gathering the wet pens from their little gooey, stained hands.

"Awwww," they all said, almost in unison.

"Who wants their face painted?" Doa announced, holding up his face paints.

"Oooh me, me, me!" Pansy said, pushing the other kids out of the way so she could be first.

"And Jason will do balloon animals for you while you wait, isn't that right?"

"Yes, Mr. Doa, it is. Who wants a dog?"

"Me, me, me, me, me," Hannah said, jumping up and down.

No sooner did we have the kids under control, when two of Kathy's maids brought the kids plates of food. Doa started to gather the girls and I went down the hall to get the boys. I was expecting to walk in on the boys fighting over the Nintendo and maybe witness a little smackdown action.

I popped my head in, "Hey, are you boys hungry?"

"No we're good thanks," the oldest boy replied, resetting the game for the next match.

"How are you doin' in here?"

"Good thanks," Randy replied, manning the controls.

Ahhh, boys. We're simple creatures. I wish I could've stayed in the game room with them while Doa sat with the girls. But I couldn't leave a fellow soldier to fight a battle alone. It wouldn't be right.

"Let me know if you need anything. Ok, boys?"

Randy half replied, "Uh-huh."

I went back to the girls' room and saw Doa and the maids were having a tough time getting the girls to sit and eat. I asked one of the maids if she could bring the boys' plates of food to them in the other room.

"Si, but Miss Hannah must eat."

"Ok. We'll do our best," I assured her.

Our best wasn't good enough. We tried and tried and tried to have the kids sit at the table and eat but they were not having it.

"I don't like squash."

"I want more gravy on my potatoes."

"I don't want to eat."

One of the maids brought Doa and I plates of food in the middle of all the eating negotiations. We were so busy we just set them down off to the side for later or to take with us.

"We want you to paint our faces again!" Hannah demanded.

"You washed off what I painted on you earlier," Doa told her.

"But I didn't like that. I want to be a princess now."

"I'll tell you what, if you let me paint your face you have to eat something, ok?"

"Ok, ok, ok, just paint my face."

"Ok, ok, ok." Doa's just a big kid himself. He's the bestest.

Doa was getting settled in to repaint all the girls. The girls started to push and shove each other to have their face painted... again. I knew it was bound to happen and eventually, Pansy pushed her younger sister, Hannah, so hard she fell and spilled Doa's face paints on the rug, as well as our plates of food.

So much for eating; I wasn't hungry anyway.

Pansy yelled at her younger sister, "Now look what you did! You're so stupid!"

Hannah started to cry and I tried to console her, "Don't cry, Hannah, it wasn't your fault." I turned my attention to Pansy. "Why did you push her? It's not like there are so many kids here you're not going to get your face painted."

With major attitude she felt inclined to tell me what really happened.

170

"I didn't push her. She fell."

What a little bitch!

I looked over at Doa to see whether he was catching all this but he was more concerned about his face paints staining the carpet. I started to clean up our food that was now on the carpet as well. The next thing Pansy said really rubbed me the wrong way and showed her true colors.

"You don't have to do that. That's what the help is for."

How sad is that? She's so spoiled rotten. I gave her my opinion on who should clean up the mess.

"You should clean it up. It's your fault this happened."

She stared at me and I could see tears welling up in her eyes. I didn't know whether she was crying because it helps her get her way and gets her out of trouble, or whether the hard truth that she has a small, black heart finally hit her.

"I'm going to tell my mom you're being mean to me!" she said, storming out of the room. She had cried to help get her out of trouble, no doubt about it.

Doa started to panic. "I don't think this is going to come out! You know this rug costs more than we both make in ten years and was probably handmade by virgins in some Middle Eastern country and is a one-of-a-kind and irreplaceable."

I love Doa and his gift for the theatrical. He always makes me laugh. We could hear Pansy coming back up the stairs, crying even harder than when she left, and telling someone her side of what happened. She entered the room with her mother in tow. I could only imagine what was going through Kathy's head as she entered the room. Not to mention the scene she walked in on. The room was a complete mess with spit-stained construction paper and beads strewn about, and two grown men with strange splatter marks on their backs, on their hands and knees cleaning up spilled food from the floor, and kids jumping on the bed hitting one another with balloon swords.

I could see Kathy needed a minute to take it all in before she spoke.

"What happened?"

"She knocked Hannah over and—" She didn't even let me finish.

"It was an accident right, Pansy? You didn't mean to push her, did you?"

"No."

You lying BITCH!

"Good. Now go play while Mummy visits with her friends. I'll send someone up with a trash bag for you two to put that in. Thanks." And she left.

Pansy gave me a look as if to say, "Ha, ha, I didn't get in trouble." She sat down and said, "I want to be a princess, Doa."

Doa got some more water for his face paints and tried once again to get some faces painted. This time he kept the water container close to him. I started to clean up our stuff and counted the minutes until we could go. The girls kept pestering us.

"What are we playing next?" Hannah asked.

"Doa and I are playing the 'we're going home' game."

"You can't go. I don't want you to," Pansy said, admiring Doa's painting job in the mirror that was a replica of the one from Snow White.

"Like the Rolling Stones say, 'You can't always get what you want,'" I replied, packing away the rest of our stuff.

Pansy looked at me with a very confused look on her face, "Who?"

"Not 'The Who,' 'The Rolling Stones'. Same area, different bands." All this was said for my own amusement mostly, but it was nice to have Doa there to appreciate it as well.

As we were leaving we got compliments from all the parents, who told us we did a good job. By this time most of them were three sheets to the wind. Tarlton walked us to the door.

"Thanks again, tell Rachel we'll be in touch. Ta-tah."

"Have a good night. Bye," Doa and I said in unison as the door was closed behind us.

"Let's hurry and get out of here before they examine the carpet!" Doa said, almost sprinting to his car.

On our way home we of course discussed the party.

172

"Can you believe we worked continuously from five to eight thirty?" I asked.

"It was like a workout. You know we were basically overpriced babysitters?"

"I know. I also know Tarlton can afford it. Did she give you a tip?"

Doa looked over at me in surprise, "No, I thought she gave you something."

"No, I thought she gave you something."

"Did she stiff us?"

"Maybe she's going to send it to the office?"

"She'd better!"

We got back to our bosses' house and the party was in full swing. When everyone noticed the two of us enter the living room they started clapping for us. Rachel ran over to us, "So, how'd it go?"

Doa and I didn't answer right away so she knew it didn't go well.

"What happened?"

We told her everything that had happened just in case someone called with a different version given to them by certain little bad girls. Rachel wasn't really shocked at the kids' behavior; she's done a lot of parties for these people and knows all the troublemakers. What did shock her was that Tarlton didn't tip us.

"Don't worry, boys, I'll make sure you get something. I'm so sorry to hear it went so badly. Why don't you sit down, eat, and come and join the party?"

Doa and I did just that. Nick came over to us while we were preparing our plates.
"Hey, you guys missed the going around the table and telling what you are thankful for."

"That's too bad. There's always next year." I didn't miss a thing.

"We're going to have the two of you stand up and tell everyone in the living room what you're thankful for, ok?"

I knew he was kidding and if he wasn't I was going to hit him in the face with a turkey leg.

"I'm just kidding. You know what though? We had a lot of criers this year and most of them were the men. Some people didn't know when to shut up."

Like I said, I didn't miss a thing.

I think Nick was getting the non-verbal hint from us that we were not really in the mood to chitchat yet.

"I'll let you guys eat, ok?"

Great guy but loves to gossip more than a group of old ladies in a sewing circle.

Doa and I sat across from each other at the end of the makeshift table that was furthest from the others in the living room. We quietly sat and ate. Every once in a while we would look at one another. I was sitting and enjoying what was turning out to be a mediocre meal compared to the spread they had the previous year. *Who made these mashed potatoes? They suck,* I thought to myself. I still ate them but I wanted to enjoy them more.

While scarfing down my food I got to thinking about the core of Thanksgiving. Thanksgiving is just like any other holiday, people like to eat and do on this day whatever it is they did when they were growing up. The happiness is in the rituals. If your family served you steak-ums and Sloppy Joes and then raped you, when you get older if you are somewhere else you're going to say, "Where's the steak-ums and Sloppy Joes? And what time do we start raping because I have to get to another Thanksgiving dinner?" If you have kids be aware that you are establishing holiday habits and idiosyncrasies that will live on *way* past your lifetime, and if you're lucky, into the next generation.

In between bites, Doa spoke, "Never again." He looked up and over to me. "I wish the fucking Indians killed all the pilgrims. Then Thanksgiving would be fun. 'Thanks for giving me a hatchet to slay those that piss me off.' Watch us not get a tip from that stupid coke-whore. Thanks for giving me a fucking headache, bitch!"

That Doa, always giving me something to think about and

making me laugh.

Thanks for giving me Doa.

Gobble gobble.

Tarlton never sent a tip and Rachel felt so bad, she tipped us each $75.

Chapter 12

Today Is Christmas

I can't believe Annette and I have only been dating for two weeks and I feel like I can't live without her! I feel so lost and confused when I'm not with her, like a part of me is missing. Her smile lights up my heart and soul and makes me feel more alive. She's so amazing! I can't believe a woman as beautiful as her wants anything to do with me. I'm truly a luck man. Last Christmas I was all alone and pathetic; this year I couldn't imagine being happier.

Normally, I hate Christmas in Los Angeles. I used to hate it more before I started doing parties; it was nice to get paid to hang out with someone's family, even if they were strangers. Family is very important to me, a trait instilled in me by my father who is as devoted as they come. "The more the merrier!" is his motto and he would do anything for family. Holidays in Los Angeles can be real lonely if you're not from here. It's like the city knows you're not an indigenous Los Angelino and wants to make sure you are aware of that fact every second you breathe in its thick, yellow, smog-infested air. But this year things are different.

Annette is Mexican, and they celebrate on Christmas Eve; since we're now dating I was invited over last night. After doing two parties as an elf and two as Santa I ran over to join in her family's festivities. It was the most fun I've had during the holiday season since moving here. I got a homecooked meal, gifts and Annette's mom sent me home with a bunch of leftovers.

The only other time I was invited to someone's house for Christmas was the very first year I moved here. Christine, a co-worker and fellow page from Paramount Studios, invited my roommates and I to her house for the day. This was a very kind proposal on her part, since there were five of us total. Two of them were Jewish; they told her they were not going to go because they don't celebrate it. She insisted and they acquiesced to her demands.

I don't know about my roomies but I felt more like a voyeur than a guest. Soon after we arrived they all went and opened their gifts, while the five of us just sat around waiting for the maids to finish the final touches on setting the table so we could eat. I felt icky. It's not like I knew any of them well enough to get why it was just so darn funny that her dad had gotten a pink golf ball from everyone for Christmas. "Ha, ha, ha!" they all laughed while we five sat around staring at one another like lobotomized drones. I would've rather stayed home, got drunk on Jack Daniel's, spun a dreidel with my Jewish roomies, and maybe jerked off. *Ah, the perfect Christmas away from home!*

I gobbled up the plate of leftovers given to me by Annette's mother and gave my family a call to wish them Merry Christmas using a C-Phone. The C-Phone is a box about the size of a VCR you hook up to your TV and your phone line so when you make a phone call you can "see" and talk to anyone else who also has one set up. The little camera on the front of the box didn't broadcast a continuous moving video stream, but rather snapshots taken at 30-second intervals. So you were seeing more of a very slow slideshow than an actual video. It was very progressive and impressive technology at the time.

Every time I hook up the C-Phone I recall how we got our little middle-class-American hands on this wonderful technology. My roommate from college, John, and I used to work together at the *Leeza* show. My mom tried to catch the show whenever she could, because she felt a connection with the show after John and I started working there. Even after I left the show she kept watching because John was still there; she loves him like a son. She saw a segment saying they were looking for people who were "dying to get to L.A." She called John and said what a great idea it would be to fly Jasmine out so I could see her. He agreed and got the producers and Leeza to go for it.

What made my ten-year-old niece, Jasmine, so special as to warrant her getting on a nationwide morning talk show? Jasmine had major reconstructive surgery on her face for a medical condition called Crouzon Syndrome. The Crouzon's Bridge of Hope Foundation defines Crouzon Syndrome as "a congenital defect, which affects the skull and facial bone area. It is a form of multi-craniosynostosis (fused bones of the skull). Portions of the skull's plates become fused, thus restricting the brain's growth in that area. The results are severe deformities to the mid-face. Problems can develop from infancy and beyond and affect breathing, feeding, vision, hearing, and brain development."

After the surgery she refused to let anyone take a photo of her. I was dying to see how the surgery went, but she was adamant—"no pictures!"

I didn't press the photo issue with Jasmine and told her, "Whenever you're ready to send me a photo I'll be waiting."

Behind my back, Mom, John, and the producers over at the *Leeza* show conspired on how they would get me to the show without me knowing what was really going on. Mom told Allison and Jasmine they were not allowed to talk to me. Love my sister and niece, but neither one of them are good at keeping secrets. The best way to get them to talk about anything is to tell them it's a secret.

John was in charge of getting me to the show under false pretenses. Getting me there was the easy part of his assignment—he told me some of the producers on the show still know me and know I'm an actor. They thought I would be the perfect person for a segment on the show for a new product they were going to feature called the "C-Phone."

"Plus, Jay, when they mentioned your name to Leeza, she loved the idea of having you back on the show. They know Leeza loves you and wouldn't be able to say no."

They played my ego to perfection. I'm an actor and needed any exposure I could get and this included yet another appearance on the *Leeza* show. I had been on the show a few times already, another reason why no red flags would go up for me. To cement the deal, the producers even offered to pay me! I was going to be a real-live working actor. I was bursting with fruit flavor and had to call home and tell my folks the good news. Unbeknownst to me, my folks already knew the real reason why I was going to be on the show. "That's great, J-Bug," my mom told me, knowing the whole time I was being set up.

Getting me to do the show, check. Now came the hard part for John; he had to keep me from discovering the real reason I was there. This meant he and I were sequestered in a small room, in the Mae West Building, next to Soundstages 26 & 27 where the show was being taped. I'm a very social butterfly and between working on the *Leeza* show, being a tour guide, and working in the mailroom at Paramount Studios, I pretty much knew everyone on the studio lot. John and I had always compared the Paramount Studio lot to a college campus. The longer you're there the more people you get to know, and before you know it you recognize every face that passes you by. I loved going to the Paramount lot just for this reason. I figured since I was there, why not walk around and say "hi" to some people? After living together for seven years, John knew this about me and he knew keeping me from being social would be the hardest part of his assignment.

John had me meet him at the show's production offices and from then on he never left my side. Leeza and the producers were afraid one of the other staff members might let it slip that I was getting surprised by seeing my niece for the first time since her operation. They made it clear to John he had to keep my interaction with ANYONE limited and brief, preferably nonexistent. Just walking me across the studio lot to the Mae West Building was a chore. I think we stopped every twenty feet to talk to someone. John knew how to cut the conversations short: "Need I remind you, Jay, that you are a working actor today and have to get to hair and makeup?"

"That's right," I would add, proud as a peacock, "Sorry I have to go, but I have to go get pretty for the camera. Not that it's going to take long. See ya 'round." And with that, John and I would continue on to our little designated hole-in-the-wall dressing room.

At Paramount they used to send the TV signal of the show being taped to everyone in the production offices on the day of the tapings. Before we entered the room John did a quick check to make sure the show's tape feed wasn't on the TV in the room, and that no one had accidentally left a shooting schedule for the day with all the guest names lying around. The coast was clear. We sat there for a few hours and waited. This is very normal for any type of production. Ninety percent of the time you sit around waiting for that ten percent when you get to do your job, and someone else is sitting around waiting for you to finish your job so they can go back to work and you can go back to waiting. During our time alone, I asked John who I was going to be talking to on the other end of the C-Phone.

"Just some people from the company back east somewhere." And then he changed the topic. Probably to movies or music, two of our favorite subjects.

Finally it was time for my segment. My friend Kristin, the stage manager in charge of the talent (that's just a fancy way of saying the guest), came into the room. "Are you ready to go, Jason?"

"Let's do this thing!"

Kristin and John escorted me to the stage where I was greeted by Leeza, who gave me a big hug, "It's so good to see you, sweetie. How are you doing?"

"Good. Thanks for having me on the show," I said as I was being shown to my seat on the set. Hair and makeup did one last check on both of us while we were sitting and getting ready to tape my segment of the show.

"Thank you for helping us out today, Jason," Leeza said with a big smile. She has a really friendly smile that lights up her whole face.

Once the cameras were rolling, Leeza introduced the C-Phone and explained what it did. She introduced me and said I was going to do a demonstration of how it worked. After some witty banter back and forth, Leeza instructed me where to look into on the C-Phone. I said, "Hello" into the camera on the box and Jasmine appeared on the TV and said, "Hello." I recognized her immediately. Even though the face looking at me was one I had never seen before, I knew the person it belonged to.

I was instantly brought to tears. I couldn't control myself. I was in shock. She looked good and very different. I thought they had sent Jasmine the other C-Phone in New Hampshire, but in actuality, she was backstage with my mom and sister. They came out and I finally got to see Jasmine's surgery results up close. I was still crying and my hands were now shaking as well. It was as if the tears couldn't get out fast enough, and gathered in my hands looking for another way out of my emotionally overloaded body.

While I sat in the shoebox of a dressing room, Leeza was interviewing Jasmine, my sister, and my mother, going over the whole story of Jasmine's surgery and how I hadn't seen her since she got it done. When it came time to bring me out they sent my family backstage. My friend Kristin, the stage manager, told me after the show everyone who worked on the show was crying.

"When I say everyone, Jay, I mean EVERYONE was in tears. Those big, burly, manly men running the cables and cameras... bawling! We told the audience before you came out to not give it away why you were here by crying before revealing Jasmine. We should've extended that to the crew."

My friend Roger came out of his office, and he never comes out of his office, just to tell me, "Dude. Your family made me cry. I've worked on this show since day one for over four years. I've seen a lot of sad shit and never cried until today. You got me, brother. You got me right here." And he pointed to his heart, located about six feet from the ground in a slim, athletic frame.

Our appearance was so popular Leeza had Jasmine, Allison, and I come back for another episode for a "guest update" show, and we were also featured on a "Favorite stories" episode that was all taped segments, so she wasn't flown out for that one. After her first appearance on the show, Jasmine became an instant celebrity to her classmates. For her second appearance, the producers had Jasmine's classmates and teacher, Mrs. Louzio, who by the way was also one of my elementary school teachers, make a video to her that aired on the show. They were now all stars as well.

Jasmine went through years of kids picking on her and making fun of the way she looked. I know her appearance on the *Leeza* show helped cut down the amount of kids that picked on her tremendously. Her classmates became very protective of her all the way through high school, and it made the rest of her school years go by more easily. I can never thank Leeza, John, and the producers who made it all possible enough. Thank you, you changed a little girl's life.

Yes, all that did go through my head while I hooked up the C-Phone to talk to my parents on this Christmas day. Of course in my head it only took a second to flash by while I was hooking up various cables. I dialed my parents' phone number on the C-Phone remote control keypad and waited for it to connect. A green fluorescent burst slowly faded to a video signal from three thousand miles away.

"How the fuck are ya, young fella? Ya still playin' stink finger with those California hotties?"

My Uncle Joe has, and has always had, a very colorful vernacular. I've never known anyone to be as creative as he is at intertwining profanities. He is a true artist at cussing. Hell, for the first fourteen years of my life I thought my name was "goddamn little pig fucker!" But he always said it with love in the tone of his voice.

"Som' bitch look at that. Hey, Jay, can you see me? It's Uncle Joe." He was standing by my parents' couch waving.

"Yup. Can you guys see me, ok?"

My Uncle Phillip chimed in, "Oh yah, we can see you real good."

So we spent a few minutes on both our ends to work out the kinks. There is a weird delay that is hard to get used to. You have to talk, wait until you hear your own voice on the other end, then they respond. It was more difficult for them since there were so many people on their end. Once you get used to it, it's fun. It was great being able to see everyone and each person wanted to chat. Luckily, there were not too many people there. I talked to Mom; Dad; my sister, Allison; my niece, Jasmine; my brother-in-law, Brian; Uncle Joe; cousin Joe-Joe; Uncle Jr.; Aunt Anita; Uncle Phillip; cousin Cory; and cousin Melissa. Small gathering this year.

We took turns watching each other open gifts. Allison and Jasmine asked me to play guitar for them. I had a request of my own and asked them to point the camera outside at the snow. I miss the seasons. Fall is my favorite, New Hampshire has amazing foliage.

Everyone said goodbye and we exchanged "I love yous" as I watched the screen go blank. I stared at the black screen filled only with the words "NO SIGNAL" in white staring back. I stared more. The more I stared, the more I missed my family. I stared a little longer. I collected myself, got up, and started to get ready to go to work. I was going to be Santa Claus. I was going to make that day very special for the children of strangers. That was my job. Spread happiness to strangers. And I did it well.

I shaved so the spirit gum I used to adhere the Santa beard and mustache to my face would have a better grip, last longer, and look more real. There are some Santas out there that don't give two shits how real they look, it's not about the kids as much as it's about the money. On the other spectrum we have the men who start growing their beards in April so it will be nice and full for the holiday season.

There's big bucks to be made in this town by looking like a real-live Santa Claus, complete with real facial hair and a real round, robust tummy. Kids' parties and personal appearances as Santa are chump change compared to what can be made doing commercials and TV shows. All those shows on TV need Santas for their holiday shows; so all the hard-core, serious Santas have their Screen Actors Guild cards and memberships paid and up to date.

My paperwork for the party that day said, "SANTA – STUFFED." So that meant they wanted a fat, "stuffed" Santa. I don't naturally possess the ginormous belly or the real facial hair associated with the picture most of the world has of Santa, but I do have the big A-Type personality that comes with being him. I personally like to look as real as I can. One of the things I do is construct an artificial belly by stuffing extra pillows I have lying around the house under my shirt. Who am I kidding? I'm a bachelor—I don't have extra pillows. I have two old, flat pillows that I have laid my head on for the past ten years.

My mom got me new pillows when I left for my freshman year in college and I haven't gotten new ones since. Every time I use them as my Santa belly, they get a little damp from my own stomach sweating on them, but don't worry—I don't sleep on them right away. I let them sit out to dry first. While they are drying I still need something soft to lay my sleepy head on at night. I ball up some of my dirty clothes in a clean towel so they don't touch my head because that would be gross, and I can make my homemade pillow as big or as small as I want. Ah, the life of a bachelor!

While I finished up with part of the grooming ritual of becoming Santa, my sister, Dawn, called from Florida to wish me Merry Christmas. I explained to her I didn't have long to talk because I had to go to work. She understood and told me she just changed jobs. The most important thing to me was that my sister sounded happy.

After our brief conversation, I finished getting ready and did a quick little run-through of my mental checklist.

Clean shaven, check.

Pillows for artificial belly, check.

Santa costume, check.

Call client, not yet.

"Hi, this is Jason, your Santa today?"

"Hi, Santa, this is Liz Maizel Gayle. You better be a "stuffed" Santa as I requested."

184

"Yes. I will be stuffed."

"Good. Now let me give you the best directions to my house. What direction are you coming from?"

She proceeded to give me, what she thought, was the best directions to her house. Usually people are not good with directions but she did really well. She told me she just wanted me to talk to the kids and hand out gifts. I asked her about other stuff I normally do at parties. She made it very clear she didn't want any balloon animals, face painting, or magic. Fine by me. I prefer to not have to do all that other shit I do on a regular basis.

"Thank you for calling, Santa. See you soon." Then her voiced changed and got very serious, "Don't be late. Bye."

Even though Liz said she didn't want any of that other, as she put it "stuff," I was going to bring it with me anyway. She is a woman, a rich woman, and they have been known to change their minds from time to time. I would rather have my bag o' tricks in my truck and not need them, than need them and not have them. I slipped on my Santa pants, grabbed my stuff, and headed out the door to go to work.

Living in Beverly Hills equals cash, living in the hills north of Beverly Hills equals even more cash. *Oh yah, Papi is going to get a nice big tip today!* Normally, I don't expect a tip but today is Christmas and I knew she had the cash to spare and then some. She could give me a thousand-dollar tip and it would be nothing but pocket change to her. To me it would be like hitting the fucking lotto. January through March are usually slow months so we kids' performers have to stock up on our funds during December, the busiest month of the year.

I wasn't scheduled to enter the house until 5pm. It was only 4:15pm. There was very little traffic because of the holiday. I found a place to park; the closest spot was around a few tree-lined corners a hundred yards from her house. I sat in my truck watching the tardy guests arrive and go around the bend that led to the house of Gayle. Around 4:40pm I started getting ready, both physically and mentally. I got out of my truck, made sure none of the guests were arriving and could see me, and put on my red Santa jacket. I heard a car coming and quickly leaped like a gazelle being chased by a pride of lionesses back into the cab of my truck. I ducked down so my very red jacket wouldn't be seen by the wandering eyes of any youngster who might ask their parents, "Why was that man dressed like Santa? Santa's not real, is he? I hate you for lying to me!" Parents don't appreciate all that I do for them.

The car passed. I sat up in my truck and applied the spirit gum to my upper and lower lips as well as my sideburn area. I always forget that the amber-colored resin adhesive that is spirit gum is alcohol based and has a strong smell. I quickly remembered as soon as I applied it to my upper lip. Carefully I pulled the fake mustache and beard over my head and lined up the mouth opening to my mouth. Once aligned, I put pressure on the appropriate places that had to be held down by the spirit gum. I once tried to put the beard on first, and then apply the spirit gum, but it's so sticky the hair gets caught up in the applicator and it's a bitch to separate them.

It's like one of those Chinese finger torture things you get at carnivals and fairs as a cheap prize. You put your two index fingers in the open ends of the tube and every time you try to pull them out, it tightens up and makes it harder to get your fingers out. When the spirit gum gets all over the hair it gets harder and harder to pull it apart and it becomes a rat's nest. It's not pretty. It's best to put the spirit gum on first then put on the beard. All this also has to be done quickly before the spirit gum gets tacky. You want it to get tacky while you are pressing down on the beard so that it dries directly to the beard.

When I'm clean-shaven and I apply everything correctly, I can talk and the beard and mustache move with my facial movements and looks real. This is what I always strive for when I do Santas—realism. I want the little bastards to question whether I'm real or not. If they question me, I've done my job.

I stuck my head out of the open window and listened for any cars. Nope. The coast was clear. I rolled up my window and hopped out of my truck. I added the last few touches to the costume. The last things I put on are the wig and the hat. Once I do this, my body temperature rises to rival that of the surface of the sun. I started to sweat as soon as I put the wig in my hand.

I don't sweat like a normal human being. This is not my observation, because it has always been "normal" for me; I have been told by many they have never seen ANYONE sweat like I do. It does come with a nice benefit though, clear skin. I am a makeup artist's dream. I have had every single makeup artist I've ever dealt with tell me, "I am so jealous, you have the most amazing skin. There's not a single blemish. You hardly need any makeup." I make their work very easy. Wardrobe departments on the other hand hate me. They have to have several wardrobe changes of the same shirts for me because I sweat right through anything they put me in. It's a blessing and a curse.

I walked the hundred yards to the house and the dark brown wooden main gate was open. The ground beyond the gate was covered in big, bluish flat stones that gave the house a castle-like feel. The reddish-brown house was hidden by a lot of trees and looked small from outside the gate, but once I got closer it seemed to pop out from the trees and say, "Hello. See how big I am?" It was like magic. I was expecting to see David Copperfield, Criss Angel, or Doug Henning jump out from the bushes and announce, "IT'S MAGIC!" But to my disappointment no one did. I like magic.

I rang the doorbell and waited. The door opened. In my BIG Santa voice I started my hour, "HO, HO—"

The woman dressed all in black at the door started to wave her arms at me and whispered, "Shhhhhh, 'day not supposed to know you 'ear yet. Come. I show you to Mrs. Liz."

I entered the house in an invisible shroud of secrecy. *Wow, this place is FUCKING HUGE!* I thought to myself as we tiptoed to a room off of the side of the main foyer. I must've slowed down to take it all in because the woman who I met at the front door grabbed me by my left arm and made me move a little faster. She acted as if she failed her mission she was going to be publicly flogged for her incompetence by the master of the house.

The room we went to was small, compared to the rest of the house, yet oddly enough it was still bigger than my apartment. Three of the four walls had tables parallel to them with just enough room for a person to squeeze in between the wall and the table. The tables were covered with red and green tablecloths that were thicker than my blankets at home, and had branches from pine trees and pine needles randomly placed throughout. One of the smaller tables had a coffee machine and an espresso machine on it, "Oh, this must be where the desserts are going to be later on."

"Yes, that is correct, Mr. Santa," my handler told me.

The door opened and judging by the way my watchdog cowered away I was guessing I was now standing in front of our hostess.

I extended my hand for her to shake, "Santa, nice to meet you."

She gave me a big fake smile and shook my hand, "You look great, Santa! I love it. Ok. So here's a list with all the info on the kids. I need you to look at this before you go in to see the children. If you look here…"

She opened the paper in my hand, arranged it so we could read it, and pointed to the top portion. There, in big, black, bold letters and all in caps, were the words "Nice" and "Naughty."

"…this is really important," she said, hitting an asterisk next to the word "Nice" with her right index finger. "I made a note here but I need to know you understand this." She didn't wait for me to acknowledge her in any way, not even with the slightest grunt, she just kept yammering on. "You'll notice I have the words 'Nice' and 'Naughty' next to the name of each child. But I don't want you to say or use the words 'Nice' or 'Naughty.' I think they have a bad or negative connotation to them, so I want you to not say them to the children. I'm only using them on the list in the traditional sense of a 'Santa's list' so you won't be confused if you needed to look down at the paper quickly to reference it when talking to the children. You can say things like, 'You were really good with that thing this year' or 'You may want to work on this thing next year.' Do you get it or is this way too confusing?"

I looked at her for a second blankly, thinking to myself, *Oh my god, she's serious!* Once she started to get a look on her face of concern that I was an idiot I answered her. "Oh yah, I get it. It's no problem." *You freak.*

"Good. I was hoping it wouldn't be a problem. I had to write really small because I wanted to keep it to one page. I thought it would be too distracting if you had to ruffle the pages looking up the kid's information. You can carry the paper with you but I prefer if you try and memorize it. Are you ready?"

I glanced down at my list, "…um…shhuure."

Liz grabbed me by the hand and led me out of the dessert room and into the insanely huge foyer. We headed toward a spiral staircase that looked right out of *Gone With The Wind*. I'm not sure if that's an appropriate comparison because I've never seen *Gone With The Wind*. I know what some of you are thinking, *GASP! EGADS! How can you call yourself an actor?* I just haven't. Have YOU seen all the classics?

I believe at one time the opportunity presented itself, but if I remember correctly, I think I chose *Die Hard* over *Gone With The Wind*. Bruce Willis is awesome! One of the highlights of my move to Los Angeles is that I once got to work in the building that was used as the "Nakatomi Plaza Building" in the movie. Every time I see it or pass by it I still say, "Yippee-Ki-Yay, motherfucker!" out loud. Love that movie!

Now, even though I've never seen *Gone With The Wind*, I have seen the episode of *The Carol Burnett Show* where they spoofed *Gone With The Wind*. And that's what Liz's staircase reminded me of.

Liz and I walked under the staircase and into an equally insanely huge living room. As we entered the room I was expecting some sort of acknowledgement of my entrance. I'm sure if the music were turned down to "11," maybe I would've heard crickets. I could see this did not make Liz happy. After a few long seconds, her frustration got the best of her and she was compelled, very loudly, to let her guests know I was there.

"HELLO! IT'S SANTA. LOOK, EVERYONE, SANTA'S HERE!"

In all honesty, she could barely be heard above the music. Silly, silly people. Let a pro show you how it's done. I leaned over to her. "Let me try." Then, at that moment, I did the unthinkable. I used my outdoor voice indoors. "HO, HO, HO, MERRY CHRISTMAS! MERRY, MERRY CHRISTMAS!!"

Everyone turned and looked at me. Not just a few, or a handful of people, everyone, including the wait staff. An old man, who looked to be in his eighties, was the first to respond once he got over the initial shock of my booming voice, "Hello, Santa! Look, kids. It's Santa."

"SANTA!" a few kids yelled in unison as they ran toward me.

I bent down on one knee to receive the hugs that were coming my way, as well as protecting the family jewels. When you've been doing this for as long as I have, protecting the jewels from the excited, flailing arms of children becomes instinctive.

"Why hello, children! How are you doing?"

They all answered me at once in a mish mosh of little voices that ran together like one long sentence. "Santa! Me! Love! Want! Barbie! Five! Reindeer! Pineapple!"

I felt a tap on my shoulder. I turned my head with a jerk, only to see an unhappy Mrs. Gayle.

"Santa, you can't start, all the kids aren't here yet."

With a child clinging to my neck, I slowly stood up, and asked, "What would you like me to do?"

Liz took the child off of me and set her down like an empty cup of cocoa. "Come now, Samantha, Santa has to go check on his reindeer. Isn't that right, Santa?"

"Oh yes, it was a long ride from the North Pole and I bet they are thirsty, just like Santa. And that would make Santa happy to get something to drink. Nothing would make Santa happier. And you kids want to see a happy Santa, right?"

"YES!!!"

"And Santa wants you to be happy while seeing a happy Santa who's happy. So I'll go get a drink and be right back."

A little brown-haired boy around six years old asked, "Santa, are you going to have a beer? My dad likes beer."

The adults in earshot started to laugh and they all looked in the direction of one extremely red-faced man, who I would guess was the beer-swilling dad in question.

Liz quickly added, "Santa doesn't like beer, Garrett, he likes water" before all the kids' perfect ideals of Santa were washed away in a flood of beer. She leaned into me and quietly said, "If you're really going to have some water, go into the kitchen because I don't want the kids to see you drinking."

Ok, that's not weird or anything. In what universe is Santa above the laws of dehydration? I wondered whether Liz was protecting the kids' visions of Santa, or her own sick, twisted ones. The bottom line is she is paying me, so for now I was in her universe, and in her universe Santa doesn't drink. Liz turned to the woman who met me at the door all dressed in black, "Mariposa, show Santa the way to the kitchen."

I was escorted into the kitchen and "dropped off" by the lovely Mariposa. She put her hand out, palm up, as if to say, "There you go." The kitchen looked like it belonged in a five-star restaurant; when I turned to ask Mariposa a question she was already gone, like dust in the wind.

All the workers were running around concentrating so hard on going about their various jobs no one noticed me, Santa, standing in the doorway. They were all giving up Christmas with their families just like me. I didn't feel bad for myself; I didn't have family out here in Los Angeles and who knows, maybe some of them didn't either. It always makes me sad to see people working on Christmas Day. Like people working at grocery stores on Christmas Day. Sad. But it's Christmas, so I hope they're all getting paid double what they would usually get paid. Plus, we should all be getting tips. It is Christmas after all.

I waved to a woman standing next to the refrigerator to get her attention. I think I startled her because she jumped when she noticed me.

"Ay, dios mio!"

"Agua, por favor. Tengo mucho sed."

"Si, si, si," she said. She opened the refrigerator, reached in, pulled out a couple of 12oz bottles of water, and handed them to me.

"Gracias. Su corazon es un arco iris."

She started laughing and shaking her head with a big smile on her face, as she repeated what I said to another woman washing dishes. "Santa dicho, 'Su corazon es un arco iris.' Loco, loco."

I'm hoping she laughed because I told her, "Thank you, your heart is a rainbow" and not because she thinks I'm crazy. I was so happy to get a chance to have some water. My portion of the party hadn't even started yet and I was already sweating bullets.

I was finishing up my second bottle of water when the door to the kitchen from the living room swung open and our hostess zeroed in on me, "Santa, most of the kids are here so we should start handing out the gifts." She looked around the kitchen with a gaze a prison guard may give to inmates working on a chain gang, just to make sure everyone was doing what they were supposed to be doing, and in the manner she wanted it done. Not one single person in that kitchen made any eye contact with "Mrs. Liz." They kept their heads down and kept working, praying she wouldn't find a reason to personally speak "at" anyone.

"Ok, Santa's ready. Let's go," I told her, walking past her standing in the doorway.

Liz led me over to a chair that was set up for me, "to do my Santa thing." The chair was positioned between a fireplace that was so big you could roast a pig on a spit in it, and three Christmas trees. That's right, not one, hell, not even two, but THREE Christmas trees. The biggest one was snug in the corner to the right of the fireplace and had to have been at least twenty feet tall. It was so close to the ceiling you couldn't fit a Christmas card in between the two. The other two trees flanked the tallest, the one to the right was half the size of the tallest and the one to the left was half the size of the one on the right. It was very Capri-esque. And in between these wondrous sights was the very plain brown chair from the dining room set I was to park my ass in for the next hour.

I sat down and Liz said, "I'll get the kids for you." And with that she was off to wrangle the kids.

Who's running this show? I thought to myself. If it were me, I would've gathered the kids and had them seated on the floor in front of the "Santa Chair" prior to dragging Santa out of the kitchen. You make Santa's arrival an event, have him enter to Christmas music and shake everyone's hand while saying, "HO, HO, HO!"

I thought Liz and I were on the same page in thinking having Santa show up to your party on Christmas Day should be special for children. Not just any day in December, but CHRISTMAS DAY! Most people think they know what they are doing when it comes to organizing and throwing a truly magical Christmas party. What do I know? Being Santa is only my job and all.

A few minutes later, a winded Liz returned with the last of the children in tow. "I think that's all of them. Why don't you have the kids sit on your lap and tell you what they want?"

"Ok. Hi, kids. Do you all know who I am?"

In unison they said, "Santa Claus!"

"I'm sorry, kids, but I'm really old and I couldn't hear you. This time say my name louder. Do you know who I am?"

Once again, in unison they yelled, "SANTA CLAUS!"

I leaned way back in the chair while they yelled my name. When they stopped I said, "Wow! That was really loud; you almost blew me out of my chair."

As the kids laughed I got ready to go into more of my shtick that I do as Santa but was interrupted by Liz. "Alright, who wants to be the first to sit on Santa's lap and tell him what they want for Christmas?" When she finished talking she mouthed the words, "the list" to me.

I nodded, acknowledging I understood what she was trying to communicate to me; I held up that precious piece of paper in my right hand to show her I had it. I wanted to say, *What? I don't know what you're talking about? OOOHHHH! The list. You mean that piece of paper with all the kids' names on it that you made a big fucking deal over earlier when I first arrived? Yah, I kinda vaguely remember you also drilling into my head that I wasn't allowed to say the words 'Naughty' and 'Nice.' Nope, don't have it. In my incompetence I must've lost it somewhere between here and the kitchen.* Man, is she a nervous, out-of-control, control freak!

When none of the kids wanted to be first Liz appointed an unknowing eight- or nine-year-old boy with the honor. "Timmy, why don't you go, you're the oldest of the kids here that's going to get a special one-on-one with Santa today? Go get on Santa's lap and tell him what you want." Parents drill into their kids' heads to be wary of strangers but are always amazed at how their child hesitates when asked to go sit on a strange man's lap. Come to think of it, I don't know whether any of these kids are Liz's.

Liz persisted with a little more authority in her voice this time, "Timmy, don't be such a baby…" There you go, Liz, nothing gets a boy up faster than attacking his manhood and possibly embarrassing him in front of his family on Christmas Day. That's more of a Thanksgiving Day maneuver but it is her party after all. "Go sit on Santa's lap and tell him what you want for Christmas."

It was clear this little boy either didn't want to be the first one up to talk to Santa, or he just didn't want to talk to Santa, period. I intervened before poor Timmy was going to be in need of some good, ol'-fashioned therapy to deal with Christmas Day from here on out. "You look like you're a big boy, Timmy, maybe too big for Santa's lap. You can just stand next to me and whisper in my ear what you want. Is that ok?" Timmy nodded his head and I motioned for him to come up next to me.

I glanced at my paper and looked for the name "Timmy." It took a little more than a few seconds because Liz didn't put the names in any type of obvious order to me. It wasn't alphabetical— the first name was "Samantha" followed by a "David"—or by age, because I knew from Liz's diatribe earlier that Timmy was the oldest and his name wasn't at the top of the list. Guess I should've studied the list like Liz had recommended.

Finally I found it. "So, Timmy, I hear you have to work on not hitting your little sister."

"Wrong Timmy, Santa!" Liz yelled across the room. "He's Timmy S. not Timmy B."

Another glance at my list revealed there were indeed two Timmys.

"So, Timmy S., I see you need to work on not playing so many video games. But I hear you are doing really well with playing with your younger brother. What would you like for Christmas?"

With his head down, quietly he said, "A video game."

"Speak up, Timmy! We can't hear you!" Liz once again yelled from across the room.

To prevent any further embarrassment, I spoke up for Timmy, "He said he wanted a video game. Maybe you should turn down the music so everyone can hear us better."

As I finished my sentence I felt something lightly touch my left shoulder. I thought it was Timmy, but both his hands were firmly stuck to his sides. I felt the tap again and this time I turned around to see a girl in her mid-teens with braces holding a wrapped gift. She was too cool to say anything to me; she motioned toward Timmy with a nod of her head and once again, tapped me with the present. If Liz has a kid, she must be it. I took it from her and handed it to Timmy.

"I think this present might be for you, Timmy."

"What do you say to Santa, Timmy?" Let me guess who that was. Yup, Liz.

"Thank you, Santa," Timmy said shyly.

"I'm having someone turn down the music. Who's next, Santa?" Liz yelled, putting the ball in my court.

"Whoever wants a present from Santa, that's who."

The hands went up now that the kids knew there were real presents involved with visiting Santa. Not like at the mall where he just makes empty promises that always disappoint on the "Big Day."

The music was finally lowered to a volume conducive to conversation.

"Why don't we have a little girl come up this time? How 'bout you, little girl?" I pointed to a little girl sitting right in front of me. She jumped into my lap and announced, "I been a good girl, Santa!"

"What's your name, little good girl?"

"Sally! I'm three!" she said, struggling to hold up four fingers on her left hand and holding her left wrist with her right hand.

"Oh, that's a lot, Sally. Let Santa help you." I helped her hold down her thumb and pinky. I continued my interrogation on Sally, "What would you like for Christmas?"

There was no hesitation in her voice; she knew what she wanted. "Big girl undies! I'm learning how to go potty. I need ma own 'cause my mom told me I can't wear hers or Daddy's."

Everyone started to laugh, all but one red-faced man. That's the second red-faced daddy we've had at this party so far. I wondered whether there would be more. Kids do say the darndest things. I got Sally her gift and sent her on her way.

I was really starting to get hot. I was next to the fireplace after all. I could feel the spirit gum on my face losing its grip on the beard and mustache. The more you sweat, the quicker it loosens up. I could see beads of sweat roll down off my eyebrows right before they would land in my eyes. By this time I started to get into a nice groove with the children. Some kids were getting so anxious to talk to me they would just yell up to me while they were sitting on the floor waiting their turn.

"Hey, Santa," yelled a boy around eight years old from the last row of children sitting on the floor in front of me, "Is Rudolph real?"

It always baffles me that most kids don't question the existence of the other eight reindeer. They always ask about Rudolph. A flying reindeer is believable, but a flying reindeer with a nose that glows red? That can't be possible. Come on, Santa, now you're pushing it.

"Of course he is, young fella. How do you think I got here today? By driving a green 1993 Ford Ranger with a standard cab and two bucket seats? Now THAT would be crazy." A few of the parents laughed, getting that I was actually talking about my real vehicle.

By this time I didn't have to ask who was going to be next; they were ready to pounce as soon as I handed the previous child their gift. Some didn't even wait that long.

"What's your name?"

"Kimberly."

"That's a beautiful name, Kimberly. How old are you?"

"I'm eight."

"Do you like the Spice Girls?"

"Yup."

"So tell me what you want, what you really, really want. I'll tell you what I want, what I really, really want."

"Santa, you're silly!" a little girl sitting on the floor yelled up to me.

"Thank you, very little," I replied. A few film fans in the group chuckled, getting my reference to a line from *Fletch*. Sometimes you have to throw the adults a bone to see whether they are going to pick it up. I turned my attention back to Kimberly. "Do you know what you want for Christmas, Kimberly?"

"I want my dad to stop smoking. If he dies, I won't feel bad. I've asked him a thousand times to stop and he won't. He must love smoking more than he loves me."

Yah, what do you say to that? I was not expecting that at all. A hush had fallen over the room. I could see all the adults' faces frozen in shock. I'm sure my face was also frozen in a state of shock, but it couldn't be seen because it was covered in a fake beard and sweat. I composed myself and did what every adult in that room wanted to do and changed the subject. I quickly referenced the list given to me by Liz and looked for a Kimberly.

"Do you like furbies, Kimberly?"

"Yup."

"That's good. I do too. Maybe you'll get one for Christmas this year since you've been so good. I think I have a gift here for you." I quickly grabbed the gift for Kimberly from my adolescent helper. "Merry Christmas, Kimberly. Ok, who's next? Is there anyone else left?"

I noticed one girl who had not been up to tell me what she wanted and she wasn't raising her hand.

"How about you, little girl? Yes you, right there. Do you want a present from Santa?"

She got a very sad look on her face. "I can't. I don't have Christmas. I'm Jewish, we have Hanukkah."

"Can Santa give you a Hanukkah gift?"

She smiled and said, "Ok!"

Liz ran up beside me and put her arm around me. "Let's hear it for Santa, everyone. He took time out of his busy schedule to come by and spend some time with us today. Let's hear it for Santa!" Everyone clapped for me as I stood up. "And what do we say to Santa, kids?"

"Thank you, Santa!" The kids were joined by most of the adults in thanking me.

After Liz left my side, kids who were trying to get in that last hug before I left, mobbed me. I was giving out hugs and walking away from my "Chair" when an older man in his seventies came over to me.

"Are you a member of the Screen Actors Guild?"

"Yes, why do you ask?"

"You can tell when a person's an actor. You're very funny… and quick. Very quick a few times there. I'm sure you know what I mean."

"I think I have an idea. I do have to think on my feet at times. You never know what kids are going to say."

"Did Liz book you through SAG?"

"No, it was through a party company." Although, now that I've met her, I could see Liz calling a party company and requesting an Oscar-nominated performer to be Santa at her party. "It was either this or wait tables. At least this way I get to perform and work on my improv skills."

"That's Hollywood for ya. Well, I just wanted to let you know you are a great Santa. I had a fun time watching you interact with the kids."

I shook his hand. "Thank you. Merry Christmas."

I escaped the grasp of the kids and found Liz at the entrance of the living room nearest to the foyer, where we originally came in. I needed to remind her there was a balance left on her bill.

She put her hand on my shoulder and said, "Thank you for sharing your Christmas with my family. Everyone loved it. They're all raving about how wonderful and entertaining you were. Feel free to change and come back for some food."

"Ok, I'll be right back." If this were a scary movie, I'd never come back, alive at least.

She must be too busy at the moment to pay me. That's cool. I guess she wanted to make sure I had a bite to eat before I left; it was Christmas after all. She probably figured if she paid me now I might leave without eating. Plus, this gave her time to listen to more praises about me from her guests and hopefully that would increase the already huge tip I should be getting.

I started making my way across the foyer and with each step, in my flooded rubber boots, getting exponentially eager to go and change, only to be stopped in my tracks by one last request.

"Santa, Santa, hold on a second!"

I turned to see a little girl around five years old holding the hand of a girl in her early teens. The older girl continued speaking, "Santa, my cousin wants to tell you one more thing. Patty, go ahead and tell him what you wanted to tell him."

Patty held her head of long, wavy brown hair down and stayed silent.

"Sorry, Santa, we were sitting in there and she started crying because she wanted to tell you something she didn't tell you when you gave her, her present. Patty, Santa's waiting for you."

Still nothing.

I figured I would give it a shot. "Hello again, Patty. You can tell me <u>anything</u> you want. Was there a present you wanted and forgot to tell me about?"

Patty shook her head and tugged on her cousin's hand, cueing her to bend down, so she could whisper something in her ear.

"Uh, huh. Ok, I'll ask," her cousin said and turned to me and asked, "She wants to know whether it's true that you can see little girls when they are bad and good?"

I bent down on one knee to get on her level to see whether I could get her to look at me and talk. By this point I was doing everything I could to keep my beard from falling off my face that was like a waterfall. "Yes, it's true, Santa can see you when you've been bad or good. Just like in the song. Have you been a good little girl?"

Once again, Patty shook her head.

"It's ok, Patty, you can tell Santa anything and he won't get mad at you. It's ok." I could see her starting to break. I needed one more thing to crack her. "Santa loves you no matter what. You can tell me."

That was it! I did it! Patty cocked her head to the side, still slightly hesitant, leaned toward me, and spoke. "Sometimes I play with my hootie. That's my vagina. Is that bad?"

That's something you don't hear every day! I was expecting to hear she hit a sibling, or didn't share her toys or something. I was truly shocked and caught off-guard while still trying to absorb what I just heard without laughing and traumatizing poor little masturbator Patty.

Her cousin started to snicker, "Patty!"

I could see Patty starting to regret she told Santa her secret. So I jumped in as quickly as I could to do damage control. "It's ok Patty, Santa's not upset with you."

Patty looked up at me, with all her hair cascading over her face resembling cousin "It" from *The Addams Family*. Behind the curtains of hair I could make out two very red, swollen brown eyes. "But I've been bad."

Must choose my words carefully. "That's not a bad thing to do, as long as you're all by yourself and in your bedroom at your home." I could see some relief on her face so I continued, "And don't worry, Santa can't see you when you do that and I won't tell anybody your secret and neither will your cousin." I looked up at her cousin. "Isn't that right?"

"Oh yah, Santa. I won't tell anyone. I promise."

I could see in her face she was lying; I glanced at her hands to see whether she had her fingers crossed. Oh yah, she was dying to tell someone. She'd most likely tell the story to her family on their way home from the party. If it does get back to Patty's parents, hopefully they are understanding people and don't throw her in a locked closet and tell her to pray for forgiveness while being squirted with holy water.

"Are you ok, Patty?" I asked.

She nodded her head. "Can I hug you, Santa?"

"You sure can." She hugged me around my chest and squeezed hard. "That's a big hug," I told her, which made her squeeze even harder.

"Merry Christmas, Santa," Patty said, letting go of me and wiping the hair out of her face, revealing a big smile.

"Thank you and Merry Christmas to you too, Patty. Santa has to hurry and get to Rudolph and the other reindeer. I'm sure they're hungry."

"Come on, Patty, let's let Santa leave." Her cousin grabbed her by the hand and pulled her back toward the living room. Patty was walking in the direction her cousin was leading her, but she was looking back at me and waving, up until she disappeared into the abyss that was the Gayle Christmas Party.

I was huffing it back to my truck very eager to disrobe. I could not rip off that suit fast enough. *AIR! I NEED AIR!* I was roasting. Everything about the Santa suit was drenched. I poured out what seemed to be a gallon of sweat from each of the heavy-duty industrial boots and watched it go down the hill along the contours of the road. A river of sweat is proof I suffer for my art. The art of being Santa.

I looked at the clock on my truck and saw I stayed longer than the hour I was hired for by almost thirty minutes. I don't keep a watch or any other timepiece on my person while doing a Santa gig.

I think it comes off as "tacky" and inconsiderate to the children. I know some Santas don't give a shit and I've heard stories of some Santas who keep an egg timer on them and set it to go off when their time is up. Can you imagine?

"What would you like for Christmas?"

"Santa, I want a—"

"BUZZZZZZZ!!!!"

"Tough shit, kid, my time's up. Good luck next year. See ya!"

I know it is the performers' decision to stay later than the time they were hired for. Anything after the agreed-upon period is us donating our time, hoping it doesn't go unnoticed by our client and that they show their gratitude monetarily. When I'm other characters, I admit to "watching the clock," but not as Santa. There is something sacred and dear to me about Santa. How could I, in good conscience, leave a party as Santa as soon as my time is up and especially on Christmas? So I stayed, because today I am Santa.

I air-dried for a moment and then changed into my civilian clothing. A pair of wrinkled light brown cargo shorts with a small tear on the right ass cheek and a psychedelic red, yellow, blue, and black long-sleeved tie-dyed thermal, I have to admit is quite eye-catching. I wasn't expecting an invitation for Christmas dinner. It was all that I had with me, my only other choice was to go back in as Santa and that was not happening.

As I approached the door to the house, it opened, and a couple in their forties stepped out. They were laughing, until they saw me.

"May I help you?" the man asked.

"I was Santa Claus."

They both looked me up and down for a minute.

The woman got a confused look on her face, "But you're skinny. The voice from Santa was a big man's voice."

I told them in my Santa voice, "Liz told Santa to change and come back in and get a bite to eat. Merry Christmas! HO, HO, HO!"

The woman covered her mouth in shock, "Oh my God! You're Santa! That's great!"

The man laughed and put his hand on my shoulder. "It looks

like we have to fatten you up, Santa. Go eat."

The woman took her hand away from in front of her mouth and touched my cheek, "Santa, you're so young."

I smiled. "Thank you. I'm going to go eat."

As they walked away, I heard the woman say, "He was really young. I would've never guessed he was Santa."

Once inside the house I made my way over to the "dessert room" where I first met Liz and popped my head in quickly. The only difference this time was that there were desserts in it. I couldn't get over the fact that there were so many desserts they got their own room. I saw the room earlier but it really didn't register in my brain because it only had a coffee machine in it at the time, and I was preoccupied by the one-way conversation Liz was having with me. The desserts looked great and I noticed they had my favorite, brownies, but first I needed sustenance. Being Santa burns a hell of a lot of calories, calories that can only be replaced by luxurious MEAT.

I turned around from the doorway of the "dessert room" where I could see into the living room where there were people sitting around eating. There were a few kids sitting on steps in the foyer eating. I noticed people coming out from a hallway to my left carrying plates of food. Plates that had meat on them. So, I went left.

There it was. I was standing in a short hallway between the "dessert room" and the kitchen and right in front of me was the main dining room. They had a spread like you read about. There was so much food it bordered on obscene. There was everything from lobster and shrimp to roast beef and chicken, pasta, fruits, and vegetables. With so many choices, where does one start? The expensive meats sound good to me. So I got a plate and loaded up on seafood and red meat.

I found a nice place on the steps in the foyer next to the kitchen door to eat. I was able to sit in peace and eat. No one bothered me or even gave me a second look, which was odd considering how I was WAY underdressed for a Christmas dinner party. Maybe they thought I was some weird relative Liz never talked about. Kind of like a family secret that crawls out its hole for special occasions to get paid off to go back into hiding for another year.

My second helping consisted of chicken and pasta. After that plate, I ended my meal the European way by finishing with a salad. Actually it was three different types of salad all mixed together on one plate. I know some folks have an aversion to different types of food touching one another, but it was all in the same food group for me—salads—and what the hell, it's all going to the same place. When I finished my salad I was stuffed and realized that when I started it, I wasn't really hungry, but was just eating for sport. Being an out-of-work actor, I never know when I'll eat like this again, that's why I chowed down. And I don't prepare small-portioned plates of food; I had piled it on and finished it all.

My Uncle Joe used to tell me when I ate at his house I was allowed to take as much as I wanted, but I'd better finish what I took. It really didn't matter because he'd finish on my plate whatever I couldn't. Sometimes he wouldn't wait for me to finish before he'd just start picking off of my plate.

After I ate it was time to get paid. I tracked down Liz.

"Thank you very much for the food, everything was wonderful. My paperwork says I have a balance to pick up from you."

She seemed shocked for a moment, then I saw a light come on in her brain reflected on her face, "Oh my, that's right! Come with me."

I followed her to yet another huge room with vaulted ceilings that looked to be an office.

"Did you get yourself something to eat?" she asked.

"Yes, thank you."

There was a ton of signed sports memorabilia all over the room—baseballs, footballs, boxing gloves, photos, and a ton of other stuff. I only recognized a few of the signatures because I was born without a sports gene. My dad always said sports were a waste of time and the energy spent playing or watching them should be used to get real work done, like splitting wood. Although we were allowed a few hours every Sunday to watch wrestling and at times we would have a houseful over, because we had one of the big-screen televisions that came out in the early 80s. It was the type that magically rose up out of a big, wooden box the size of a VW beetle and took up most of the space in the living room. If you came late or were a little kid and had to sit to the side of the TV it was impossible to see what was on the screen. To really see well you had to sit directly in front of it and that space was reserved for the adults. Dad liked when people came over because the time we lost cutting wood was made up by everyone sticking around after the entertainment to help out getting work done around the house.

My dad wasn't a big sports buff but he did like to watch movies and that was why my folks got the big TV in the first place. The only other times sports played on the TV, was when Mom wanted to watch the Super Bowl or if the Red Sox were in the playoffs.

If Liz's intention was to impress me with all the sports-related stuff in the office it was wasted. She grabbed a checkbook out of one of the drawers from a desk the size of an airline carrier.

"What do I owe you?"

I showed her the paperwork and read her the balance, so there would be no mistake in the amount due. "One hundred and forty-five dollars."

Liz made some small talk while she wrote out the check, "So the list I made for you seemed to come in handy."

"Yup, thanks, that was a great idea. And very helpful. How was it organized?"

"By family," she said, scribbling on the check and not looking up.

I was thinking to myself, *Yeah, baby, make it a Merry Christmas for Santa!*

She folded the check and handed it to me, "Thank you so much, Merry Christmas."

I didn't look at the check, because I thought it would've been tacky to do so in front of her. We left the office and she went back to her guests and I went into the foyer. I made sure no one was looking and I unfolded the check.

"One hundred forty-five and zero cents."

I looked up, puzzled. Then looked back down at the check, to see whether it had miraculously changed to a larger amount. It was still for "One hundred forty-five and zero cents." I rubbed the corner of the check thinking maybe she had given me two checks—one for me and one for the party company she hired me through.

Nope. There was only one check and it was made out for the exact amount, "One hundred forty-five and zero cents." Did she forget it's Christmas? What a fucking Scrooge!

I folded the embarrassing check and put it into my pocket. Calmly I walked into the kitchen. In my very broken, childlike Spanish, I asked the lady who had given me water earlier if there were any paper plates I could have. They looked around and finally found some.

"How many do you want?"

"How many do you have?"

"Ten or twelve."

"I'll take them all please."

I thanked them and went to the buffet. I loaded up three plates of food. I filled one plate up with seafood, another with beef, and another with chicken. I placed an empty plate on each one of the full ones and walked to my truck and set the plates down on the floor of the passenger side. I secured the top and bottom of my three sets of plates with duct tape that I had in my truck that I use on occasion to make any quick fix on costumes. Ahhh, the magic that is duct tape with its multiple functions! I locked my truck up and went back into the house.

I grabbed the last of the paper plates and did one with pasta and the other with desserts. I like brownies.

I took the plates to my truck. When I opened the door to my truck it smelled like a fancy restaurant and it kind of made me hungry again, hungry for retribution. I duct-taped the plates and put them on top of the other plates that were already on the floor. I locked my truck and went back into the house.

I needed beverages.

I was trying to strategically place the beverages in my arms to get the most I could. I had a two-liter bottle of coke and a two-liter bottle of sprite. I really couldn't grab anything else.

"I guess I'll have to make another trip."

I noticed one of the workers who was cleaning up around the buffet looking at me. He had seen me load up on the food both times.

"Mucho trabajo, poco dinero," I said.

He laughed and held up his index finger, "Un momento."

He went into the kitchen and came back with a brown paper bag. I didn't have to say anything to him; he put the two two-liter bottles into the bag.

"Cerveza, senor?"

"Si, papi. Mucho cervezas! Tengo mucha sed."

He handed me the bag with the soda in it and went and grabbed another one. When he came back he put six beers into it for me. He motioned to the wine as if to ask me if I wanted some bottles of that as well. I hate wine. So I only asked for two bottles. Two bottles of red and two bottles of white.

"Gracias. Viva el gato!" I told him.

He shook his head, smiled, and said, "Su corazon es un arco iris, Santa," and continued about his work.

I heard a voice with a thick Spanish accent say behind me, "We are all talkin' about how funny you are, Santa."

I turned around to see the woman dressed all in black who was the first one to greet me when I arrived at the party.

"Dat's how he knew wha you say earlier. We have all been laughin' about it all night. Thank you for giving us all laughs when we have to work on Christmas. You are good person."

"No, no, thank you," I said, holding up my two bags filled with beverages. I took my bags of goodies and left.

It was a Christmas miracle—the universe found a way to give Santa a "tip" for all his hard work.

I always aim to please the clients and I gave Liz what she wanted. She specifically wanted a "Santa – Stuffed." And that I was. First I stuffed pillows under my shirt, then I stuffed my face full of food and lastly, I stuffed my truck with what ended up being a week's worth of groceries.

I was dying to get home to call Annette and tell her about my party. She was happy to hear from me and couldn't believe my story.

"I love you." I was so overwhelmed with emotion I can't believe I said it!

"I love you too."

Merry Christmas.

Chapter 13

I'll Entertain Your Kids While You Entertain The World: Part Two

"Oh my God, you were Fred Flintstone!"

"Yah, that was me." That party will forever haunt me.

Here I am sitting at my friend Conner's second wedding reception unable to escape the grip and influence Mr. Steven Spielberg has on the people of this town.

"You were also a referee or something at Sasha's birthday party. I knew you looked familiar. I just knew it!" Jacob said, addressing our table at this fine authentic Chinese wedding.

It was so authentic that on the way home later that evening Annette—who is now my fiancée—made me stop at an In-N-Out Burger. I proposed to her unoffically three weeks into our relationship after I was rushed to the hospital on New Year's Day, for what turned out to be a very bad case of hemorrhoids. That much blood should never come out of a person's ass. I offically proposed on Valentine's Day in front of the castle at Disneyland. I couldn't imagine life without her and was happy to hear she felt the same way.

Surprisingly, our families were very supportive of our quick engagement. When I told my Mom I did it because *I just knew she was the one*, she told me my paternal grandparents gave her their wedding and engagement rings for me when the time came. Annette's Mom insisted I come around more often so she could get to know me better. The look on her Dad's face when I told him I was an actor who dressed up for kids' parties was priceless! I'm sure he was hoping she'd marry a doctor, lawyer or rocket scientist.

For the first time in my life I really cared about my personal wellbeing and about the future, the future we were going to build together. I was excited to have family here in a city that always made me feel so lonely. Love had come to me once I stopped looking for it. A peace had come over me I had never felt before and I welcomed it. Annette was my good luck charm; soon after we got engaged I got a commercial agent and started auditioning for commercials. I booked one so quickly I couldn't believe it.

Jacob had been eyeballing me at the wedding from the moment we sat at the table. After a while of hanging out and talking he started to say, "You look familiar, have we met before?" and "I know I've seen you from somewhere before, I just can't place where from."

"I was in a commercial recently but my face was covered. Other than that I've done mostly extra work and a few things for the *Leeza* show."

Nope, that wasn't it. We continued to figuratively dance the verbal dance done at weddings where you are obviously seated with the leftover "where do we seat these people and with who?" crowd that usually end up seated in the furthest rear corner behind a giant pillar surrounded by a bunch of strangers trying to find something in common, or at least something interesting to talk about. I had been to many weddings as a solo act so this wasn't new to me. I usually didn't have a date so that part was new. It was during our *Ring Around the Rosie* conversation of "So…how do you know the bride or groom?" that Jacob finally pieced together how he knew me.

It turned out Jacob works with Conner over at Dreamworks SKG for Mr. Steven Spielberg and Company. From time to time his job consisted of editing Steven and Kate's home videos, including the kids' birthday parties. As soon as I told him I entertained the kids at their parties he put it together where he knew me from. He didn't know I played Friendly Prehistoric Man Type at Sawyer's party until I told him.

"You have to tell everyone about that party! We laughed so hard in the editing room at that part where you fell. We kept playing it over and over. Sometimes in slow motion both backwards and forwards; it was one of the funniest things I've ever seen in my life. You gotta tell the story, come on!"

I told my version of the story and Jacob added to it for me. "I'm telling you, the first time we watched it we thought you were dead. It was friggin' hysterical. You fell against the wall, slid down it, and once you hit the ground there's a moment where you didn't move at all and if you listen closely on the tape you can hear Kate say to someone, 'Is he ok?' And you can tell she was genuinely concerned. It was friggin' awesome! You're friggin' awesome! Let me just thank you for making that part of my job bearable. Every time we saw you pop up on one of the kids' birthday party videos we knew you were going to make us laugh somehow. Just think, you're on a shitload of his family's home videos. You're a funny dude!"

"I wish he'd think that and hire me to act," I replied, half-hoping he would put in a good word for me to Steven.

It turned out Jacob is an aspiring director working on his first independent feature film. It gets very frustrating when people in this town tell you how talented you are, yet won't hire you for their projects or even help you out. Jacob also felt this common Hollywood sting when he asked Mr. Spielberg for advice on his little independent project and Steven told him, "I don't know anything about the independent filmmaking world, I can't help you."

I give Jacob credit for having the balls to even ask Steven for advice. Most people would be afraid to—take my bosses, Nick and Rachel, for example. They brag about all the Hollywood big shots they know and always say they are "one day" going to ask all their connections to help them out with their idea for a kids' show. They, like a lot of other people in this town, enjoy talking about what they are going to do without actually ever doing anything. I too was in this category for longer than I would like to confess, and put my fate in the hands of others way too often. I eventually got tired of listening to others "talk" and became friends with people that actually had some sort of follow-through.

I told Jacob he'll be seeing me again soon because I've got another Spielberg gig coming up this week. Normally I don't find out if I'm doing a gig at the Spielbergs until the last minute, but Rachel was approached by Steven's daughter, Sasha, a month earlier at another event and she specifically asked her if I was going to be at Destry's party. Rachel called me ASAP to make sure I was available. It was the first time any of the Spielberg kids personally requested a performer to be at a party. Nice to be wanted.

I woke up excited for my party at the Spielbergs today. Then everything changed with one phone call. Rachel called to tell me Christian was also doing the party with us and he would pick me up.

Christian. Why did it have to be Christian? He's so fucking weird! Normally, I welcome weird but Christian is scary weird. If he came to my door to get me and pulled out a ten-inch butcher knife, stuck it in my heart, and danced around my body in the nude, oddly it wouldn't surprise me. It's Christian.

The first time I met Christian was at the office and my first thought was, *Wow, what a really nice guy!* He seemed completely normal; your average six-foot-tall, skinny, good-looking guy with reddish-brown hair trying to make it as an actor in Hollywood. He reminded me of a real-life, good-looking version of Howdy Doody.

A few weeks after our first meeting at the office I ran into Christian at an audition. The room was packed with actors going over their lines and I thought I saw him from across the room but there was something different. His whole demeanor was different. His hair was now blonde but it was more than that. I caught his attention from across the room and waved. He looked at me as if I was crazy.

I thought to myself, *Maybe he didn't see me or he can't see me because he needs glasses and isn't wearing them. Or he just doesn't remember me.*

I decided to go over to him and say hi. "Hey, Christian, it's me Jason. I met you over at Fun Entertainment."

He looked at me as if I was crazy and we had never met and said, "Excuse me?"

Slightly offended, I reintroduced myself, "I'm Jason, I work over at Fun Entertainment for Nick and Rachel. I met you there a few weeks ago when you were picking up costumes for the weekend."

Still staring at me with zero recognition in his eyes he said, "I don't work for any Fun Entertainment. My name's Dirk, Dirk Winnecka."

Now I was looking at him like he was crazy. I have met a few actors and actresses that are so self-involved they always play the, "I don't know who you are and I'm going to act like we've never met" game, but this was taking it to the extreme.

I gave him another chance to redeem himself, "You're not Christian who I met a few weeks ago?"

Stone-faced, he replied, "No. I am not."

"I could've sworn you were him. You look just like him."

"I must have one of those faces."

Game on now, buddy, you don't know who you're fucking with! "Well, you don't look exactly like him now that I see you up close. He's kinda goofy looking. He's also an actor, except a lot less good-looking than us. And I hear his wife is super hot. My boss, Nick, said she's got a face any man would love to jizz on." Still nothing. I thought for sure that last comment would get a reaction.

The casting director came out, looked at the sign-in sheet, and said, "Dirk, Dirk Winnecka, you're up."

"That's me." Christian stood up and addressed me, "It was nice meeting you, good luck at your audition."

After he walked away I went over and checked the sign-in sheet. There it was in big, bold letters, "DIRK WINNECKA." *Son-of-a-bitch, am I going crazy? That was Christian, I know it was! There is no fucking way two complete strangers look and sound that much alike.*

I went in, did my audition and it went well. I was sitting in my truck changing out of my audition clothes when there was a knock at my window. It was Christian, reddish-brown hair and all. He had a wide, shit-eating grin on his face and was waving to me.

"Jason, Jason!" His voice was slightly muffled due to my window being all the way up.

I rolled down my window, "Do I know you?"

He put his hand on his stomach and arched backward with laughter, "HA, HA, HA!!! You've never met Dirk before."

Why does this just keep getting weirder? "No, I haven't."

"Yah, he's a good guy, speaking of good guys, how are you doing?"

Oh, I was not going to let that little episode back there go untalked about, no fucking way it was too weird. "So, who's Dirk?" I asked, bracing myself for the strangeness I knew was coming.

"He's one of my characters I use to audition with."

"One of your characters you use to audition with?" Now I get it, he's a freak who takes on other personalities to audition with. I was scared but it had to be asked, "So, Sybil, how many do you have?"

"Sybil, that's funny. I have three right now but recently I met a fourth."

This just keeps getting better every time he opens his mouth. I'm already in the rabbit hole so what the fuck, let's keep going. "Really? Where did you meet him?"

"Well, I was at a swinger's party…"

Did I not say it keeps getting better?

"… and there was this guy that looked a lot like the Mike Myers character Dieter Sprockets, from *SNL*. You know, all in black with black hair and glasses."

I nodded my head in recognition of what he was talking about, while at the same time having no idea what he was talking about.

"What's his name?" I asked because I couldn't help myself.

"Florio Covello."

"So he's Italian?"

"Well, he's half-Italian."

"Which half would that be, the top or the bottom?"

"The top or the bottom, that's funny. No, his dad is from Florence, Italy, and his mom is American. They met while she was studying art abroad during her junior year in college."

He had this guy's whole back story and went on and on with the story until it came to a head with him asking me, "Do you want to meet him?"

"Sure." I didn't even hesitate; it was like my own personal episode of *The Twilight Zone.*

I walked with Christian to his car, letting him walk in front of me; I didn't trust him enough to allow him to walk behind me. He opened the trunk of his green Ford Escort and lying there very neatly were four plastic bags. On each bag was an index card, and on each card in big, black, bold letters was a name; **DIRK, CHAD, FLORIO** and **CHRISTIAN**.

Christian reached for the bag marked **DIRK**. He pulled out a blonde wig and some headshots of himself dressed like Dirk. At the bottom of the headshot was the name Dirk Winnecka. "Everybody has their headshots and other stuff they need for auditions, including me."

I had to, had to, had to ask, I would've not been able to sleep if I hadn't. "Can I ask Dirk how his audition went?"

Christian's face lit up, "Sure, I think he would like that. Hold on."

He took the bag in his hands and went into his car and not only put on the wig but full-on changed his clothes and emerged from the car as Dirk.

"Hey, Dirk, how did the audition go?"

"Well, well. It went very well, thanks for asking," Dirk replied with his well- groomed, composed self.

"Do you have any more today or is that it?" This was fun.

"Nah, I'm all done. Yourself?"

"That's it for me. What's the rest of your plans today?"

"You know, the usual."

"Hanging with Christian today, are you?"

"Nah, I'm gonna do my own thing, you know. Maybe meet up with some friends."

Now I was dying to meet Florio and Chad. "That's cool. Well, I'll see you later; I need to ask Christian a few things before I take off. It was good seeing you."

"Yah, you too, man. Later." And with that he went back into the car and came out as Christian.

"He's cool. I like Dirk." I was totally lying; he was too trendy for me.

"He is, isn't he? He has a lot of friends; everyone seems to like him and are really drawn to him. He's very charismatic."

"You could say that. Can I meet Florio and Chad?"

Once again he beamed like a lighthouse on a dark, stormy night, "Sure!" He put Dirk back in the trunk and took Florio and Chad into the car with him.

First up was Chad. A self-described dork in taped-up glasses wearing a white shirt with thin vertical stripes that were red, orange, and yellow and tan pants that were hiked up as far as they could go, exposing his socks and giving him a mean camel toe. But the topper was a set of fake crooked teeth Christian had personally ordered, made by a special effects makeup artist. They were incredible and must've cost a pretty penny. They fit perfectly and you couldn't even tell they were not real. Chad got the most auditions out of all the boys, he told me.

Next up, Florio. Dressed all in black from head to toe, including his underwear (I caught an unfortunate glimpse of Christian's white, white ass as he was changing, ewwww). He had on a jet black bob wig that accentuated a pair of very artsy black glasses. He was very artsy in all his mannerisms and speech. Visually, he reminded me of a beatnik sans soul patch. Christian later confessed he was struggling with the idea to give Florio a mustache or soul patch, he didn't want Florio to be TOO cliché. Oh no, he wouldn't want to make him weird or anything. Wow. That's all I had to say was wow!

My intercom system alerted me someone was now at my door and snapped me out of my flashback.

"Hello?" I asked the stained light brown box next to my door.

"Hey, Jay, it's Christian, I'm here to pick you up for our party."

"Can Dirk drive? He's a better driver than you."

"Ha, ha, ha, that's funny. He can't drive today; he left his driver's license at home."

I met Christian out front and could see he had our Alien Baby costumes in the back of his truck. I was happy he was driving. It was raining out and I hate driving in the rain in L.A. It would be fun if Christian got into a fight with himself on the way to the party; it'd help make the trip go by faster and be more interesting. He didn't get into an argument with himself unfortunately, all we did was talk about our recent auditions and how the "acting" thing was going for us, typical actor conversation stuff.

When we arrived at the Spielberg compound Nick and Rachel had gotten there late (no surprise there, I would've been more surprised if they had been there on time) and needed our help to hurry and set up. To add insult to injury Lauren, Rachel's assistant, was very late (another non-shocker, since in my opinion, Lauren wishes she were Rachel and is slowly morphing herself into a younger version of Rachel, kind of like a Rachel 2.0, right down to the always-late personality trait) and showed up just in time to throw on an Alien Baby costume and start the show.

Due to it raining outside we had to have the party in the screening room. I want to have a screening room in my house when I grow up!

We were the four "Alien Babies"; I personally got to be the purple one with the purse who people always questioned the sexuality of. Sweet! I love controversy. We were scheduled to perform for an hour-and-a-half but I knew the gig would go longer; it always did, but especially for the Spielbergs. I never minded; who would want to be in a hurry to leave the Spielbergs and go back to their dingy, ol', tiny, screening room-less apartment? Not I, said the Purple Alien Baby, while holding up his purse.

It was hot and humid and I was sweating bullets in my costume and we hadn't even started the party yet. We changed in the projection room of the screening room. Rachel was the "Master of Ceremonies" and once she started the show we all came out of the projection room dancing to the "Alien Baby" music. Destry, who was turning two and her sister Mikaela, who was almost three, were having a blast and wanted to dance with us the whole time. They are very sweet children and it's a very age-appropriate party for a two-year-old. Believe me, not all celeb offspring are sweet.

Sawyer Spielberg and Chester Hanks both showed up to get balloon animals. Chester came over to me with his little brother, Truman, and told him, "When you ask the Teletubbies for a balloon make sure you say please and thank you."

I was very impressed with young Chester and his politeness. While making Truman a blue dog, Chester was trying to figure out who was inside all the Alien Baby costumes. He came up to me while I was kneeling down and looked into the eyeholes to see whether he could see who was inside the hood. He not only did this to me but to all of us at one point or another. This got a little annoying after a while because he was always in our way and those Alien Baby costumes are not easy to maneuver around in with their oversized heads.

"Jason, is that you in there? I remember you! You were Fred Flintstone."

That party will forever haunt me. It's funny to me that all the kids in this little group, no matter how many times they've seen me, always remember me best for being Fred Flintstone. I've done parties for other friends of Sawyer's and they all say to me, "You were Fred Flintstone at Sawyer's birthday party."

I never took off my hood that day so I'm not sure how they all know that was me. This gig as a Purple Alien Baby is the first hood I have done for a party at the Spielbergs since I did Fred Flintstone. I guess the kids just put it together on their own, because it's been Nick and I at every party since then and Sawyer knew right away back then that Nick was Barney Rubble. I never realized that falling against a stucco wall would make such an impression—I should fall more often, not only at parties, but in life in general.

"Ok, kids," Rachel said, "Let's go get some juice. And that goes for you as well, Teletubbies."

I looked around to see where I could go for a water break. Nick was waving us over to him, while Rachel led the kids out of the screening room. The three of us Alien Babies gathered around Nick who had four water bottles in his arms. "We're going to duck into the projection room for a minute for a breather, c'mon."

Like brightly colored lemmings we followed Nick into the projection room. He held the door open and handed out the water to each of us as we entered. Lauren was first to enter so she took her water and moved to the furthest end of the room. Christian took his water and made his way toward Lauren and planted himself on the floor in between the two projectors. I took my water and sat on the steps in front of the door that led up to the projectors. Once we were all in, Nick closed the door and made his way past me and sat on a stool. Almost in unison, we all removed the oversized Alien Baby heads and left the rest of the costume on while we chugged down our bottles of water.

"Wow, it's hot!" Nick said.

"The humidity isn't helping," I added, pouring water on my head.

"This room is awesome. I wonder whether they've ever shown porn in here?" Christian said in between sips of water.

We were all a few sips into our water before the projection room door opened. Instinctually, we all leaped toward our heads to throw them on in case it was a child. It was not a child, but an adult—"the" adult, actually.

"How are you guys doing?" Steven asked as he entered the room.

None of us responded quickly. Steven hardly ever had time to talk to us and we were all a little thrown off. It took what seem liked hours, but in reality it was seconds, for us to respond.

Nick was the first to answer. "Fine, a little hot, but fine."

"Good, Mr. Spielberg, sir. Like, thanks for asking," Lauren responded awkwardly.

"Peachy," Christian said true to form.

"Good, thank you. The kids seem to be having fun," I said, keeping it short and simple.

Steven walked further into the room. As the door closed behind him, he put his left foot up on the first step in front of where I was sitting and we were almost face to face. He adopted the arms akimbo pose and looked right at me.

"Why do you think kids love the Teletubbies so much?"

I almost wanted to look around to make sure he was talking to me but I didn't have to—it was quite obvious who he was addressing. Without missing a beat I answered, "Well, Steven, funny you should ask, I've actually thought about that myself and I have a few theories on the subject."

Here I was half-dressed as the controversial, ambiguously gay purple Alien Baby, unshaven, wearing a bandana soaked in sweat, and discussing the popularity and psychology of the "Alien Babies" with Mr. Steven Spielberg!

There was no way I was letting this surreal moment pass. "The main characters are bright colors, so that gets the children's attention right away. They don't even wear clothes; they just have big TVs in the middle of their bellies."

Steven added, "And they don't really say much. They have a limited vocabulary that the youngsters can relate to, and they repeat everything over and over."

"…and over and over and over," I augmented and he chuckled.

I made Steven Spielberg chuckle!

He must see my comical genius, he must! WHY DON'T YOU SEE IT?

Is this conversation really happening? I thought to myself.

I continued with our, and when I say "our" I mean the dialogue Mr. Steven Spielberg initiated with me on dissecting this latest kids' sensation, "The trippiest thing about them is that creepy baby face on the sun. So if it's raining, is the rain the baby's drool? Creepy and yucky!"

220

There are a few things I didn't want to share with him on the subject. Such as, my stoner friends loved to watch the Alien Babies as well. For the same reasons that kids do—they are simple and trippy. This is an example of it paying off that I did my research. I could have this conversation with Mr. Steven Spielberg because unlike my fellow Alien Babies, I have actually watched the show on a few occasions. Nick is like his wife, Rachel, in the fact and it is fact—Rachel has told me on more than one of her wine-induced, drunken occasions—that neither of them has EVER watched any of the characters they portray at parties. She loves to boast, "I don't watch TV." Like it's beneath her, which is fine, unless it's the business you want to break into. It's like saying you want to be a vet but you hate animals and can't stand being around them.

Rachel opened the door, almost hitting Steven, and popped her head in. "Hey, guys…" Then she noticed she almost hit Steven with the door. "Oops, sorry about that."

"It's ok, I need to get back out there anyway." He turned back to us before departing, "Thanks again for everything, you guys are doing great."

"Are you ready to come back out and finish up?" Rachel was not so much asking as she was telling us, regardless of whether we were ready or not.

"Ya, ya, we're done. We'll be right out," Nick said as the mouthpiece for all of us.

Rachel closed the door while we finished our bottles of water, took a few more deep breaths, put back on our heads, and went back out to finish the party. There wasn't much more left for us to do. We gathered around the birthday girl and sang *Happy Birthday*, made a few more balloon animals, said our goodbyes and that was that. Before I knew it, I was back in the projection room changing into my civilian clothes and helping clean up our stuff.

"Jason, would you like a piece of cake?"

I turned around to see who was addressing me. It was Sasha with a slice of cake on a party plate.

"Sure, thank you. How are you?" I asked her, taking the plate.

"Good," she replied.

"I don't get a piece?" Christian said, coming over to me and peering over my shoulder.

Sasha gave him a nasty look and said, "I don't know you."

Good girl.

"I'm Christian. Now you know me," Christian said.

"Hope you like the cake, Jason, I've got to get back to the kitchen. Bye." She turned and almost ran away.

I don't blame her, I know Christian and he still creeps me out. Actually, I think the more you get to know him the creepier he gets. Hell, I wanted to run away!

"Guess I don't get cake," Christian said, eyeballing my piece.

"Guess not. You're free to watch me eat mine," I said, hoisting the cake toward my mouth and taking a huge bite. With a mouthful of chocolate cake I added, "And it's good too."

"Asshole!"

"Yup, that's me," I said, finishing my cake.

Nick and Rachel once again had something to do after the party so Christian offered to give me a ride home. It was still raining after the party was over, so that meant our ride home would be longer than normal. It doesn't matter where you are in L.A. your commute doubles when it rains. Lucky me. We weren't even out of sight of the front gate before Christian spoke.

"Hey, Jason, can you believe we were at Steven Spielberg's house?"

"Yah, it was fun. It's always fun, that's why I like doing parties for them. They're good people and more importantly the kids are not little shits."

"How cool would it be if Steven hired us as actors based on our performance at one of his kids' birthday parties? Do you think he'd ever do that?" Christian asked hopefully as if I had some inside "info."

"Well, I heard from Nick that one of his maids asked him for an autograph and she was fired immediately."

"So I guess me bringing a headshot the next time I do a party for them would be a bad thing?"

"I'm going to agree. Rachel has always told me we are to never mention we are actors unless we're asked. Then it's fair game. But, hey, it's Hollywood, this is where anything is possible and dreams are made—that's one of the reasons why we're all here. There was a story in Hollywood lore when I was a Page at Paramount Studios we used to tell on our tours. The story went something like this: A studio exec at the time was getting frustrated with an actor on set, and he told the actor anyone could do the role. The actor said, 'I dare you to find someone else for this role.'

So the exec left to do just that. Actors used to wait in a line by the main gate of Paramount to sign up to do extra work. The exec walked to the main gate and went up to a man who used to be a coal miner in Pennsylvania. 'What's your name, kid?' 'Charlie Buchinsky, sir.' 'No, that won't do. It's too ethnic, we have to change it.' The exec looked at the name of the street of the gate where they were standing. Bronson was the name of the street, and that man was known from that moment on as Charles Bronson."

"Is that true?" Christian asked.

"That's what we were told."

"How cool of a story would it be if Steven Spielberg discovered great talent at one of his kids' birthday parties?"

"I think the press would eat it up. And it would be even better if it was me he discovered."

Then things got weird. And it's too bad; up to that point I was having a halfway decent, un-creepy conversation with Christian.

"You know, if we thought it out well enough, we could probably kidnap one of Spielberg's kids if we wanted to."

I looked over at Christian in shock trying to figure out whether or not he was joking. He was looking right at me and smirking. Almost as if testing the waters to see whether I was in on his evil plan. The fact that thought even crossed his mind was just so wrong to me on soooo many levels.

With my lack of a response he continued, "It'd be easy. We snatch one of the kids or, hell, we might even be able to grab two of them. I even have an idea of how we would do it."

I didn't like how he kept saying "WE"; there is no "WE" in his sick, twisted plot. I didn't, and couldn't, respond to him or what he was saying. I could not get over that he was even thinking about all that stuff. I can admit I've had fantasies or delusions about being discovered while doing a party for Steven and Kate and I know everyone else who has ever done a party for them, or any celeb for that matter, has thought the same thing. This was the first time I've heard anyone take it to this dark place. I wanted to get out of his car and walk home in the rain.

"If there were going to be any kids we nabbed, they would be the best ones to get. Wow, traffic really sucks, don't you think?"

Christian was always a little off to me, and this was the final confirmation that, yes, he is a freak. "Yah, there is a lot of traffic. I don't know about you but I'm beat, I'm going to take advantage of being a passenger for once and nap. Wake me when we get to the other side of the hill." I closed my eyes but I'll tell you, I didn't sleep. I was afraid if I did Christian may try to cop a feel or something.

I couldn't get home fast enough and thanks to the rain it took longer than normal. It was a painful ride; I just wanted to get away from Christian as soon as I could. I got home and had to shower because I felt so dirty from Christian's comments. After my shower I sat on my couch in my bath towel, having a beer and staring at the phone. I was debating whether or not to call Nick and Rachel and tell them about all the stuff Christian had said.

I had once brought to their attention that I suspected one of their performers might be a pedophile (he was always eager to play tag with the boys of eight and older at parties and his "tags" lingered longer than I felt appropriate, bordering on uncomfortable). Big charges I know, but I wanted to make them aware of the situation to keep an eye on him. That's it. They didn't use him for a while but then he was back. Here I was, yet again, with another "situation." I had to do it. If anything were ever to happen to the Spielberg children, at least I would know I did my part.

I called Nick and Rachel to tell them about the whole thing so they would have knowledge of it. As per their normal M.O., they didn't pick up the phone and I had to leave a message.

"Hey, guys, give me a call when you get in. It's kinda important."

They didn't call me for two days. That's what my "important" means to them.

"Hey, Jay, I was wondering whether you could come over today to help prep for the weekend."

I was waiting for the part where he asked me about the message I left. Nothing.

Nick continued, "I know it's only Thursday but we want to get a jump on things because after this weekend it's going to get super busy."

"Did you get my message?"

There was a pause before he answered.

"Ah, yah, what's up?"

He has no idea what I'm talking about, as usual. I don't know why I'm shocked.

"I wanted to give you a heads up about the conversation I had with Christian on the way home on Tuesday." I proceeded to go into full detail about what Christian had said to me on the way home from Destry's party.

He laughed and asked, "Do you think he was kidding?"

"I don't know. But don't you think that's fucking weird?"

"I'm sure he was just kiddin' around. So can you come over today and work?"

I went over to their house and Rachel asked me about what Christian had said. She seemed to take it a little more seriously than Nick had. She agreed with me it was wrong for him to even think about kidnapping the Spielberg children.

Rachel took a sip of wine and a puff off her cigarette, "Guess Christian won't be doing any more parties at the Spielbergs. I'll have a talk with him, thanks for the heads up, JJ."

I never did hear whether she had a talk with him or not; knowing her, most likely not.

A month-and-a-half after Destry's party Christian had a mental breakdown and tried to commit suicide. He did everything he normally does on a Friday. He picked up his costumes, got his information for the weekend from Fun Entertainment, went home and called all his parties to confirm the information he was given.

On Saturday morning he loaded up his car with all his costumes, kissed his wife goodbye and left to go do his parties. On the way to his first party, he just decided he wanted to die and stopped into a home supply store, picked up a garden hose and duct tape. He went somewhere remote, parked his car, placed one end of the garden hose to the exhaust pipe and the other end went into the passenger side window he had cracked open. Once he secured both ends of the hose with duct tape, he got into his car and started it up.

A few minutes later he called his wife to tell her goodbye. She was on the phone with him and his other personalities for three hours talking "them" out of doing it. She would get him to get out of the car but then he would go back into it. His wife was talking to Christian who was bouncing in and out of his other personalities—finally she requested to talk to Dirk and played on his narcissism.

"Dirk, you don't want to die, do you?" she asked.

"No."

"Then don't. Please tell me where you are."

Dirk disclosed "their" location.

When the paramedics arrived Christian was sitting in his car in a Purple Dino costume sobbing. He ended up going to his parents' house in another state to get some help. He was gone for a little over a month before he came back to Los Angeles and jumped back into doing kids' parties for Fun Entertainment.

Or maybe…it was Dirk? Or Florio? Or Chad?

Chapter 14

Cue The Fat Lady

"I deserve a raise!" I stated brazenly.

"I totally agree, J.J.," Rachel responded.

This is very out of character for me; I'm usually never this bold, especially when it comes to my own interests. I'm the type that would rather make someone else happy at the expense of my own happiness—a "people pleaser" if you will. After all this time working for Nick and Rachel I was their "main" performer they pimped out, yet I was still making the same per party as when I first started.

I was only asking for ten dollars more per party. Between Nick and Rachel, Nick is the one who deals with the money. So why was I talking to Rachel? Because Rachel is the one who deals with Nick. Nick is very non-confrontational. If he was asked for more money, he'd turn it into a raunchy sex joke and avoid the issue altogether. I know this from experience. I decided to go above his head, so to speak, and go to the real boss. Knowing Nick, I know he likes his money, ten dollars more a party for me, is ten dollars less for him.

I'm extremely grateful to them for giving me a job in the first place, especially during a difficult time in my life, and I didn't want to "bother" or pester them about my pay. I am loyal to a fault and figure if a person paying me thinks I deserve a raise I would get one. That's how it works in the real world, right?

Rachel agreed with me it was about time and she was going to let all the other party companies they subcontract through know as well.

Being engaged to Annette, who is a very strong, confident woman, was rubbing off on me and giving me a new confidence in myself and my skills. She showed me in this town, or in life in general, if you allow people to step on you, they will and they'll do it with a smile. It also helped I was becoming a working actor in television commercials and was less and less financially dependent on doing kids' birthday parties. Doing parties was only supposed to be a temporary gig while I strived to make a living being a working actor. And it finally happened. The commercial money was great but I decided to continue doing parties to pay for our wedding.

I left Rachel feeling very good about myself and our little so-called, "business meeting." I was expecting a little more negotiating and had built a case to support my cause, but she seemed to be in agreement with me. Through all her faults she does defend and support her perfomers.

The amount of parties I was getting went down. I thought enough of the companies subcontracting me through Rachel and Nick knew my work and knew I was worth my new rate. Plus I'm not stupid; I saw most companies had raised their rates as well, and would still be making a good chunk of change even with my new rate. I got worried because I was getting married in May and needed every penny I could make. After a month I decided to talk to Rachel to find out what was going on.

"Well, JJ, it seems since we started informing the other companies of your increased rate, they only want to use you if no one else is available."

"Really?" I was shocked. I had been doing this for years and built a reputation as an excellent performer and entertainer who was always professional, and thought the transition into my new rate was going to be seamless. I'm not really that business savvy, I'm more a creative type, but I learned a lesson the hard way that in business quantity beats quality. And these business owners would rather save ten bucks than give their clients a product that was proven to be worth the money they were paying.

"I know if you're really hurting for cash we can get you more work if you lower your rate," Rachel added.

"Mmmmm… no. Someone will get desperate and they'll force themselves to spend the extra ten bucks and they'll see I'm worth it. Thanks though."

I think Rachel was waiting for me to cave in and lower my rate. They were still using me but not as much. When I asked her about their business she said it had been so slow for them there was barely enough work for her and Nick via their personal clients.

Then things got worse.

The Screen Actors Guild went on strike over their commercial contract with the Producers Guild. I did one more commercial the week before the strike officially started. Not knowing how long this actors' strike would last I was forced to lower my rate for doing kids' parties for the other companies. Nick and Rachel did continue to pay me my higher rate for all the parties I did for them directly, but they seemed to be putting me on a lot more parties for other companies. My wedding was a month away so I was happy to have anything coming in financially.

It was back to business as usual. And I hated it. I became really bitter. I had a taste of the sweet life of a working actor and then it was gone. I felt like I was going backward in my career, while my personal life was moving full-steam ahead. *I'm getting married in a month!* I kept saying to myself over and over, while I schlepped my ass bitterly from one party to the next. I kept myself in check rationalizing that it was "the stress from the wedding" making me so sour.

Our wedding day was amazing and ended with fireworks in front of the castle at Disneyland where I had proposed. Annette went back to work at the balloon store where we met and I went back to doing parties. My frustration finally got the best of me. I was a Purple Dino Type at a Chinese restaurant for a two-year-old's birthday. There was no room to do any games or activities so my gig consisted mostly of balloon animals, face painting, and posing for pictures, which was fine by me. Under that big Purple Dino hood I was saying to myself, *Whatever, at this point I really don't give a flying fuck!*

I was going through the motions and this one boy behind me kept poking me with chopsticks, pulling my tail, and saying "Hey, Barney, Barney!"

I would turn around and in my Purple Dino voice I would ask, "What?"

He would look at me, smile, and say, "Nothin'."

Every time he did something I would turn around and give him a "death stare." It had zero effect on getting him to stop. It almost seemed to fuel him more. I didn't get it; there were no other kids his age to impress or anything else I could see to motivate his behavior. He was just being a pain in the ass to be a pain in the ass. Over my years of doing parties I have run into plenty of pains in the ass, but what I did next I had NEVER done before and I couldn't control myself.

He poked me and pulled my tail. I turned around and said in my Dino voice, "Listen, fatso, why don't you go over to the buffet and leave me alone?"

He just stared at me and got an uncomfortable smile on his face.

"I don't know why you're smiling there, chub-o; you keep stuffing that fat face of yours and no one will ever love you. I hope you don't like girls because they don't like to kiss big, fat faces like yours. I'm going to teach you some words that will come in handy for you in life—'No thank you. I'm full.' Try saying it once in a while."

His smile disappeared and he cowered away.

I went back to business not giving what I had just said to this kid a second thought. All I knew was he was now gone and no one was bothering me anymore. Like a convict, I did my time and left. Outside while getting out of costume and loading up my truck I realized what I had done. I sat in my truck and stared into space.

What have I done?

When I was his age I too was overweight and confused about life in general, and can honestly say I wasn't a pleasant teenager. I had no idea what came over me. That had never happened to that extent before. For the most part I have always been able to let stuff slide off me, but what I said was truly hurtful. The more I thought about it, the more I realized I was done. I was no longer having fun and it was now "just a job." I knew it was time to quit. I had always promised myself the moment I ceased to have fun it was time to stop. I didn't think I would ever let it get to that point though. Lucky for me, and any other bothersome fat kids, it was Sunday and I didn't have any more parties that weekend.

I dropped my stuff off at the office and told Rachel and Nick what had happened. Nick laughed because he'd been there before emotionally. Rachel understood and said, "I think every performer has a weak moment and that one was yours."

I told them I was going to take advantage of the Screen Actors Guild strike and find a production assistant job, since I didn't have to worry about leaving for auditions until the strike was over. I figured it would give me a nice break from doing parties and I could return to them hopefully refreshed. They completely understood and told me they would continue putting me on gigs until I found a production job. I went home and started calling everyone I knew to let them know I was looking for a new job.

Ask and you shall receive.

I just didn't expect to receive so quickly—it had only been a week since my verbal assault on the fat kid when I got a call for a job.

"Hey, Jason, I hear you're looking for a P.A. job. Is that true?"

It was my friend Antonio, and he told me he was working as a production coordinator on a show called *House Calls*, about a psychologist who went to people's houses and gave them marital advice and was in need of a production assistant.

"Are you kiddin'? I would love to do it. When can I start?"

"What are you doing right now?"

Yah, it was that quick. That's how it happens in this biz at times. I still needed to go and meet with the executive producers for a formal interview but as Antonio told me, "It's just a formality, don't worry you're as good as in. I really talked you up to them. Just be your charming self. If you need help with that let me know, I'm the king of charming." Antonio thinks very highly of himself.

He's one of those people that deep down inside really wants to be an actor. He grew up in L.A. and "tried" acting for a while. I have found a lot of people "try" acting but then realize they don't like being poor, so they get jobs within the industry to be close to and involved with the process. The entertainment industry is full of "colorful" people, so what's one more? I find most people in the industry started out wanting to be actors and actresses. On average, people get headshots taken, maybe take a class, then after three months of not becoming a "STAR" and watching their bank accounts slowly deplete, they quit "acting" and get a job with one of those…what do they call it? Oh yah, a weekly paycheck and steady job. I've had so few it's hard to remember what it's called.

I went in and met with the big wigs at the production office. I could tell the show was just starting up because there was no furniture in the offices, resumes were strewn about the floor, and the staff was bare minimum. There were the four executive producers, an executive in charge of production (the money man), my friend Antonio, and now me. I think I got the job because I own a truck and my first assignment was to go pick up a desk and chairs from a warehouse. I learned a long time ago if you want to stack the odds in your favor to get a production assistant job, get a truck and put it on your resume that you have one.

Antonio was so happy that they hired me on the spot. "It makes me look good that you were so impressive they had to hire you right away."

Antonio and I had worked together before so he knew I was an actor. Once it was official I was on board he told me, "When the actors' strike is over we'll figure out a way that you can still make it to your auditions, ok?"

I couldn't believe it. A steady gig that would let me take off for auditions, it's almost unheard of and in the world of actors it's as mythical as unicorns and leprechauns. Amazing what a little change in attitude will do. It was official, this was the perfect job. I was on cloud nine again.

At the end of my first week, Antonio said our bosses were very happy with me and the head honcho, Susan, told him, "That Jason sure is a workhorse and really smart to boot." They were impressed with my handyman skills and felt I was worth more than I was getting.

"Jason, can you come into my office for a minute?" Susan called to me from the intercom system I helped set up.

I was so happy. It was nice to be at a job that I was happy with again.

Susan was sitting behind her desk that I built earlier in the week when I entered her office.

"Hey, Jason, I wanted to let you know we have decided to give you a raise. It's not much but we feel you're worth it. Go see Jack so he can get the paperwork part of it done, so your new rate can be reflected in your next check."

I took the opportunity to ask them to interview my wife for a position. The show is about a psychologist and my wife studied psychology at UCLA, so I figured *why not?* I had nothing to lose.

"Annette, my wife, is a psych major at UCLA and really good on the phones."

"Sure, give us her resume. Now go see Jack."

I did parties for five years and never got a raise—I was there for a week and "BAM" I got one. It was a nice, little ego boost after my last job started to make me feel unappreciated. And the day kept getting better.

I went and saw Jack; he made my raise retroactive and factored it in from my previous check. I like Jack.

Jack used to be a rocket scientist before he got into the entertainment industry. I was so happy to be able to tell people I was friends with a real-life rocket scientist. "You know my friend Jack, the rocket scientist, he said…" I couldn't wait to bring it up in conversations.

Jack said he always had an interest in the arts and got a production assistant job on *The Howling*. Perhaps one of my all-time favorite films, I found myself regularly asking him questions about his experience working on it. Lucky for me, he loved to talk about it. I eventually got out of him that he is also an Oscar winner. "Of course he did, he's Jack." Modestly Jack would add, "It was a technical Oscar but an Oscar nonetheless."

Not knowing how long this job was going to last, I kept myself on the schedule to do kids' parties on the weekends. A week after I started, the big wigs brought my wife in for an interview and hired her a week after that as an associate producer. During those few weeks I was working every day of the week between the two jobs. Life for us wasn't good—it was great! Here we were a newly married couple in the industry and we were both working and making steady money. That's almost unheard of, especially when one of those involved is an actor. Annette and I were able to carpool into work every day, also unheard of in Los Angeles.

After Annette had been working for a week we were driving into work and sitting on the 405 in L.A. traffic when she said, "You should quit doing parties while we're both working."

I agreed. I had been noticing, especially in the past few months, my patience was wearing thin at the parties that were bad. If I had a good party, I had no problems. My patience level was in direct correlation to how the party was going. As a party got worse, my patience would follow exponentially. This concerned me. That was not the real me. I don't know whether it was because I got a taste of what it was like to be a working actor and felt way underappreciated, or I was just plain getting burned out. Most likely it was a combination of both.

People who own their own companies don't get quite as burnt out, because they see all the money from the parties they do, as well as their cut from the parties their employees do. I often compare it to being a stripper—the money is so good it's hard to stop. I've seen the kids' party business change people and most times it wasn't for the better. Me, I was changing, and I didn't like it.

So after several long years of indentured servitude, I quit.

Rachel and Nick told me I was more than welcome to come back to work for them anytime I needed or wanted to. I was hoping

I wouldn't have to. Rachel already had me booked for the following weekend as well as one party during the week on Thursday, and asked if I was still interested in doing them.

I didn't want to leave them hanging, plus I wanted to do them, knowing, as of that point, they were the last parties I was ever going to do.

Now I had to let Antonio know I had a party during the week I had committed to. When I told Antonio I had a party on a Thursday, he was a little hesitant to let me go, until I told him who the party was for.

"It's for Cindy Crawford. I can't let Cindy down." I knew Antonio was a big one on name-dropping so he told me I had to do it. Antonio brags to people his girlfriend's family was friends with John Wayne. The first time I took a leak in her house Antonio said, "You realize John Wayne used to also piss in that bathroom? Hee, hee, hee!" Antonio is a HUGE name-dropper.

"We can't let Cindy down, now can we?" Antonio said and I could see him mentally adding one more name to his "name-dropping bucket." He continued, "Have fun, we'll see you when you get back. On your way back drop this paperwork off for us. Thanks."

Antonio told all the higher-ups in the office where I was going. He said it was best we be honest with them, plus it was an opportunity for him to drop the new celebrity name he acquisitioned from me. They all thought it was very interesting I did kids' birthday parties—it's not an occupation you hear often, even here in L.A., so it always catches people's attention. Add into the mix I do a lot of parties for celebrities and the job gets even more fascinating.

The party for Cindy was only for an hour from 12:30-1:30pm so I made it part of my lunch hour. I left the office and everyone was eager for my return, so I could fill them in on the party and how Cindy was "in person."

Cindy's house was relatively close to the production office so I have plenty of time to find the house, look over the paperwork, and prepare myself mentally—just the way I like it. I was going to be a Red Furry Monster Type for Cindy's son, Presley's, first birthday, that much I knew. What I didn't know was Kenny G was the one who referred Cindy to my company. I also noticed she had a list of special preferences for the performer of the party. Cindy's request: *Make sure Elmo does singing, dancing, bubbles, puppets, parachute, and Ring Around the Rosie. He also needs to be very gentle and make sure the performer can do the Elmo voice.* To the left of these notes was another note written in red pen specifically for me. *JJ, does this sound like you or what? Thanks! Rachel.*

The Elmo voice is not one of the easier voices to do in my profession, or what was soon to be my old profession. I can do it very well and, if I had to, I could do it for ten hours straight. Granted, my throat would be extremely sore and my voice would be shot for a day or two, but if I absolutely had to do it, I could.

Fifteen minutes before I was scheduled to start I rang the bell at the gate.

"Hello," the static-y voice said.

"Hi, I'm from Fun Entertainment. I'm here for the party."

"Great, come on in."

The big gate opened. I drove down the driveway to the house and was met by someone waving me down. *Is that Cindy?* It can't be. I'm never met at celebrities' houses by the actual celebrities, except for the occasional time over at the Spielbergs, but other than that, never. It's always an assistant, nanny, or some other form of hired help that well…helps me.

"Hi, are you our Elmo?"

Son-of-a-bitch, it is her!

"Yah, that's me. I'm Jason."

"I'm Cindy."

Like I didn't know. Sweet. She extended her hand and I extended mine and we shook hands. Yes people, I TOUCHED Cindy Crawford. Little ol' me, Jason Lassen from a farm in the hills of New Hampshire, touched The Cindy Crawford. Normally, celebs don't affect me this way, but to be honest she is absolutely stunning in person. I've never even been a big fan of Cindy's either, yet I couldn't get over how unbelievably attractive she is in person. Plus she seems really down to earth and you know that always boosts a person's looks. An ugly person, or any living creature for that matter, is more attractive when they, or it, have a good personality. Now take a person or creature, make them beautiful, AND add in a good personality and you have someone/something irresistible—you have Cindy Crawford.

"You can park over there and I have a room inside for you if you need it to change into Elmo."

"Thank you, I love you" is what I wanted to say. It came out as, "Thanks."

I parked my truck, grabbed my stuff, and allowed Cindy to escort me to my "private performers' suite" (a guestroom inside of her house).

"We'll be outside under a tree when you're ready, Elmo. If you need anything else just let me or someone know. See you out there."

"I love you" is what I wanted to say again, but it came out as, "Ok, thanks." As I watched her close the door behind her, I promised myself—no, I challenged myself—to find a way to tell Cindy I love her.

When it was time, I met the party outside and they were under a tree as Cindy told me they would be. I knew she wouldn't lie to me. She loves me. I entered carrying my boom box playing *Elmo's Song*, while singing and dancing along with the music. I kept in mind the whole time that she requested I be very gentle with the children. This is usually code for, "We don't want a six-foot-tall Elmo freaking the kids out." After all the years of doing this I have perfected reading kids, and know when and if they want me to get closer or stay far away. At times parents can't read their own children and force them on the character—this is not a good thing. Can you say, "Up all night with your kid while they have severe night terrors?"

Cindy was the best; she played with us the whole time. It's more common that parents, much less celebrity parents, don't play with me and their children.

I started out dancing and doing bubbles and Cindy held on to Presley for both activities. I got out the parachute and played a few games with it, before we sat on it for singing and puppets, during which Presley stayed on Cindy's lap where I wish I could be.

While singing, Cindy asked Presley, "Do you love Elmo, baby?"

This was it! This was my opportunity to tell Cindy how I feel. So I took advantage of it before that door closed.

"Elmo love Presley," I said, working my way up to my true target.

"See baby, Elmo loves you."

NOW! NOW! NOW! DO IT! DO IT NOW!

"And Elmo loves Cindy too. Does Cindy love Elmo?"

"Of course I do, Elmo."

He shoots and he SCORES! No fucking way! Not only did I get to tell her how I feel, but I got her to profess her love for me. Ok, it's for the character of Elmo but at this moment I'm Elmo so at this moment she loves me. I couldn't wait to tell my wife Cindy Crawford told me she loves me and that I got her to tell me the same.

After we were done singing with the puppets Cindy said, "I think everyone needs to take a break and get a drink of water, right, Elmo?"

"Elmo agree with Cindy. It sure is hot out today."

"Let me take you inside so you can get a drink too, Elmo."

"Elmo follow you anywhere."

Cindy handed Presley to one of the nannies and led me inside the house to the kitchen.

"Is water ok, Elmo?"

"Water just fine."

"It's safe for you to take off your head and use your normal voice in here."

I took the Elmo head off and still in my Elmo voice I said, "Elmo thank you for water."

Cindy laughed while handing me a glass of water. "It's amazing how well you can do that voice."

I was waiting for the line I usually hear after someone compliments my ability to do character voices. "You should get into voiceovers." But it didn't come.

"You're doing great. The kids are having so much fun and Presley's not even scared of you. I can't thank you enough for being so gentle with all the children, you truly have a gift. Help yourself to the water and take as long as you need before you come back out."

Cindy turned and started to head back outside. I quickly swallowed my mouthful of water getting a drop or two in my windpipe.

"Thank you," I said, half-choking.

She turned, saying nothing, only shooting me a smile that said it all.

After a few more glasses of water I returned to the party and finished up with bubbles, balloon animals, and singing *Happy Birthday*. If this was a weekend party and I didn't need to get back to a "normal" job, I would've stayed longer. I went over to Cindy, put my hand on her shoulder and said, "Elmo have to go back to Sesame Street now. Do you want to take any more pictures before Elmo go?"

"Sure, Elmo. Squeeze in here next to us in front of the cake."

I posed for a few more photos while everyone was eating cake.

"I think that's good. Thanks, Elmo, you were great," Cindy said to me before addressing the rest of the party, "Ok, everybody, say goodbye and thank you to Elmo for playing with us today. He's got to go back to Sesame Street."

All the kids waved and said goodbye as I walked away and made my way back to my changing room. As soon as I got into the room and closed the door I couldn't get my Red Furry Monster Type head off fast enough. Southern California in the middle of July gets hot and it's even hotter in a giant, furry red suit. I had only taken a few deep cleansing breaths before there was a knock at the door.

"KNOCK, KNOCK!"

Instinctually, I hurried and put my head back on. You never know who's going to come into the room.

"Hold on a minute," I said in my Red Furry Monster Type voice, while I adjusted myself and opened the door.

"Mr. Elmo, this is for you." One of the nice ladies working the party handed me a glass of ice water.

"Elmo very appreciative. Thank you," I said, taking the ice cold glass anticipating the moment the door closed so I could chug it down. Sweet relief.

"Mrs. Cindy wanted me to make sure you saw she left you something on the bed."

I turned around and saw a white envelope on the bed with the words, "FOR ELMO" written on it in bold, red letters.

"Elmo see. Tell her Elmo say thank you. And thank you for the water."

She said nothing and walked away as I closed the door behind her. I ripped my head off and started to chug water, making my way over to the envelope on the bed. Inside there was forty dollars and a note that simply said, "Thank you."

As I drove away from Cindy's house on my way back to the production offices of my new job, it hit me. *That was my last party; I don't do kids' parties anymore!* After several years and eight hundred and forty parties, that was my last one. I thought about all the people I met over the years, everyone I entertained along the way and all the cake I had eaten. And that's a lot of fucking cake. *That was my last party; I don't do kids' parties anymore.* I kept repeating it over and over and it didn't seem real to me. It was an odd feeling, one I knew would come one day, but never knew when or what the circumstances were going to be.

I'm a completely different person now from the person I was when I started working the kids' party circuit. Back then, I was single, lost, and a very lonely twenty-five-year-old whose world was crumbling down around him. I felt like my life was spinning out of control and I questioned my very existence. I was in the process of learning that this town changes people, and not always for the better.

My core group of support was friends and they were morphing. Family members may change but they will always be family—when friends change it doesn't mean they will always be friends. For example, Nick had changed toward me soon after my wedding. I learned through a friend he was upset I didn't include him as a groomsman in my wedding. At times, I found myself in a room full of "friends" and still felt completely alone. It's not a good feeling. Some of my friends became self-absorbed; verging on obsessive, doing whatever it took to succeed out here, even at the expense of their friends. Other friends, I watched leave L.A. altogether, after the realities of just how hard the entertainment business can be, especially on those who want to be actors, hit them. It's brutal.

I too, in a moment of vulnerability and weakness, was almost another L.A. crushed-dream victim. Thanks to a woman who knew me better than I knew myself, I stayed, toughed it out and saw my dream become reality. If I had left, I wouldn't have what I have now and would've never met the woman who completes me, my wife. Thanks, Mom, for believing in me.

Isn't it said that a person's greatest quality is also their weakest? I'm loyal to a fault and want to help people as much as I can, whenever I can. What I was seeing and living around me at the time made my heart very sad. With an unstable support system, I felt like everyone and everything didn't care about me, and was against me being here and I almost called it quits. Not only on L.A., but on life as well. If I said I never thought about taking my own life after I moved to L.A., I would be lying.

Seeing the aftermath of my roommate, who succeeded in killing himself and how it affected his family and friends, I decided to take another road. I tried to drink the pain away and lived my life with reckless abandon. How dramatically stereotypical is that of an actor? I hate following the norm and that's one of the reasons why I took the job of entertaining at kids' parties in the first place.

Now, here I was, a new man, a happily married man, a man with confidence in himself and in the world around him in ways I had never dreamt possible. My wife showed me I'm worth loving;

when I look at myself through her eyes, I finally understand what it means to truly love oneself. She always compliments me on being able to recognize my own faults and to not hate myself for them, but strive to change them and make myself a better person. We are all works in progess. Love is not something a person only has so much of and then it's gone—we have an unlimited supply and we can decide how many people we give it to and its intensity. It's not only limited to people; hell, I love my pets more than I care about most humans.

Working as a children's party performer ran its course and had its purpose—it was now all over just as quickly as it had started. *That was my last party; I don't do kids' parties anymore.* That chapter of my life is now closed and I'm on my way to another adventure but this time I'm not alone.

Everyone I have come to know, who owns his or her own company, does very well and makes a good living doing it. I've seen people whose business started out of a spare room, moved to the garage, and eventually settled in an office space or warehouse. Each step was the result of a dramatic jump in revenue. As their businesses grew, so did the need for space to amply provide for its growth. There's so much money to be made in the party entertainment business out here in L.A. I'm surprised Donald Trump hasn't tried to get a piece of the action yet, by opening his own company or buying out an existing one.

However, all this success comes with a price. A price I was not willing to pay. I watched many people get so wrapped up in the business that all the hopes and dreams they first had when they moved to Hollywood faded away. I didn't want that to happen to me. I moved to L.A. with a mission and I wasn't going to let anything stop me. I'm a firm believer that you don't have to be a cog in the blue-collar machine. I didn't want to clock in, do my eight hours, clock out, and go home. I wanted my job to be such a passion and joy that it didn't feel like a job. To me, that is the American Dream—getting paid to do something you love to do. It's not to say that along my journey I haven't strayed from my idealistic values. Hunger and overall survival has a way of trumping idealism.

Waiting for traffic to ease up so I could cross the road and enter the office parking lot, I had time to think a little more. I thought about this production assistant job and whether it really was too good to be true. What if it ended tomorrow? Then I thought, *If it does it does, so be it. I have family out here now and that makes for a strong support system. We help each other through the hard times because those times will pass and will be followed by good times. As far as my career, I take it one day at a time and hope when this SAG strike is over I can get back to doing commercials and hopefully on to more acting gigs.*

As I pulled into the parking lot of the office ready to regale my co-workers with stories of the lives of the rich and famous, I thought about all the parties I had done over the years—so many memories, both good and bad. A part of me will always be a Hollywood Clown.

Maybe one day I'll write a book about all my experiences.
Now that would be an adventure!

Acknowledgements

If I had known what I was in for when I first started writing this book, I would've quit before typing the first word. This shit is not easy! I know some people, as well as some fellow writers, bag on authors and the "acknowledgements" section of their books. The irritating name-dropping of anyone they know who is famous in any way, shape or form. The splurges of gratitude, for every single person at the writer's agency and publishing house, right down to the janitors. And especially for the spouse who gave up med school just so the author could keep writing while they both ate watered-down tomato soup to help cut the cost of living. All I have to say is, it's my book and I'll thank who I want to. So here we go -

I would have never set out on this journey if not for Ward Grant. Ward served as Director of Media and Public Relations for Bob Hope at Hope Enterprises Inc. since 1973, as well as doing public relations for Dorothy Lamour, Fess Parker, Eva Gabor and Phyllis Diller. The man would tell me he knew talent and saw it in me "from day one." He always had high hopes of my book being turned into a film or TV show and helping me with my acting career. I'm sad he'll never get a chance to read what he had me start. He passed away in 2007.

This is my first venture into the literary world and I couldn't have navigated it without help from the few people I knew, or got to know along the way. Bart Baker and Michael Loynd, thanks for the bottomless guidance, endless encouragement and for having such faith in my story. Thanks for selflessly offering words of wisdom and insight when I really needed it.

Lisa Cron, Michael Kostroff and Stacy Sparrow Lellos; the only people I know who have experience in the literary world, thanks for your "insider info."

Looking over the corrections my copyeditor/proofreader, Jessica Keet, made was like a writing class all its own—thanks for making my writing that much better.

Barbara Deutsch, who showed me I'm a writer who acts, not an actor who writes, and for always being my personal champion. And for sharing in my addiction to physically hold our respective books in our hands.

A big debt of gratitude goes out to all the people who, at one time or another, read my manuscript during one of its many edits, and gave me the feedback I needed to make it the best it could possibly be. They read a lot of crap so you didn't have to. Thanks Buffy Hornung, Doug Spearman, Jen Moreno, John "Doa" Farrentine, Mark Allen Ruegg, Melony Denise Valencia, Michael Santorico, Natasha Rhodes and Patty Valencia.

To my English teachers, Pam Peterson, Dan Henry, and Katherine Pixley; thanks for accepting my idiosyncratic style of expressing myself with my writing and nurturing the seed for a love of storytelling I never knew I had.

Maria Whitworth, thanks for opening the door of possibility for me and for letting me know I needed to write a book at some point in my life.

Sadie, Roxie, Kona & Phoenix, my four-legged friends who sat by my side allowing me to read my daily writings to them. The only critques they ever gave was that my writing was "ruff". Thanks for keeping me company during this adventure.

I also want to send a shout-out to my cousin's daughter, Abbey Bailey, whose talent helped me design and create my vision that became my book's cover. I couldn't have done it without you!

Naddy Ziekursch, whose talents designed and built The Hollywood Clown website. Thanks for helping me give people a place to go online for all things The Hollywood Clown.

I'm eternally grateful to my parents, Albert and Dottie Lassen, for instilling such a fierce work ethic in me that quitting anything is not an option. Big hugs to my sisters, Dawn Wilkins and Allison Girard, for setting such a great example of those ethics, and for softening up our parents for me so I could get away with more than they did while growing up.

Lastly, I can't thank my wife, Annette, enough for all her understanding, support and honesty. No, she didn't have to quit med school so I could write my book but she did support my every decision along the way so I could do what I had to, to get it done. Annette, you are my best friend.

And to our two lovely, spirited children, Isabel and Evan: Thanks for giving me a second childhood and the extra push and insight I needed to finish writing this book.

Proof

Made in the USA
Charleston, SC
13 September 2013